Successful Strategie

Fortune in Real Estate

PHIL JONES & DAVID LEON

Best selling author of ***How to Get Rich Rewards in Real Estate in 3 Years***

WITH ANDREA CRABB AND MATTHEW GILLIGAN

RICHMASTERY

Educators Investors Experts

Disclaimer

Although every effort has been made to ensure the accuracy of information contained in this book, the publisher and authors hold no responsibility for the correctness of contributed material, or for any negative consequences resulting from the use of this book.

Published by Richmastery Limited

www.richmastery.com

ISBN 0-9582669-2-1

First published 2006

Contents

Special Rewards

To help you get the most out of this book we provide you with the following five Special Rewards. Please make sure you use them and enjoy them.

1. FREE Real Estate Investing Pack worth $249

The pack contains:

- Real Estate Toolbox on CD
- House Plan & Landscaping Software
- Buy or Rent Calculator
- Richmastery Newsletter
- Ebook – How to Create Multiple Streams of Income
- Report – How to Master and Repair Your Credit
- Home Inspection Kit ... and more

Go to: www.richmastery.com/fortune and get your FREE $249 Pack now!

2. FREE Bonus Downloads worth $199

These *essential agreements and documents* enable you to correctly execute many of the strategies contained in this book. You MUST download these agreements as they will increase the rate of your investing success and reduce your risk significantly. Go to: www.richmastery.com/fortune

---

3. FREE Online Investor Support

Join the Richmastery Forums at www.richmasteryforums.com, a live, fun online meeting place used by thousands of investors to meet, chat, support, share information and help one another achieve investing success.

---

4. FREE Property Analysis Software

The number 1 tool that EVERY successful investor should be using is RevIQ Property Analysis Software, a critical decision making tool that can save or make you thousands when buying, selling, renovating, flipping or doing lease options. Download a free 14 day trial from: www.reviq.com/bonus

---

5. FREE Live Event

We want to give you two tickets valued at $79.90 to Richmastery's four-hour *How to Profit from Property* Live Event so you can build on the exciting knowledge you gain from this book. If you'd rather watch the DVD of this event, there's $20 off its price. For your FREE tickets and DVD Discount go to: www.richmastery.com/fortune

---

Introduction

BY PHIL JONES AND DAVID LEON

In writing this book we wanted to achieve two goals...

The first is to initiate the beginner into the amazing world of real estate investing. Plus we wanted to make this book an interesting and practical read instead of the usually dry and somewhat stagnant theoretical real estate books that gather dust on many book shelves. This book is a rich tool that new investors will treasure and from which they will gain much insight. We encourage you to also read the other books in the Richmastery series.

Our second goal is to fire up more experienced investors with new, fresh and innovative ideas to run their property-investing businesses more profitably and more effectively. This book gives you detailed instructions on how to use 22 fantastic strategies, with a summary of steps at the end of each chapter that guide you to successful implementation and results.

Richmastery has always taught that 'success comes from doing things differently' and the ground-breaking techniques contained in this treasure trove are guaranteed to have you thinking outside the box like you never have before!

The power of real estate – turning dreams into reality

Real estate can provide you with the vehicle to propel you to achieve all the things you have dreamt of. However, in order for your dreams and goals to become a reality you have to follow this simple plan.

Step 1

You need to know what your goals really are. Do you want to go on a great holiday? Spend more time with your loved ones? Give more to charity or to sponsor more underprivileged children? Play lots of golf; serve others in your church or cultural group? Whatever your dream outcome is, define it clearly.

Step 2

Write your goals and dreams down. Describe the outcome you want in explicit written detail. We do this because manifested written goals are **a hundred times more powerful** than ideas floating around in our heads.

Step 3

Define the specific income in annual dollars that you need to create for your written dreams and goals to become a reality.

Step 4

Now identify when (write a specific time and date) you MUST have created this annual passive income. What time, date and year do you want to commence living your dream?

Lastly: make your plan!

By now you have the dream, the goals, the amount required to enjoy it and the time line you need in which to achieve it. Now read this book and then sit down and design a detailed financial plan using the strategies in this book that will carry you to your desired financial destination. This will become your success road map, which should be reviewed, adjusted and updated at least every six months.

Investing in real estate is one of the easiest and safest ways for you to achieve true financial freedom. You can obtain and transform your financial position with cashflow or massive dollops of profit through executing different real estate strategies such as buy and hold or buy and sell.

It has been recorded that 80% of the world's millionaires made their fortunes in real estate. Maybe it's time you did too! The difference between those who achieve serious wealth and those who don't is discipline, education and application. Join the winners' circle and take the wisdom of this book, use it ... and make your dreams come true.

Has the horse bolted and real estate profits gone?

Some of you may have some doubts or concerns about the real estate market in Australasia. You may ask yourself whether it is a safe property market to invest in and whether it will provide you with good returns. The answer, in both cases, is a resounding **yes!** This is why David moved to New Zealand and has sold most his his portfolio in Spain and England to concentrate on real estate investing in New Zealand and Australia. These markets are strong, emerging and exciting markets stacked with a myriad of money-making opportunities for educated investors who know what to do and when to do it.

You just have to look at real estate markets in other areas of the world where the market is more mature, more advanced and still booming. Take, for example, Spain, David's country of birth. The average salary for a first-time buyer in Spain is roughly €15,000 and the average price of a property for a first-time property buyer is about €180,000. If we divide the average property price for first time buyers by the average salary we come up with a Wages versus Value Ratio, which is one of the key indicators anyone should use to measure a market's progressiveness. In Spain the Wages versus Value Ratio is currently about 12. If you look at other countries like the United Kingdom, United States and most of Europe the Wages versus Value Ratio also consistently sits at around 12.

However, here is where things get exciting...

- In New Zealand the median house price is $310,000 and the average salary is $37,000.
- In Australia the median house price is $319,000 and the average salary is $52,000.

This leaves New Zealand with a ratio of 8.4, which is only two-thirds that of most other Western or European countries. This means that it is a third as easy for Aussie and Kiwi investors or first-home buyers to purchase property than it is for the citizens of many other countries! This confirms that the real estate markets in Australia and New Zealand are robust, strong and healthy compared with many other international investing locations.

So we know New Zealand and Australia present excellent investing value but what about cities and regions within them? That's where the bonanza is and where the grunt in this book is really going to benefit you. Different real estate areas and phases of the property cycle require the execution and customisation of different strategies. That's why we packed 22 very good ones into this book!

Experienced investors, who make the most money, select the right strategy for the right area and the right property. This book is designed to give you a huge amount of insight into exactly how to do that.

Australasia is a premium real estate paradise just waiting for you to come and pick the fruit. You literally have an opportunity of a lifetime right on your doorstep. Have you ever stopped and wondered why so many foreigners (like David) are putting so much money into real estate in Australia and New Zealand? Something to think about, isn't it?

If you want more information on reading and understanding the real estate market indicators in each area, visit the Richmastery website at: www.richmastery.com or post a question in the Forums under the Community tab on the Richmastery website.

The only regret most property investors have is that they did not get started sooner. It is easier to live with failure than with regret.

Do yourself a favour and re-read these last two sentences – they changed our lives and hopefully they could do the same for you. These two sentences will make perfect sense when you read Chapter 37 on Goal Setting. But remember the best time to start investing in real estate was three years ago; the second best time is NOW!

The strategies and concepts we discuss in this book work today where you live. Like any other investment strategy they will become obsolete over time and some new and even more exciting ones will eventually replace them. For this reason we want to stress the need to talk to other investors and to have a great network of professionals, such as mortgage brokers and accountants, to advise you and who will push you into going further and learning more about your business. If you don't do this you'll probably be doomed to be a mediocre investor who may lose as much money as you make. Make a habit of visiting Phil's Richmastery website (www.richmastery.com) and David's website (www.david-leon.com) so you can be kept informed and up to date with new strategies and tools as they become available for you to use in the current market.

Risks – don't allow yourself to be scared!

Some of you will already be thinking about the risks associated with real estate investing and we haven't even started explaining anything about it yet! If you're a risk-averse investor, take a deep breath and understand this: life is risky. Crossing the road can kill you, if you get hit by a bus. The reality is there is risk in EVERYTHING you do and that includes real estate investing.

If someone tells you that an investment is risk free, they are being less than truthful. You can't eliminate risk but you can control it and minimise it through intelligent investing, structures and planning. And that's exactly what we aim to educate you to do through this book and the other resources available at www.richmastery.com

The funny thing is that the risk-free life that many people believe they are living is in fact considerably more risky than the life of the informed real estate investor. Do you think your pension or superannuation will provide you with enough money to live a decent life? Do you have a direct benefit or direct contribution pension? Will there even be a pension when you reach retirement? Nothing is certain in life and in our experience you are much wiser to have *control* over your own financial future than *hope* that others will provide it. Many people who choose not to invest in real estate will end up dependent on their families when they retire.

Statistics say:

- On average only one in 100 Kiwis or Aussies will be financially free at the age of 65.
- 24 will be dead.
- 54 will rely on their pension or welfare to survive.
- 16 will still be working.
- 5 will be financially independent.

Sadly if you don't plan for your retirement – NO ONE ELSE WILL! And who said retirement starts at 65? For many of the students we have taught it started at 35! Read Richmastery's book *How to get Rich Rewards in Real Estate in 3 Years* for more than a few examples or check out the Success Stories Section of the Richmastery website.

The more you learn about real estate investing, the more your risk level decreases and you therefore become a safer, more informed and more knowledgeable investor.

Ignorance is always more expensive than education.

Tax, the thing we love to hate

In Chapter 8, tax and structures expert Matthew Gilligan from Gilligan Rowe and Associates will guide you through this constantly changing and critically important area. Matthew and his team are asset planning and structures experts who we personally use and endorse.

Failing to plan is planning to fail.

We have lost count of the number of investors who have cost themselves tens of thousands of dollars and received wicked migraines all because they didn't take the time to set up a simple asset-purchasing structure from a *good* asset planner like Gilligan Rowe and Associates. In the desire to save yourself a few dollars you can cost yourself a fortune by not taking professional advice BEFORE you start investing.

An effective structure is essential to success in property investing and MINIMISES and CONTROLS your RISK.

Do not invest in real estate solely because of the tax advantages (and there are heaps); invest in a property solely because it makes strong financial sense to do so. Tax benefits are a bonus but they should never be the only reason you purchase a property. Governments have a habit of changing tax rules so don't build your future on outcomes that could change.

That's why professionals like Gilligan Rowe and Associates are worth their weight in gold. Their job is to keep you ahead of the game and any impending law changes while saving you the maximum tax and protecting you so that you enjoy minimum risk.

Tip: Use an accountant who is a specialist asset planning expert in real estate and is an active property investor themselves.

We hear horror stories all the time where investors are poorly advised by garden-variety accountants who specialise in nothing and generalise in everything. In a recent case a client of ours was selling his property and was wrongly advised by his accountant of the depreciation claw back on the property. The result was that the sale of the property left him with a huge tax bill, which he was not expecting and therefore did not budget for.

Make sure you surround yourself with a group of advisors who are smarter than you and who are experts in their field. Doing this will increase the momentum of your investing, enable you to make more accurate decisions and do larger, more complex deals. Investors who do multi-million-dollar deals daily don't have more intellectual horsepower than you; they have just built a quality team of advisors around them. And that makes doing bigger deals easy.

Be a generalist with a good grounded knowledge on most subjects and use experts to give you the grunt, detail and quality advice on difficult technical areas you are unsure of.

How property investing changed David Leon's life

How did David get into property investing and how has it changed his life? His three specialities are property investing, public speaking and sales. He wanted to share with you the small tricks and strategies he has learnt during the last few years, and to show you how they have been extremely profitable for him and how they could be for you too if you apply everything in this book and mix it with lots of the other great advice and education provided by Richmastery.

David started investing with a consumer debt of around $15,000, no savings and just a monthly salary. His first four deals were no-money-down deals. He just had enough courage and knowledge to go out there, put offers in and start making some real money. He says: 'You can get started in real estate investing regardless of your economic situation or any other obstacles that you may think of. Property investing can be profitable for anyone if you follow some simple steps.'

Reading this book will definitely assist you to generate the income you need to achieve all your exciting goals and dreams in life.

The money David has made from real estate investing has changed the quality of his life radically. He can do the things he always wanted to do. He spends a huge amount of quality time with his partner, and together they have travelled all over the world and have lived and thrived in three different countries in the last few years. He donates a big part of his earnings to several charities. Property investing has empowered David to free himself to do the things he feels passionate about, like teaching other people how to obtain the results he has obtained.

The key to your future

Real estate is the key that can unlock the door to a whole new future. It's worked for us and we are sure it can work for you!

Right now think of the things you have always wanted to do, but have been unable to because of time and money constraints. Take a moment and write these down! They will become your goals. Goals that will push you to achieve amazing results. If you don't write your goals down they remain as unrealised ideas that, more often than not, stay as unrealised dreams. **A written goal is a real goal! A real target for a real investor.**

Thank you for choosing this book. Dive into it and enjoy the concepts, strategies and the wonderful world of real estate. May you be inspired, encouraged and empowered by the knowledge provided in this book. Happy investing!

Phil Jones

www.philjonesblog.com

David Leon

Acknowledgements

David Leon

There are some special people I wish to dedicate this book to:

- My father, who showed me that a man is always measured by the respect he gets from his peers. Through his wisdom I have obtained respect through hard work, honesty and values.
- Greg and Charlotte Keenan for showing me the first steps of the way.
- Gill Fielding and Kevin Green for always believing in me. Your energy is contagious and I feel lucky to have received some of it.
- Rohan Weerasinghe and Mark Dalton for your calm words of wisdom and good advice throughout the last few years.
- Thomas Muller for showing me how to run a business effectively and how to manage others.
- Alyssa Hardy for taking the time to make this book readable.
- Lastly and most importantly, I would like to thank my true inspiration and reason for everything – my partner Christina who has always pushed me to go a step further. Without you, I would never have achieved what I have and reached where I am today, and you deserve all the credit for everything we have accomplished in the last few years.

Phil Jones

- The publishing team (Renée Lang, Brian O'Flaherty and Julie McDermid) for their tireless work and professionalism assisting with the production and publication of this book.
- Andrea Crabb for the time and energy she invested crafting this book into its final form.
- John Bedggood for polishing the manuscript of this book and injecting his knowledge, expertise and skill. We have done a significant amount together in recent years and his contribution and guidance on this project has been huge and is recognised.

- I'd like to thank and acknowledge the support, inspiration and love of my deeply cherished wife Corinna who makes me smile every day and is my best friend, mentor, lover, business partner and the most amazing person I know. My life's journey with her gets better every day as our love and understanding reaches new heights with one another. To my two incredible children, Cheinnelle and Jack, thank you for the lessons you teach me every day, for your laughter, smiles, love and understanding. I'm dedicated to being the best dad I can be and I love you both very, very much. May my parenting result in you being smarter, wealthier and wiser than me.
- To the members of the Richmastery Team who strive every day to help our treasured customers get insights and results: thank you for your dedication, energy, professionalism and service.
- And finally to my brother Andrew, a man who is a silent hero but is often not acknowledged or recognised. Your patience, humour, friendship and unwavering love in the tough times of my life got me through when many others were hoping I'd fall. I owe much of my success to you and the journey we both shared starting in an Auckland seminar room one night many years ago. Though our business paths have been different, I will always be indebted to you for the unique times we shared in Coolum and the mighty strength and belief you showed in me when few others would. Words cannot convey the appreciation and love I have for you and how much of my success has been forged in your inspiration, support and love. Thank you for being the great man you are. I wish you every happiness and will always be there for you as you have been for me!

PART ONE

The power of real estate

Chapter 1

Real estate

WHY IT'S A GREAT INVESTMENT

'Property investments have produced more self-made millionaires than the rest of all investment vehicles combined.'

— Anonymous

The power of real estate investing

Real estate investing has created more self-made millionaires than all the other investment strategies put together. This fact alone should be enough to enlighten you to its power, but let's elaborate so the analytical (or 'anal-ytical') people will feel completely at ease. If you compare real estate investing to a few other investments, you can evaluate its pros and cons.

Real estate compared with savings accounts

Let's start by comparing real estate investing to a savings account. If you are lucky with a savings account you will get around 7% gross return. Once tax on your money invested and inflation are taken into account, in most cases your 'savings' are making you a pittance or potentially even losing ground.

Using savings accounts is a strategy often used by risk-free investors that sadly generates a terrible financial result.

Here's an example that explains this concept (see chart opposite):

If you were to invest $20,000 for retirement and deposit the full amount in a savings account, providing a 7% gross return, you will really be receiving around 4.5% net return after tax is taken into consideration. This will leave you with only $900 of real profit and a 4.5% yield on the investment.

$20,000 To Invest For Retirement

In a Bank Deposit @4.5% interest

One Year Earnings:	**$900**
Yield:	**4.5%**

As a deposit on $100,000 Flat **@13.5%***
(*Average NZ Capital Growth Rate last 12 months)

One year Earnings:	**$13,500**
Yield:	**67.5%**

Not counting Positive Cashflow, Tax Benefits and Debt Reduction

On the other hand, if you purchase a property worth $100,000 with a deposit of $20,000 and take into consideration the average capital growth in New Zealand in recent years of 13.5%, you will achieve $13,500 in capital growth. This is a 67.5% yield with the same starting investment of $20,000.

Three ways to wealth

The above example compares real estate investing with the low-risk, low-return investment of bank savings. How does real estate investing rate when compared with other recognised high-earning investments?

There are three key ways to create wealth that everyone can practise. They are:

- Real estate
- Shares/stocks
- Business

So let's have a look at these investment strategies.

Real estate

Investing in real estate is something that, with some good education, anyone can be successful in. It is something you can choose to invest in full time or part time alongside another career. If you are paying tax in business or through a salary you can offset this against your real estate investments, thereby increasing your income and cashflow dramatically.

If you follow simple rules and invest well, real estate investing is comparatively low risk compared to investing in stocks or setting up a business. Possibly the most attractive thing about investing in real estate is that you can use other people's money (OPIUM) to do it and create leverage while doing this. (We are not talking about the illegal substance, this acronym stands for *Other People's Inactive Unused Money*). With business or shares, on the other hand, you must have a much higher level of investment capital or cash to begin with.

Stock market

The stock market is a great alternative to real estate investing, but it requires lots of training and time if you are to make serious money from it. The advantage of the stock market is that it gives you liquidity, which basically means that you can convert assets into cash quickly. Stock-trading transactions take place in split seconds of time. You don't have this in real estate investing because as you probably know buying and selling property transactions take quite a bit longer than a split second.

The stock market is a great investment tool that should be used once you have established a large, self-sufficient property portfolio. At this point you should spread your financial risk and invest as follows:

- 50% in real estate
- 30% in businesses
- 20% in shares/stocks and options

When we speak about investing in the stock market, we do not mean buying mutual funds or the so-called 'blue chips' (well-known company shares like Microsoft) and hoping they go up in price. (Interestingly, a blue chip is the highest-valued chip when betting in a casino. Do you want to be a gambler or an investor?)

If you are 'hoping' and 'waiting' for this to happen you are not an investor but a gambler. Stocks do not always go up in value as many investors in mutual funds know, and business disasters like Enron can have a nasty effect on your stock market wealth plan. Enron workers had to learn the hard way by losing everything. (Enron management used the employees' pension funds to secure company debt. When the business went down, the employees lost their pensions.)

What we mean by investing in the stock market is buying company shares/stocks that go up in value AND that pay a monthly cashflow profit when we use the stock-market strategies of a sophisticated investor. These are the strategies that you need to understand well before you invest in the stock market.

Business investing

Another viable means to generate wealth is investing in a business, which can be very profitable if you know what you are doing. Once again, you will need to be an expert in the business itself and will not get as much leverage when purchasing a business as you can in real estate investing. You will also have the added risk that you are investing in people and ideas, which usually are not as solid as bricks and mortar.

Most business owners do not really own a business; they just own a JOB (Just Over Broke). And they actually work for the worst boss of all, themselves! It is amazing to speak to business owners who have to invest so much of their time in the business each month just so they can come out about even. Why, then, would you want to own a business? Unless you want to work more hours, be more stressed and make less money, you have no real reason to do so.

The aim of a business is to create a profitable commercial enterprise that works without you. You want to own a business and grow it quickly to the stage where you can take off for a three-month holiday while the business keeps growing and thriving. Once again, you will need a lot of training and skill to be able to accomplish this. If you are looking to improve your business skills or education, visit the Richmastery Business website for a range of tools, books and resources. Richmastery's Business Academy (www.richmasterybusinessacademy.com) could also be the ideal way of getting you started into any kind of business. This comprehensive seminar covers a broad range of business topics and offers a line-up of outstanding speakers.

The three-laned investment motorway

Business and the stock market are the only two viable alternatives to real estate investing. Both of them can and should be incorporated into a balanced investment strategy, although the timing on when to embark on each of them needs to be accurate, appropriate and carefully planned.

The road to wealth is not just a boring one-way road. You have a three-laned motorway that can take you to your destination. Real estate, business and the stock market make up the three lanes of this motorway, and across the course of your life you should master all three of them to achieve real financial success. On the motorway, there is a right lane (known as the fast lane), left lane (known as the 'slow' lane) and the middle lane is for drivers who stay comfortably at the speed limit.

You have to identify which investment will be your left-hand lane, the stable and steady one that will eventually take you to your destiny; your middle lane, where you feel comfortable but where you can still accelerate; and your right-hand lane, which can take you to your destination more quickly and put you on the fast track.

This is a perfect analogy for the world of investing and you should master all lanes of 'your investment motorway'.

SUMMARY

Investing in real estate is the safest and least risky of the three key paths to wealth creation. As long as you educate yourself in this area, it is something which anyone can be successful in, whether you are self-employed, salaried, a business owner or a full-time property investor. The 22 strategies outlined in Part Three of this book will provide you with a toolbox of exciting and creative ways to massively increase your success in real estate.

Invest in yourself and attend one of Richmastery's educational events. Then get out on the Wealth Highway and savour the results real estate can deliver you and your family.

Chapter 2

Leverage

THE SECRET TO SUCCESS

'Madness is doing the same thing more than once and expecting a different result.'

— Albert Einstein

Discipline and leverage

Real estate is a powerful investment method because it offers you, the investor, the most leverage. Why is this important? Because there are two secrets to creating wealth:

- Discipline
- Leverage

All wealth is generated using these two powers.

Ever more with ever less

Leverage is simply creating ever more with ever less! For example, we have written this book once and will be getting paid from its sales many times. You just need to master this in all areas of your life. Leverage your time, your expertise, your relationships and your money.

In real estate investing, leverage has many forms but one of the most commonly used is using other people's money (leverage) to generate equity and cash for yourself. This is how most people get started and the richest investors use the same concept with larger numbers and so get larger returns!

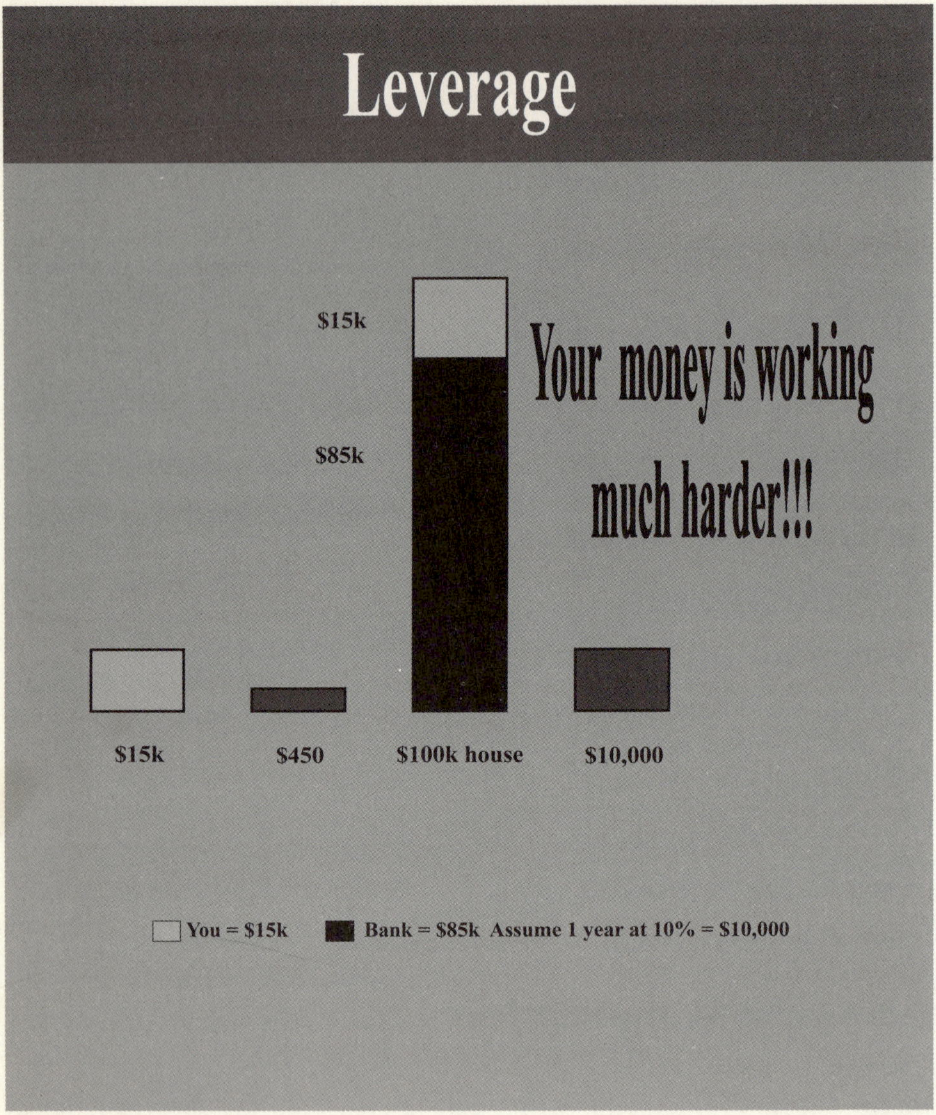

In the graph above you can see the power of leverage.

- The bar on the far left represents the money that you have available to invest ($15,000).
- The next bar represents the profit you can expect yearly from a savings account if you invested that $15,000, assuming you obtained a 3% after-

tax return on your investment. You can see that you will be making only $450 with your $15,000 investment.

- The third bar represents the deposit ($15,000) plus what the bank lends you ($85,000) to buy a $100,000 property, calculated at an 85% loan-to-value ratio (LVR). (Loan-to-value ratio is the amount of money the bank will lend you as a percentage of the property market value.)
- The fourth bar represents the capital growth you will obtain yearly – $10,000. (We took 10% as an example, not average in the property market, but we are used to seeing around 30% growth in strong markets.)

Compounding capital growth

Capital growth is just the increase in value of the property as a whole. You don't have to be a mathematician to know which amount you would rather have: $450 or $10,000. This difference gets even bigger when you take into consideration the compounding effect that will be experienced in coming years. The percentages of property-value increases are usually calculated on a yearly basis. 10% of $100,000 is $10,000 but 10% of $110,000, which is what the property will be worth in the second year, will give you $11,000 of capital growth. This capital growth component will keep increasing every year. Now, if you still want to open a savings account you must be from another planet where restraining jackets are fashionable.

Exploding real estate portfolio

Get up and take a few big deep breaths because understanding the concept of leverage is probably the most important thing with real estate investing. If you have not understood, read over the concept and the example again and then look at the diagrams on the following pages.

When you put nothing of your own pocket into an investment, your cash-on-cash return becomes infinite. (To work out your cash-on-cash return, divide how much profit you obtained annually by how much money you put into the deal – also see Chapter 7.) From this you can see the real power of leverage and why property investing is such a powerful method of achieving wealth.

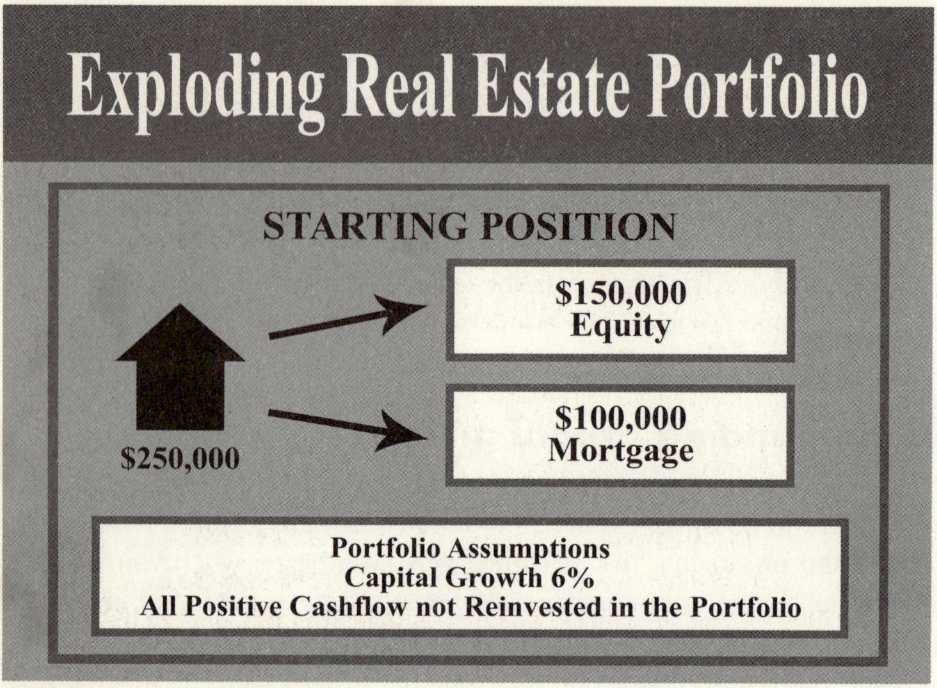
Exploding Real Estate Portfolio
STARTING POSITION
$250,000
$150,000
Equity
$100,000
Mortgage
Portfolio Assumptions
Capital Growth 6%
All Positive Cashflow not Reinvested in the Portfolio

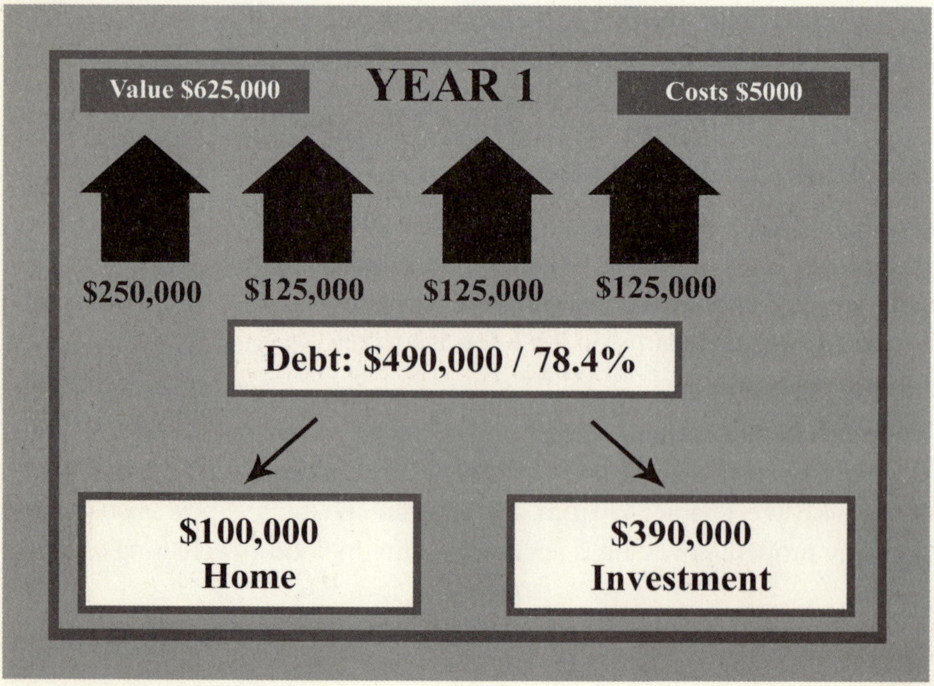
Value $625,000
YEAR 1
Costs $5000
$250,000
$125,000
$125,000
$125,000
Debt: $490,000 / 78.4%
$100,000
Home
$390,000
Investment

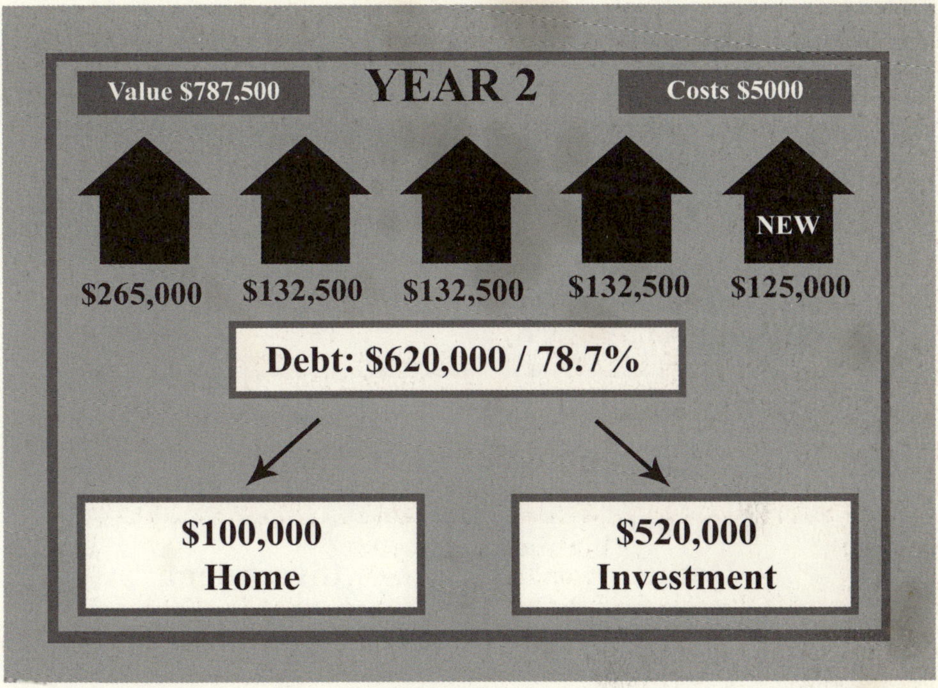
Value $787,500
YEAR 2
Costs $5000
NEW
$265,000
$132,500
$132,500
$132,500
$125,000
Debt: $620,000 / 78.7%
$100,000
Home
$520,000
Investment

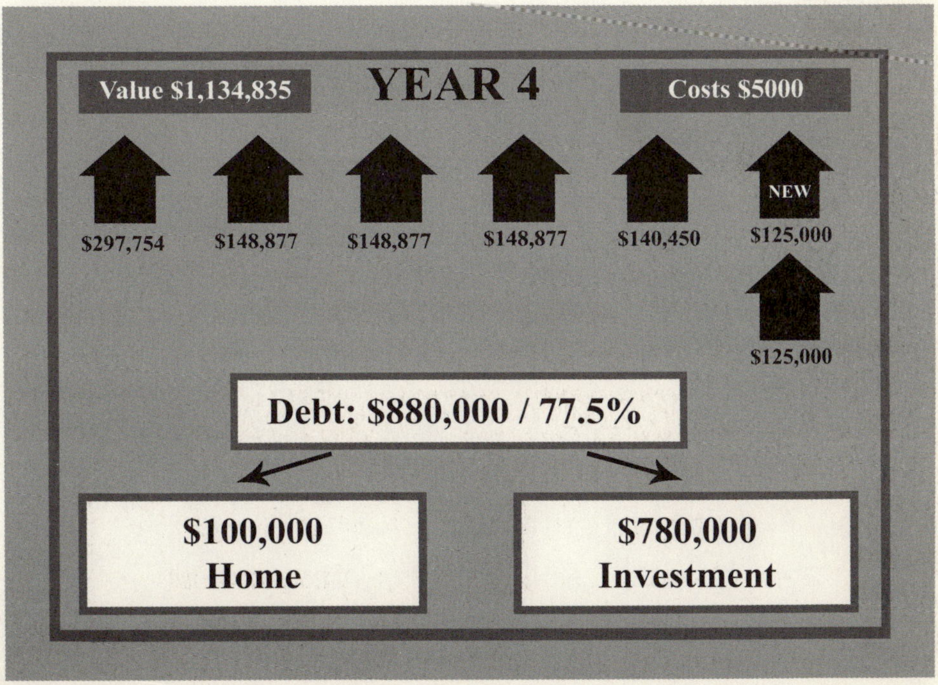
Value $1,134,835
YEAR 4
Costs $5000
NEW
$297,754
$148,877
$148,877
$148,877
$140,450
$125,000
$125,000
Debt: $880,000 / 77.5%
$100,000
Home
$780,000
Investment

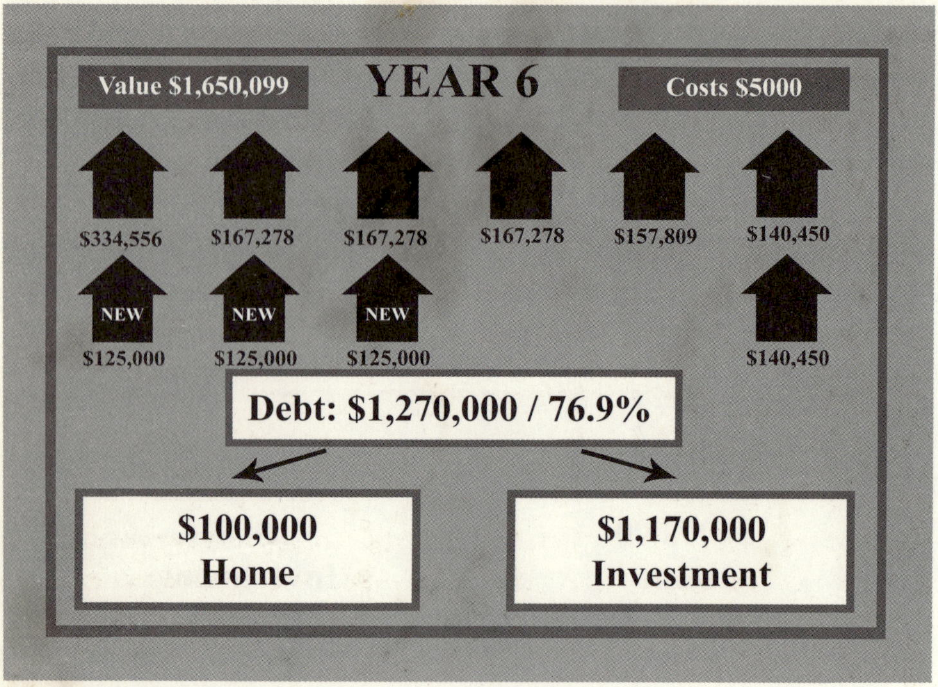
Value $1,650,099
YEAR 6
Costs $5000
$334,556
$167,278
$167,278
$167,278
$157,809
$140,450
NEW
$125,000
NEW
$125,000
NEW
$125,000
$140,450
Debt: $1,270,000 / 76.9%
$100,000
Home
$1,170,000
Investment

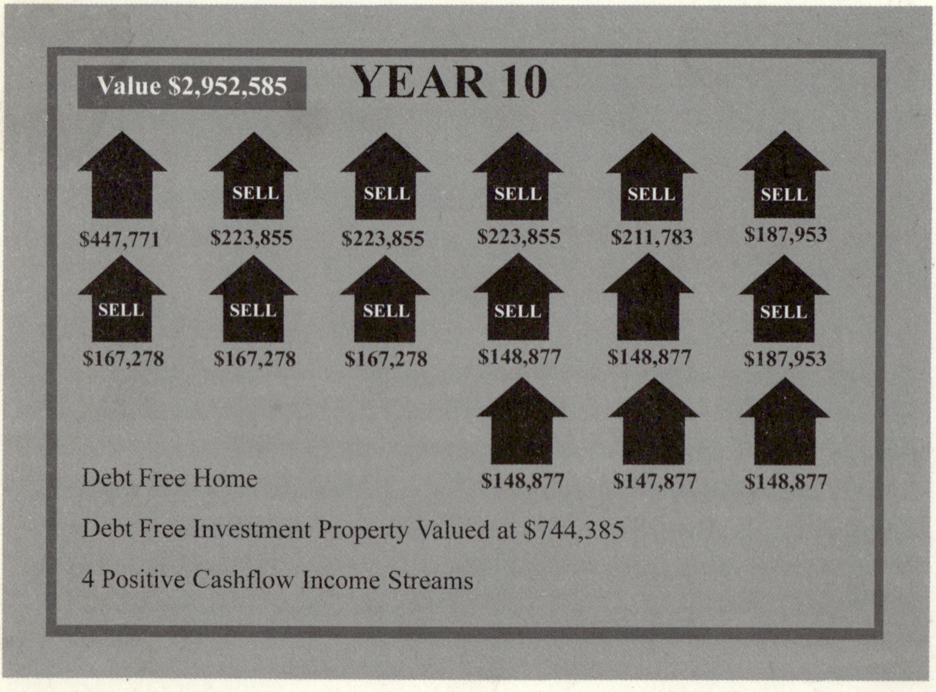
Value $2,952,585
YEAR 10
$447,771
SELL
$223,855
SELL
$223,855
SELL
$223,855
SELL
$211,783
SELL
$187,953
SELL
$167,278
SELL
$167,278
SELL
$167,278
SELL
$148,877
$148,877
SELL
$187,953
$148,877
$147,877
$148,877
Debt Free Home
Debt Free Investment Property Valued at $744,385
4 Positive Cashflow Income Streams

The concept of leverage can be seen by exploring the starting position illustrated in the previous diagrams where we are investing $150,000 in property. In this case we have a property worth $250,000 which means we have a loan to value ratio (LVR) of only 40% (very little leverage). If you did nothing your returns over 10 years would be:

Your own money invested	$150k
Property value today	$250k
Property value in 10 years @ 6% pa growth	$422k
Resulting increase in wealth	**$272k**

This beats the banks but is nothing exciting. ***Let's apply more leverage*** ... increase your mortgage to $200,000, which gives you $100,000 to use as a deposit to buy more property. You now purchase a further $500,000 worth of investment property, taking your total portfolio to $750,000 with 80% LVR. If you did nothing more your returns over the next 10 years would be:

Your own money invested	$150k
Property value today	$750k
Property value in 10 years @ 6% pa growth	$1.25 million
Resulting increase in wealth	**$1.1 million!**

By applying a little leverage we get two very different results based on the same starting position.

SUMMARY

Leverage is getting ever more with ever less. It is the key to wealth in real estate investing. Use lots of OPIUM (Other People's Inactive Underused Money). The more OPIUM you use, the better and more profitable your investment career will be. Leverage all your investments to the maximum.

Chapter 3

Finance

WAYS TO FUND YOUR PROPERTY DEALS

'If you always do what you have always done you will always get what you always got.'

— Phil Jones

Income to repay loans

There are many different types of lenders from which to source the finance you need both to buy a property, and to fund any renovations. These include banks, building societies, solicitors, credit unions and finance companies.

It can be a somewhat time-consuming task to find finance that works for you, so be prepared to clock up a few hours. In fact, it can sometimes take more time than finding the property itself.

When you are first starting out, your personal income will be taken into account in your ability to service the debt. This can really help if you are buying a property that is underperforming rent-wise, as your income can be used to make up the difference. However, once you have a few properties under your belt, your income will not come into the equation, so you will need the property to pay for itself if you are buying to hold. If you plan on selling quickly you will need to convince the bank that you can make the repayments until you sell the property for a profit and pay back the loan.

If you need to boost your income so that the bank will lend you money, you could always sell one of your other properties. The profit you make will be counted as part your income for that year and you will be looking much healthier from a lender's perspective. Your new higher income will indicate to them that you are indeed capable of making the loan repayments.

Organise your personal finances

It is important to get your personal finances in order first before you race off to the bank to borrow hundreds of thousands of dollars. Once you get your personal finances under control you can start making offers.

Your financial information

You need to know your net worth – you may be surprised how many people don't! To do this, calculate the net value of your assets minus your debt and you will have your net worth.

Work out exactly what your income and expenses are, as well as your assets and liabilities, as this is information your lender will need. Financiers will be much more impressed, and therefore willing to lend you money, if you can present this information in an orderly fashion. If you are vague and disorganised, a lender will most likely be less than keen to give you large amounts of money. The RevIQ Real Estate Software offers a range of forms, tools, calculators and schedules to help you organise your financial information. It is an essential tool for real estate investors for analysing deals and managing your finances. Get a free 14-day trial at www.reviq.com.

Prepare budgets

You will also need to do budgets to work out the money you need for the purchase of the property as well as any planned renovations.

Keep your finances as simple as you possibly can – all sorts of blunders can happen when things get overly complicated. At the very least make sure you understand all your financing arrangements fully.

Know your credit rating

You need to know what your credit rating is before you apply for finance. A company like Baycorp will have this information on file, and you are entitled to access it. Your credit file will show how many times you have applied for finance and every time you have defaulted. It will not say whether the finance you applied for was approved or declined, or whether you accepted it or not.

If you have applied for finance frequently, as is necessary when you are investing in property, your lender may be a little concerned, so it pays to know in advance so you can explain yourself!

Preparing to see the lender

Be very well prepared when you go to see a lender. You will need all the information you have about the property you are planning to purchase, as well as details about your own personal financial situation.

Lenders can be a little wary of properties that need work, especially the more run-down ones. They will, however, be impressed by thorough research, especially if it backs up your claims that the property will make a profit and their money will be safe. You need to show them also that you are in a position to make the loan payments.

Present all this information in a professional manner – that does not mean scribbled on the back of a paper napkin! If you just waltz in without documenting what you are planning to do to the property and how this will increase its value or rental income, the bank may baulk at the idea of you buying something that is so obviously in desperate need of renovations work. You need to make your lender feel confident about lending you money – or they are unlikely to give you a cent. You can use the RevIQ software for details on what to prepare for your financier. For more information go to www.reviq.com.

Getting finance

Get pre-approval for finance

Aim to get pre-approval for finance. Once you have your finance pre-approved by your lender, you can go and look for property. Just remember, pre-approval does not guarantee you will get the money – there may be something about the property the lender doesn't like which will mean your loan will not be approved.

Fees

To prevent any nasty surprises, get the fees for the loan in writing. Also remember that fees are negotiable. Almost every fee that any lender demands can be negotiated. You don't just have to lie down and accept them! Make sure you never pay fees up front before a loan is approved. You don't have to, and the lender is being very cheeky in asking!

Check the loan's features

You must check them because different loans will have different features, and you need to do some research to find out what will work best for you. Quite often you will find that a loan with low or no entry fees will not have features that are important to you, so check it out. (And remember our previous point that fees are negotiable!)

Many lenders will offer better deals to people who will be living in the property they want to borrow money for. This is one advantage of using the live-in-while-you-renovate strategy.

Shop around for interest rates

Always shop around for interest rates. It is a good idea to compare the interest rates various lenders are offering, so you know what is available, and so you can negotiate with a lender you like (see our point below). Interest rates can also differ between different branches of the same bank, so it pays to do your research. You can find this information on the Internet, or if you are using a mortgage broker they will be able to compare rates for you.

Believe it or not, interest rates are negotiable too. Do your research so you know what the other lenders are offering and use this information to negotiate. The lender may disguise a reduction in interest rate as a decrease in, or waiver of, fees, but over the term of the loan you will have to pay less so it equates to a lower interest rate.

State your intentions, even if you change them later

State your position at the time when applying for finance – and know you can change your mind later. For example, you can say when you apply for the loan that you are going to rent the property out so that the rental income will be taken into account with regard to your ability to service the loan. If you happen to change your mind after you have received the money and decide to sell the property after renovating, it is no skin off the lender's nose, as long as you make the required payments until you sell and discharge the loan.

Remember, however, not to intentionally pull the wool over your lender's eyes, as you will be caught out (especially if you can't make payments) and your credit rating will be – to put it bluntly – stuffed.

Avoid the one-bank trap

A bank manager's goal is to keep you as a valued customer and to stop you from going to other banks. However, it is much easier to borrow $1 million from five banks than it is from one, so don't be sucked in by their overtures. If you stay with one bank all your collateral property will be with them. You will find yourself stuck and unable to buy more property when they have lent you the maximum amount they are comfortable with.

If you are with a great bank but have reached your maximum borrowing limit with them, ask if they will make more loans available to you if you discharge some of the debt to other lenders. (If it is such a great bank, the answer should be yes!)

Loan strategies

Have loans maturing at different times

Have the loans for different properties maturing at different times, so that you spread your risk over time. If they all mature at once, and it just happens to be a time when the interest rates are experiencing a temporary high, you could be in for a bit of strife!

Personal guarantees for loans

All loans will require some sort of personal guarantee. However, you can limit this to the debt level, rather than an unlimited level. It is best not to request this when applying for the loan, though, as your lender may have some resistance to the idea. You don't want them to think that perhaps they shouldn't be lending you the money in the first place. Instead, your lawyer can approach the bank once the documents have been received. The bank will be much more agreeable to limiting the guarantee to the loan amount if it is approached from a legal perspective.

Borrow up to 80% of purchase price

As a general rule, borrow up to 80% of the purchase price on every property you buy. (You may be able to borrow up to 95% or even 100% on your first purchase, but loans above 80% will sometimes require you to pay a low-equity fee.)

Avoid using equity in one property as security for another

Avoid using equity in one property as security over another. This is a trap many people fall into. Rather than using the equity in one property as security over another, you are better to take the equity out as cash and put that into the next property. If you don't, you can find yourself getting into all sorts of difficulties and restricting your options, because when you sell one property, the profit will have to be used to reduce the debt of the other one.

Use revolving credit

Take advantage of revolving-credit facilities – otherwise known as a line-of-credit loan. This means that you can access any extra equity whenever you like, so you can fund your next purchase. For example, if you have a property worth $400,000 and you are able to borrow up to 80%, the amount available to you will be $320,000. If you only use $200,000 of this for your mortgage, you have the extra $120,000 to play with. If you then put this on a revolving line of credit you can use it to fund your next property purchase(s).

The great thing is you can borrow the balance that you will need from any lender – it doesn't have to be from the same bank with which you have the redraw facility. Line-of-credit loans are very flexible – you can add new property as security, and every time you have a new valuation, you will be able to add the extra equity to the fund. Although they generally have a slightly higher interest rate than other loans, you will save a lot of money by not having to pay fees when you discharge the loan at the time you sell or refinance.

Because you need to have a valuation done on your property in order to get a loan, you should apply for line-of-credit loans at the same time as you apply for your mortgage. That way you will avoid having to value the property twice, once for each loan.

The option of vendor finance

Vendor financing, where finance is provided by the vendor, is a great option, because you can customise your loan payments and negotiate great terms (e.g. low interest rate, no pre-payment penalty, long term). You will generally need to have a motivated vendor to make this work, however, and they will often want a large down payment. You may on the odd occasion be able to get 100% financing from a vendor, but you will most likely have to sacrifice some of your profit to do so.

If you are going to use vendor financing, make sure you have worked out in advance how you are going to pay the vendor and refinance at the end of the term of the loan (which can sometimes be quite short). You must do this even if you are planning on selling the property, in case there are no buyers about at the time. (This is covered in more depth later in the book in Part Three, Chapter 24.)

So you need 100% – other sources of finance

In the event that you do not have enough money for a deposit and vendor financing is not going to work, you will need 100% financing to be able to buy a property. There are quite a few options available to you if you need to do this – just be a little creative! If the option you do choose has a high interest rate attached to it, make sure you factor this into your costings and repay the loan as fast as possible.

If the bank will not loan you 100%, you could consider selling something, such as your car, to create the required additional funds.

Credit cards

Credit cards are also a possibility. You can use your credit card not to buy a house, but for your deposit. Be very sure that you can make the monthly payments before you decide on this course of action.

Private investors

A private investor could be another source of finance if you can't persuade the bank that you are a good risk. A private investor may even just lend you enough for a deposit, which may be all you need. Also friends and family, if they cannot lend you the hard cash, may be willing to offer you a guarantee or provide collateral so you are able to get a loan. They may also be generous enough to give you the money for your deposit or, in exceptional circumstances, the money for the whole property. Speak nicely to them!

Partnerships and joint ventures

Partnerships and joint venture partnerships (which are similar but different) are another way of getting finance if the bank is not interested in you on your own. Either one can provide a means of completing a project that you couldn't do by yourself. Partnerships generally have unlimited risk for the partners, whereas in joint ventures the risk can be restricted. In a partnership each partner needs to find their own finance, but in a joint venture financing can be arranged together.

You will need to set up the structure and agreements for either type of partnership very carefully, detailing who is responsible for what, how the profit will be divided and what to do if one partner is not pulling their weight or wants out. Use a lawyer to draw up the agreement and to give you advice on which sort of partnership will suit your needs, and the needs of your partner(s), best.

Partnerships and joint ventures not only provide the extra finance you may need, they are also a great way for people of like minds but different skills to work together. For example, you may provide the renovations skill and your partner the money. A partnership is also an excellent way to go if your partner is more experienced than you, because they will be able to guide you through the process and you will learn a huge amount while gaining valuable experience. Use partners for a single project at a time – it is unlikely that you will want to be joined at the hip for life!

Second mortgages

As mentioned, if you are making your first property purchase, you may even be able to borrow the entire purchase price from the bank, if you meet its criteria. Generally if you borrow over 80% you will be required to pay lender's mortgage insurance, so be sure to add this into your costings.

However, if it is not your first property (or you don't fit the bank's desired mould), family and friends are not forthcoming and the other options are not open to you, you will need to consider a second mortgage. You can sometimes get these from the same bank with which you have your first mortgage, or you may need to go to another lender, such as a finance company.

Second mortgages are expensive because the interest rates are high (though not as high as your credit card – bear this in mind), so make sure you have one for only a short period of time. A second mortgage may be enough to tide you over while you complete your renovations, after which you will be able to sell for a profit, or refinance on the new increased value and get rid of the loan.

Please note, however, that lenders are more likely to give finance to people who are committed to a property. In their eyes, commitment means putting in some of your own money. Just thought we'd better let you know in case you were planning on 100% financing everything!

Refinancing

Remember, you will be able to refinance your loan every time you get a new valuation for the properties you are holding on to – as long as it is higher than the last one! You should get your first new valuation done after you have completed your renovations, and then probably every year after that. If your original loan was for 80% of the property's value, each time you revalue you should be able to refinance to 80% of the new improved value. Then you can use this extra money to fund more property purchases – and the empire building will have begun!

If you have financed your property other than through a normal lending institution (e.g. partnership, very kind and trusting father, private mortgage) and you want to hold on to it rather than sell, you should be able to refinance on the new valuation (especially if the rent has increased to cover the outgoings) from a conventional lender.

Recycle your deposit

Work to recycle your deposit. (By recycling we mean that the increase in value of a property will allow you to refinance and use the new equity as a deposit for the next property.) The fastest way we know of to recycle your deposit is to add value to a property with cosmetic renovations. Cosmetic renovations are by far the quickest and easiest, and may allow you to get your deposit back out in a month or so – which by property standards is pretty darn fast work! Make sure you take before and after photos to show the bank so they will be impressed and keen to refinance the loan for you.

Beware of thinking that you are adding value through renovations when you are really not doing anything of the sort. This is where doing thorough research before you launch full blast into a project will really pay off. For example, you may think that adding a few rooms and turning a house into a rent-by-the-room property is an excellent idea because you will be able to get more rent. If you haven't done your research properly, what you won't know is that the bank will most likely see this as student accommodation and they will not consider you have added value from a lending point of view. What this means is that you won't be able to top up your mortgage to fund the next project because they won't give you any more money. Research is essential!

Mortgage brokers

Good leverage of your time

Use a mortgage broker unless you are experienced at finding finance, or you enjoy the challenge. It can be a complicated and tiring process finding the funds you require, and the knock-backs can be disheartening. A mortgage broker can take all this stress away from you, as it is their job to find the finance for you. They know where to look and have great bargaining power with the banks. You can tell a mortgage broker everything about your situation and they will know how much to tell lenders and, more importantly, when. (If you tell the bank far too much at the beginning, which many people are inclined to do, it can result in a resounding 'No' to your loan request.)

All this can make a huge difference to your success rate and go a long way to reducing your tension levels! Finding finance can be incredibly time-consuming, so a mortgage broker can be very good leverage of your time.

Finding a broker

If you are going to use a mortgage broker, they will need to be good at what they do. You will want to find one who has been in business for at least five years and who has a great deal of experience with investors like you. Often, but not always, you will find that small- to medium-sized companies are better than one-man-bands or huge firms. Find out how they evaluate loans and if they have relationships with all the major lenders.

One of the best ways to find a good broker is to ask other (successful!) investors for referrals. You don't have to stick to just one mortgage broker and you are not obliged to accept money they find for you if you don't think it's a good deal. Don't be coerced into signing an agreement with them that states otherwise.

We highly recommend finding a quality mortgage broker who will work very closely with you and who understands property investment. Check out the recommended suppliers page at www.richmastery.com. The brokers on the Richmastery site are familiar with investors' needs, the strategies in this book and how best to structure your lending to assist you to achieve the best possible result.

Having a great broker in your team can make you a lot of money so treat them well if they do a good job. A good way of judging whether a mortgage broker will be good for you or not is if, when you call them, you can talk to them at least 80% of the time. A good broker will let you know about the best products in the market and will offer you advice on the possibilities of restructuring your portfolio borrowings. A good connection is necessary with this member of your team – a point that we cannot stress enough.

SUMMARY

It is important to get your personal finances in order first before approaching the bank to borrow hundreds of thousands of dollars for real estate investment.

Before meeting with your mortgage broker or your preferred lender make sure you are organised and that you have all the information they will require to decide whether to loan you the money. This will show them that you are serious, prepared and have worked out that you can service the loan.

Make sure you find a great mortgage broker who understands what you are trying to achieve. Using a mortgage broker is highly recommended and they will save you a lot of time and money through their contacts and knowledge of the industry. They will become a very important part of your power team.

Remember that all terms are negotiable, and that you should get the mortgage that fits your strategy.

Aim to get pre-approval of finance before you make offers.

Follow the different strategies outlined above to obtain a high loan-to-value ratio on your investment portfolio – leverage is important for a healthy portfolio and long-term success.

Chapter 4

Types of mortgages

CHOOSE ONE THAT SUITS YOUR STRATEGY

'Borrow money when you can get it, not when you need it.'

— CEO of American Airlines

Interest-only vs. capital-repayment mortgages

Firstly, let's explain the difference between interest-only mortgages and capital-repayment mortgages. With capital-repayment mortgages your monthly payment will be divided into two pots. The first pot is the one where you pay the bank the interest at the rate that you agree when you take on the loan. The second pot is where you repay the capital that you originally borrowed.

In an interest-only mortgage you only have one pot, the one where you pay interest to the bank. Interest-only payments are significantly smaller than capital-repayment ones, but in an interest-only mortgage at the end of the term you will still owe the same amount that you first borrowed.

Advantages of an interest-only loan

Why would you take an interest-only mortgage? The main reason is for tax purposes since you can offset the total amount of the mortgage payment against the rental income you obtain. On a capital-repayment mortgage you can only offset one of the pots – the capital being repaid cannot be offset. Another reason is to get as much cash monthly as possible out of your investments and having smaller mortgage repayments will really help out. By reducing your repayments you are creating cashflow, not getting a liability.

Most people who invest in property (including us) opt for this kind of mortgage because our intention is not to repay the loan. We know that historically, on average, a property doubles in value every seven years, and once a property has done this there will be several options, such as refinancing or selling. When you are not too tight on monthly cashflow you can do more investing and this will give you more capital growth, which is where you make your money.

Having properties cost you money will mean that your borrowing ability will be limited very quickly. On the other hand, if you buy cashflow properties (i.e. properties where the mortgage interest repayments and other expenses are less than the total rents you receive) your borrowing ability will actually increase.

We recommend you balance a number of positive-cashflow properties for every one negative-cashflow property. The only reason you would buy a negative-cashflow property is because it is a high capital growth property, i.e. you expect to create quite a lot of equity from owning it through capital growth.

Loan-to-value ratio (LVR)

Let's explain the concept of loan-to-value ratio (LVR). This is the amount the bank will lend you on the evaluated market price of the property. As investors, you want the LVR to be as high as possible so that you can use the concept of leverage in your favour. The banks will be more inclined to give you a higher LVR if you have capital to cover the payment of these mortgages. You can show that you have capital with several tools:

- A well-paid job.
- Accounts statements if you are self-employed.
- Rental income from other properties, or equity (revalorisation) from other properties.
- You can also form a partnership with somebody else who has the earnings so that the banks will see this as a security on the loan.

Fixed or variable interest rates?

Lastly, let's talk about the eternal dilemma: fixed or variable interest rates on a mortgage? Let us explain what they mean first.

A fixed-rate mortgage will keep the same interest rate throughout the period that the mortgage is fixed for. A variable-rate mortgage will increase or decrease depending on the base rate. How do you know then what will happen with the base rate in the future? Nobody knows this, so trying to guess is like gambling. If you do not particularly like risks, you will be better off with a fixed mortgage, and the opposite will be true if you enjoy paragliding and jumping off bridges with a piece of bendy cord tied around your ankles.

Fixed rates – break costs

Generally, fixed rates are lower than the floating rates, and that is unusual as in most parts of the world it is the other way around. A break cost, also known as a redemption penalty, is the penalty that you have to pay the lender if you repay a fixed-term mortgage early. Break costs can be quite high. This is the only reason you should not get a fixed mortgage, just in case the base rate drops and you are stuck with the old rate for a while. But if the numbers work at the fixed rate, who cares!

Fixed rates – certainty

Who cares whether the base rate drops or not? If it drops low enough you may even consider paying the penalty to take advantage of the drop. It is definitely a very small down side to obtain a mortgage where you will know the exact amount you will need to repay each month in interest for a fixed period and can base your figures around this.

There is even a fixed mortgage that will not go up but will go down if the base rate drops (a capped-rate loan). In Australia and New Zealand the base rate tends to decrease or increase slowly so that it can be more in line with the rest of the Western world. In Europe the base rate is below 3% and you can get mortgages for under 3.4%. In the United States the base rate is even lower and in England it's about 5%, but still lower than Australia and New Zealand.

In general, it is best to get fixed interest rate loans, especially if you are planning to hold on to a property – this way your loan repayments are the same for the period of the loan and won't give you a nasty surprise by increasing to the point that the property is no longer profitable. For this reason fix the loan for as long as you can.

Variable loans when renovating

When you are renovating a property it can sometimes be to your advantage to use variable rate loans – but only for a short time. This will be the case if the variable interest rate is lower than the fixed interest rate. Lenders will also frequently offer a 'teaser' rate, lower than the market interest rate, for a short period. So, if you are going to sell or refinance after your renovations (we are talking quick renos here, not the live-in two-year variety!), take advantage of any lower rates offered by a variable-rate loan while you make your improvements

Check before you start that there are no penalty fees for discharging the loan if you are going to sell the property immediately after the renovations. If you find you will have to pay early-repayment penalties for repaying a fixed-rate mortgage before the term is up, use a variable interest rate loan so you can avoid the fees, as they can be quite hefty.

Interest-only for investment properties

For investment properties, interest-only loans are the way to go because the interest you pay is tax deductible. (Principal payments are not.) Interest-only loans are generally only available for short periods (e.g. up to five years), after which you will need to refinance. They also mean your outgoings are less than if you were forking out to reduce the principal as well (in which case it would be hard to find investment property where the rent would cover the payments you would have to make).

If you are planning to sell straight away, you may be able to take advantage of a lower interest rate on a longer term principal and interest loan, but, as in the point that follows, make sure you are not going to be penalised when you sell the property and pay the loan back.

Low-documentation (low-doc) loans

A low-documentation (low-doc) loan is a mortgage. However, these loans require less paper work and have less stringent borrowing requirements.

Less paper work

Low-doc loans are available through many financiers, including some banks. They are ideal for when you fall outside the bank's normal lending criteria (e.g. if you are self-employed, which can send some bank managers scurrying for cover). Basically you do not have to provide documentation as proof of income, only a declaration.

Lenders will not require much paper work, if any. They believe what you tell them your earnings are expected to be. Remember, though, not to lie about what you expect to make. Just plan well how many properties you need to sell or source during the year to come up with enough cashflow to be able to obtain your next mortgage.

Interest rates competitive

Sometimes the interest rate on a low-doc loan may be a little higher (up to 1%) than you could get with a traditional bank, but they are becoming more and more competitive. If you are unable to get finance from a traditional lender, these types of loans can be brilliant when you are investing. Even if the interest rate is higher, it is a much better option than not being able to borrow money to finance your property purchase at all.

The interest rates and LVR ratios are becoming increasingly similar to main bank interest rates and LVR ratios. This makes low-doc loans extremely sexy to investors. If you have ever obtained a mortgage, you know just how much hassle obtaining and providing the documentation can be. This mortgage product will be a great time saver that has the potential to transform your investing potential.

Do your research

Low-doc loans are becoming more and more popular. Get a good broker who can inform you of the current lenders, rates and interest rates. Always do your figures and invest wisely – if you do, low-doc loans can save you time and push your investing career to new heights.

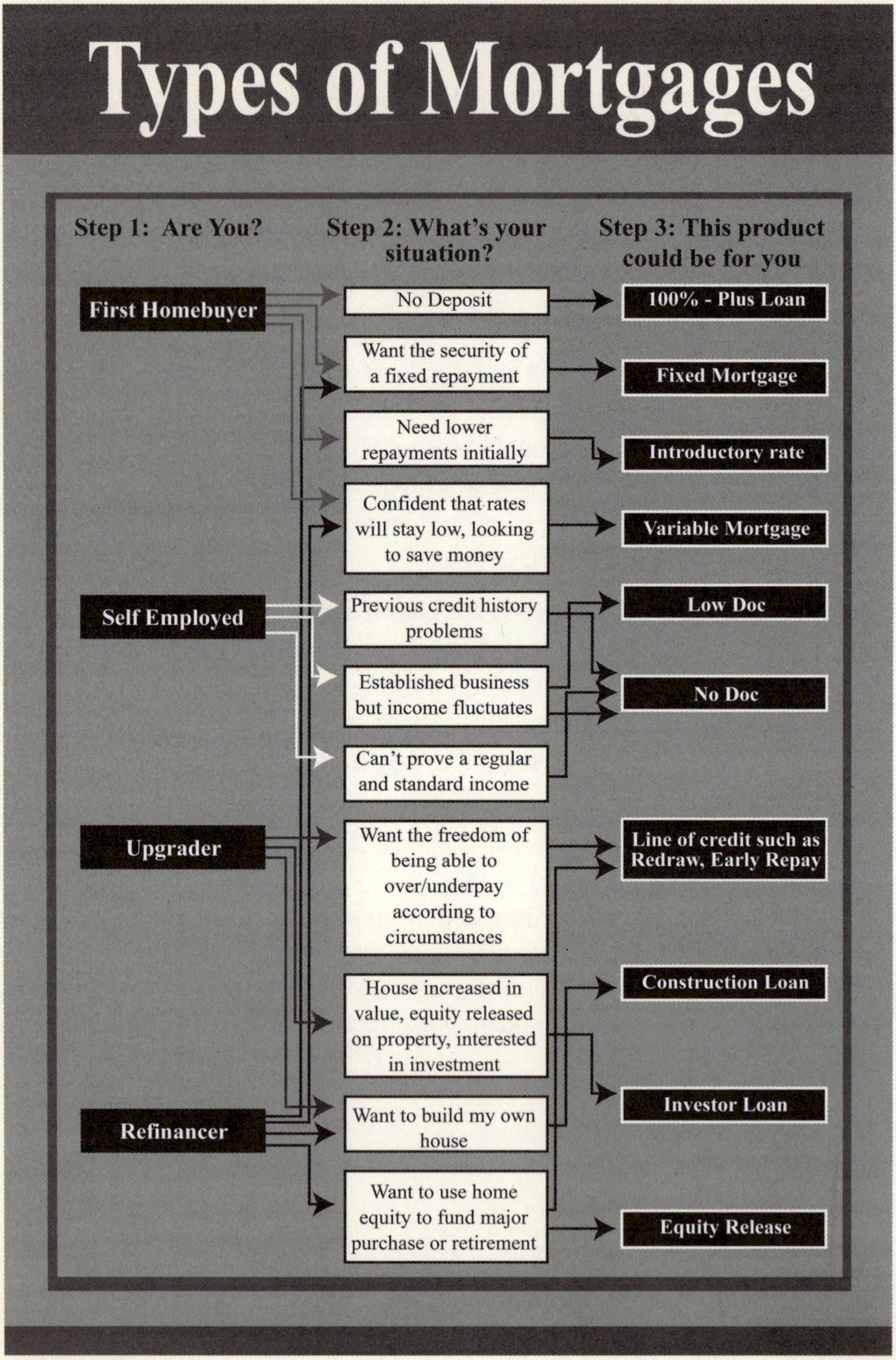
Types of Mortgages
Step 1: Are You?
Step 2: What's your situation?
Step 3: This product could be for you
First Homebuyer
Self Employed
Upgrader
Refinancer
No Deposit
Want the security of a fixed repayment
Need lower repayments initially
Confident that rates will stay low, looking to save money
Previous credit history problems
Established business but income fluctuates
Can't prove a regular and standard income
Want the freedom of being able to over/underpay according to circumstances
House increased in value, equity released on property, interested in investment
Want to build my own house
Want to use home equity to fund major purchase or retirement
100% - Plus Loan
Fixed Mortgage
Introductory rate
Variable Mortgage
Low Doc
No Doc
Line of credit such as Redraw, Early Repay
Construction Loan
Investor Loan
Equity Release

SUMMARY

Understanding the different mortgage products available and being able to negotiate the right terms on your mortgage is integral to success in real estate investing. A good mortgage broker can lead the way with this, educating you about different products and helping you find a mortgage that fits your strategy and one that you are comfortable with.

Chapter 5

Buy and hold

UNDERSTANDING THE STRATEGY'S POWER

'The policy of being too cautious is the greatest risk of all.'

— Jawaharlal Nehru, Indian Prime Minister 1947–64

Buy and hold for capital growth

The meaning of the buy-and-hold concept is often misinterpreted. We use a buy-and-hold strategy to maximise the amount of equity growth we make while minimising the risk associated with the investment. So we use a buy-and-hold strategy for capital growth and not for cashflow as it is often interpreted.

Most people who invest with a buy-and-hold strategy do so to pocket the difference between their rental income and their mortgage repayments. Some investors use buy-and-hold investments as a way to replace their salary. This means you keep purchasing buy-and-hold properties until the difference between rents and mortgages makes you the same amount per week as your salary does in your full-time job.

If this was the only way to replace your income, most investors would give up because they would need to buy many properties or would have to find extraordinarily cheap deals. As property prices have increased dramatically in the last few years and rents have not increased by the same amount, yields have come down drastically and the ability to buy enough positive-cashflow property to replace your income has become very difficult to achieve. To produce $35,000 worth of after-tax cashflow each year you would need to purchase at least $1.5 million worth of property averaging at least a 9% yield.

This main reason we purchase buy-and-hold investments is for the long-term capital growth they will provide. The cashflow is the bonus.

Capital growth and property cycles

Capital growth is the increase in value that a property will experience which is usually measured using percentages and on a yearly basis. On average, property prices double every seven years. This means that on average you can expect around a 10% increase in capital growth yearly.

As in any other investment you will have good years and bad years. Good years will be more abundant and the rises will also be higher than the losses. This is well shown in the graph below.

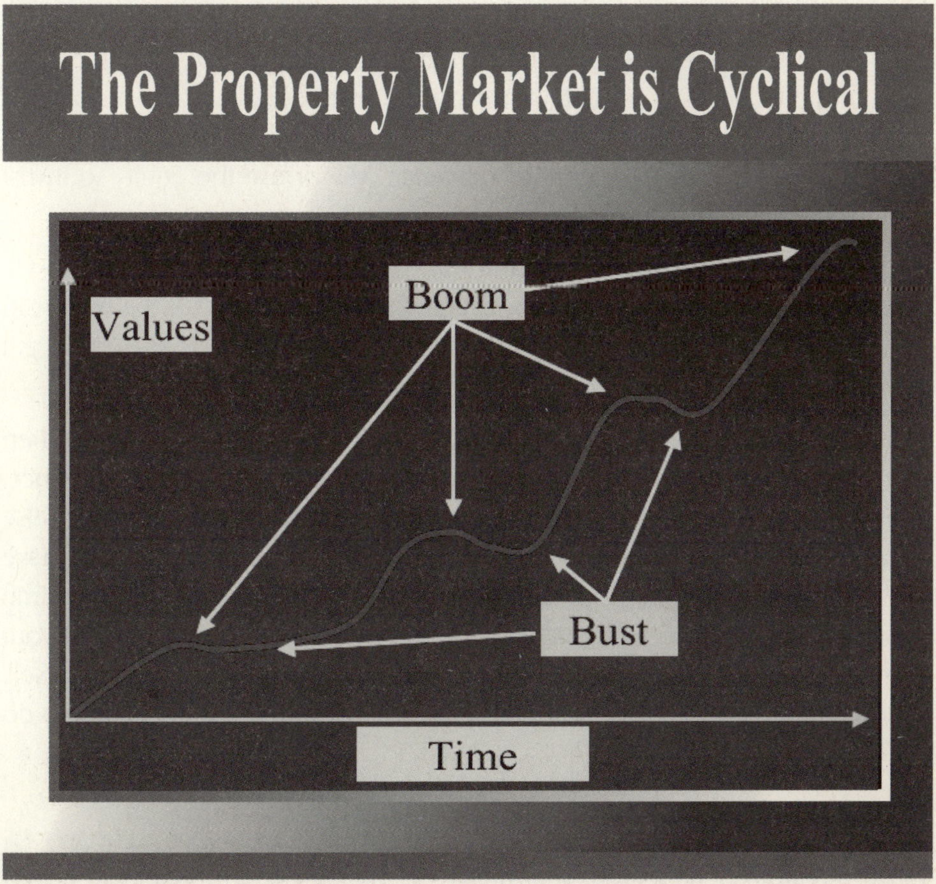

Property is an appreciating asset unlike cars, computers and other stuff that loses a lot of its value as soon as you take it out of the shop and which continues to lose value over time. Property will gain value with time.

For this reason, when you are trying to look at the profit you will make, you have to take into consideration this average capital growth. The positive difference between rent and mortgage payments is only the cherry on top of the cake. The real value of this positive difference is that because of it you will never have to sell the property because someone else is paying for the mortgage you acquired.

Cashflow vs. capital gain

You will find a lot of properties out there that pay for themselves and give you a little extra on the side. Remember that you will incur maintenance expenses and that little extra on the side could become a nothing on the side. Over time, property prices will continue to go up, as they have done historically, and so will rents. It is the property value increase that will make you some real money, as you will then be able to refinance, sell or use the equity to invest somewhere else.

The cashflow that you obtain through a buy-and-hold strategy is just a mattress that you build up and you can always fall back on it. What we mean is that someone else is paying for the debt that you acquire when you get the mortgage.

The only time that you can lose money in property investing is when you *have to* sell. The verb 'have to' has to be emphasised in this sentence. If you do not have to sell and property prices go down but someone else is paying for your debt, you are not really losing any money. You just have to wait until property prices go up again as they have always done over time through history. On the other hand, if property prices take a small dip and your mortgage payments are not covered by your rents you may be forced to sell, in which case you may take a big financial hit. This is why it is important to do the figures before you buy.

Compounding growth example

If you buy a property portfolio worth $1 million with an average yield higher than 9%, you will be making about $25,000 per year after tax for the next five years. This will give you a grand total of $125,000 after-tax income at the end of five years.

- Let's say the same $1 million property portfolio will increase by $70,000 in the first year, a modest annual capital growth rate of around 7%.
- In year two, with the same 7% annual capital growth you will obtain $74,900 in increased value. When added to the $70,000 capital growth obtained in year one this already surpasses the $125,000 you would have obtained after five years of cashflow.
- In year three, you will get $80,430 in capital growth on the same portfolio. You can see that the compounding growth of your portfolio will make a massive difference within a short few years.
- Year four will provide you with $85,773 in capital growth.
- In year five your portfolio will increase a further $91,777.

That is a grand total for the five years of $402,880. That is an increase of over 40% in your initial property portfolio value in five years. When you compare this to the 12.5% that you will get in cashflow you are making over 300% more on capital growth. This should be enough to show you just how powerful capital growth is in relation to cashflow.

SUMMARY

The real reason we buy and hold property is to gain from the compounding capital growth. The cashflow is the icing on the cake and a safety blanket. Remember the only time you can lose money in property investing is when you have to sell. If you do not ever have to sell because you have purchased property with positive cashflow, someone else is taking care of the mortgage and expenses.

Chapter 6

Sourcing agents

How they can save you time and money

'Never, ever, ever buy on emotion; numbers are all that matter.'

— Phil Jones

What is a sourcing agent?

A sourcing agent or finder is simply a person who will pass on a property deal to you. You can become a sourcing agent by getting hot deals for other property investors with the knowledge you will gain after reading this book.

Sourcing deals is a great way of getting involved in real estate investing when you do not have much capital to get started. You will get to know people and you will get to work out great strategies that you will be able to implement once you start investing in property yourself. There are a lot of people who only source property and don't invest or hold property long term. Remember, if you want to generate a passive income stream, sourcing property for others will not provide this for you.

Who can be a sourcing agent?

Anyone can be a sourcing agent. You may decide to be a sourcing agent for other investors. Richmastery.com offers some great opportunities in this area. If you are looking for a sourcing agent, the sorts of people who might become sourcing agents to help you find property can include the following:

- Your parents or other family members who will probably know people in their neighbourhood who are thinking of selling their property.

- A solicitor who deals with inheritance issues.
- Friends who know other friends thinking of selling.
- Neighbours in the areas you are targeting.
- Estate agents who know what you are looking for (remember that estate agents by law cannot take any sourcing fees; they get paid only by the vendor).
- Accountants who know when customers are going to sell property.
- Mortgage brokers who know when clients are applying for mortgages and are selling property.
- Bank managers who know of other clients who are in trouble and are about to go into mortgagee sale.
- Anyone else who is prepared to give you valuable information for the purpose of you finding hot deals.

Sourcing agent fees

If you are the sourcing agent you will be able to charge different fees depending on the service you provide and how good the deal is. If you just let people know of someone interested in selling their property, you will not be able to charge a lot – say around 0.5% of the value of the property. However, if you do the negotiation and work out a strategy for them, you will be able to charge at least double this fee, at a rate of around 1% to 2% of the property value. These are prices that we have charged and paid and which are reasonable for the amount of work involved in looking for these deals.

We always pay our sourcing agents after we complete the deal, never before. Completing means when the purchase transaction goes unconditional. Otherwise you can run into problems with people taking their sourcing fees too quickly and then at the last minute the whole deal breaks down and is lost.

Sourcing agents can be a great asset in your investing career so do not be cheap with them when they get you a great deal. Just remember that you will be making way more money than the small sourcing fee you give them. Do not look at the price of the shovel when you are digging for gold.

Passing on deals

You will probably find some deals that will not fit your strategy at the time. Don't let them go – try to pass them on to another fellow investor who will be happy to pay you a good fee to get a property that will fit their portfolio. You can pass on the deals that the sourcing agent passes you to other investors for either an extra fee or an IOU. They will then hopefully be compelled in turn to pass you back a good deal when they can't buy or if it doesn't fit their portfolio at the time.

Please read the Quick Flip Strategy explained in Part Three, Chapter 16 to get more details on sourcing properties.

Warning

The real estate industry is heavily regulated and sourcing agents that do not carefully follow very tight criteria and mode of operation expose themselves to significant risk and litigation as they may be deemed to operate as an unlicensed real estate agent. This is not want you want!

To reduce your risk and take advantage of this wealth strategy, consider partnering with larger reputable companies like Richmastery Ltd.

Become a Richmastery sourcing agent

A key part of the Richmastery business is sourcing and negotiating property purchases, which are then offered to our customers on our website, www.richmastery.com. We have a rapidly increasing customer base numbering tens of thousands of customers.

Richmastery sourcing agents are known as Property Researchers. These people earn a fee for every property they source that is sold, plus they benefit from the systems, expertise, coaching and national brand power of Richmastery and its client base.

Of course, if you want to be an active investor, what better way is there to find and keep the best deals for your own portfolio? There may also be the opportunity to participate in or facilitate other Richmastery events and activities such as Personal Property or Business Mentoring Groups, Games Nights, Software Demonstration nights and other great activities from time to time. If you are interested in becoming a Richmastery Property Researcher and want more information, check out the 'Opportunities' section on our website, www.richmastery.com.

SUMMARY

As you can see by the examples given in this chapter, you can and should have sourcing agents working for you. You can benefit from being a sourcing agent and from having sourcing agents passing deals on to you. You will become a sourcing agent if you value money more than your own time; in other words, when you have to trade time to make money. On the other hand, you will use sourcing agents when you want to save time by paying money to others to find deals for you. This second option of getting others to source deals on your behalf is the one that successful property investors use. Successful property investors know that they can always create more money but they cannot make any more time.

Chapter 7

Investment formulas

WAYS TO MEASURE YOUR PROFIT

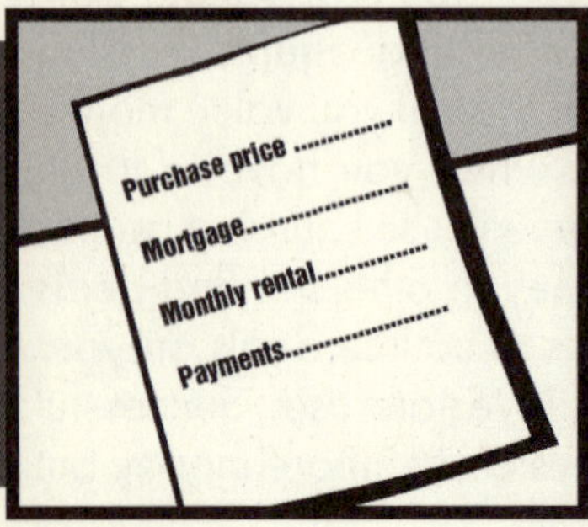

'An error doesn't become a mistake until you refuse to correct it.'

— Anonymous

Not so useful formulas

There are quite a few ways of measuring prospective earnings in an investment. Most of them are a waste of time but we will still discuss them so that you can tell the difference between an investor and a person who likes their calculator just a little too much. Let's go by a very simple thought: Show me the money! You should just want to know how much money you will be making monthly and yearly, and the rest is unimportant.

Gross yield

This is the king of useless formulas:

Gross yield = Purchase price ÷ Rents receivable (annual)

(This is usually expressed as a percentage, e.g. \$100,000 ÷ \$15,000 = 6.6%)

Who cares what the gross yield percentage is? It tells you nothing about your property-management costs and other expenses and how much you will make out of the deal. An 8% yield can be great if you get a mortgage at a 3% interest rate but it would be suicidal if you were to pay 10% interest on it.

More useful formulas

Net yield

The net yield formula is much more useful because it takes into account your expenses. Instead of just taking the receivable rents figure you subtract all the property expenses, such as mortgage interest, council rates, insurance, property management and maintenance etc., so that you get a much more realistic percentage that you can really use to compare with other properties.

Cash on cash return

Here are a couple of very useful formulas that we always use:

Cash on cash return = Cash out of deal ÷ Cash into deal x 100

(e.g. $200,000 ÷ 150,000 = 1.33 x 100 = 133%)

This is the reason why no-money-down deals are so great, because if you divide something by 0 you will end up with an infinite cash on cash return. Are you excited about infinite returns?

You can express this as a percentage (as above) and on a yearly basis, but it is even more practical in this format:

Cash on cash return = Cash out – Cash in

(e.g. $200,000 – $150,000 = $50,000)

This formula is good, practical and it follows the KISS principle (Keep It Simple Stupid). Property investing is not rocket science, is it? By the way, what happens if you do not put any cash into the deal? You get an infinite return, and that is good.

Monthly cashflow

Use this simple formula to calculate real monthly cashflow.

Monthly cash flow = Rent – mortgage payment – 15% of rent – rates and regional council rates

We will now look at some of the component parts of this formula.

- **Monthly rental:** You usually under-calculate the amount of rent you will obtain monthly because you assume that the month has only four weeks. Use this formula to come up with the real number:

  Monthly rent = (weekly rent x 52) ÷ 12

- **Interest-only mortgage:** Calculating an interest-only mortgage monthly payment is very easy:

  Mortgage payment = (Amount of mortgage you have x interest rate you pay) ÷ 12

- **Property management and maintenance fees:** Remember to subtract 10–15% of the rent (this is usually 8 or 9% for property management plus around 1–7% for maintenance, depending on your risk level and the age of the property). We make this deduction because we use property managers, and to allow for extra things going wrong. Remember that letting agent fees are fully tax deductible and that they do a professional job 24 hours a day, 365 days a year. They also have more experience than you do in checking prospective tenants.

Leveraging

Some of you will decide to manage your properties yourselves to save the money, but before you do this, ask this question – how much do you make an hour? If you make over $40 an hour, why not get a property manager to take care of your properties? Then you won't have to deal with any tenants, unless of course you really like managing your own properties and thrive on it.

Here's another point. Do you clean your house? If you do and you make more than $15 an hour you are wasting your time and you should be getting a cleaner to do it for you. There are lots of people that we meet in our seminars that tell us that they cannot afford to invest in property because they do not have the time. The real issue is that they have very poor time-management skills and that is the reason they struggle to become successful investors. The cleaner example should be applied to anything you do in life. If you can pay someone to do it for you while you produce more money in any other way you will start growing exponentially. Give it a go; it is a completely empowering experience.

Basic calculation formula

This is a simple but accurate formula to use when you are working out whether or not a property is a good investment. (Note pcm = per calendar month.)

Purchase price	$100,000
Mortgage (80%)	$80,000
Monthly rental	$800 pcm
Payments @ 7.5% (interest only): 80,000 x 0.075 = $6000 ÷ 12 =	$500 pcm
Other costs	$XXX
Letting & management fees	$80 pcm
MOE (Monthly operating expenses)	$40 pcm
(Seller finance?)	
Net cash flow	+$180

You will be able to calculate monthly mortgage payments almost in a heart beat as soon as you do a few of these calculations.

We usually take 10% of the monthly rental as an easy way to measure letting and management fees. The usual rate is around 6 to 8% but it is good to be conservative in your figures.

Also take around up to 5% of rental income to cover all the other incidentals in the property (monthly operating expenses). This should cover repairs and other costs associated with property investing.

In other costs you should add rates and any other annual expense that you will have as a direct result of owning the property.

SUMMARY

There are several formulas to measure profits and success, but the best and most simple is the Basic Calculation Formula. It will tell you how much money you will be clearing monthly, and despite its simplicity it is extremely accurate. You will soon find that, with a little practice, you can do it in your head very quickly when you are viewing properties.

Another very accurate way to do your figures is to use the RevIQ property analysis software. It is sophisticated, simplifies the whole numbers process and also gives you online access to valuable real estate data and statistics. Check out www.reviq.com.

Part Two

The buying process step by step

Chapter 8

Asset planning

ADVICE FROM MATTHEW GILLIGAN

'To move the world, we must first move ourselves.'

— Socrates

What is asset planning?

Asset planning is the process of devising asset ownership structures for private and business assets. The aim of an effective asset plan is to arrive at a structure that provides a mix of asset protection, effective estate planning and tax minimisation, and caters for any relationship property considerations. Looking at each of these elements in turn:

- Asset protection describes taking measures to protect your assets from personal and business risk. For example, if you have a business with five employees, you do not want to see your family home lost if the negligence of an employee causes a claim to result against the business.
- Estate planning looks at how assets are to be distributed from one generation to the next.
- Tax minimisation speaks for itself. While we all recognise an obligation to pay our fair share of tax, we are also allowed to structure our affairs so that they are efficient from a tax perspective.
- Relationship property issues are relevant in almost every structure I have ever put together. In some cases the solution is straightforward, but in others structures need to cater for spouses or de facto partners wanting to maintain separate assets.

Conflicts between accountants and lawyers

You can get asset-planning advice from both accountants and lawyers. However, what I have found in practice is that many practitioners in both of these fields do not offer a holistic point of view. For example, you are looking to buy an investment property and go to your lawyer for advice on the appropriate asset-ownership structure for the property. Your lawyer will quite correctly point out that you should consider protecting this asset from personal and business risk and, furthermore, as you are single, you should seek to protect the property from relationship property claims. Following this, your lawyer will recommend that you establish a trust and the rental property be settled into the ownership of the trust.

You then go and see your accountant and pose the same question to them. They consider your circumstances and note that your salary of $80,000 per annum subjects a portion of your income to the top personal marginal tax rate of 39%. Following this, your accountant suggests that you would be better off holding the property personally in order to gain access to any tax losses, so that such tax losses can be offset against your salary to produce tax credits.

Both your lawyer and accountant have raised some valid points and proposed a structure to address them. However, neither has considered the holistic picture and provided a structure that caters for asset protection, estate planning, tax and relationship property issues. This is the secret to an effective asset-planning structure.

As an investor you need to surround yourself with advisors that have a background and experience across both disciplines. If you go and see a lawyer who specialises in trusts and asset-protection structures, you will get advice that effectively protects your investment from risk, but you will not necessarily make the best use of any tax benefits that arise. On the other hand, if you see an accountant who specialises in tax, you will have an effective tax outcome, but your assets may not be protected from risk.

The basics – trusts

A trust is best described as a legal relationship created by a settlor whereby persons (the trustees) hold assets for the benefit of beneficiaries. Note that a trust has the following characteristics:

- Title to trust assets is held in the name of the trustees. Trustees are either people or companies.
- Despite holding assets, the assets of a trust do not form part of the trustee's own estate.
- Having entered into the agreement to hold the assets for the benefit of beneficiaries, trustees are then subject to various rules and obligations.

Trusts are most commonly used for asset-protection purposes, although as we will discover later in the chapter they can also be used for trading purposes. The asset-protection benefit arises from the fact that when a trustee holds an asset subject to a trust and a beneficiary enjoys the use of the asset, neither of them holds legal ownership of the asset.

Applying this to a common everyday example, take the situation where Mr and Mrs Smith jointly own their own home. They wish to protect the home from being exposed to the risks of the family business. To do so, they will establish a family trust of which they will be the trustees along with an independent trustee. The beneficiaries of the trust will be themselves, other family members and potentially trusts set up for any of these people. The Smiths will then enter into a sale and purchase agreement whereby they sell the home to the trustees of the trust and commence a gifting programme. As trustees of the trust, they resolve to allow themselves to occupy the home as beneficiaries.

In the future, should a problem arise in the business that means Mr and Mrs Smith are personally exposed to a claim, their house is protected as they no longer personally own it. This is the practice of **'controlling everything but owning nothing'** that is taught by Richmastery.

Who are the parties to a trust?

1. **The settlor(s)** – this is the person or people who create the trust by setting out the terms and making the initial settlement of property to be held by the trustees.
2. **Trustees** – these are either individuals or companies who hold assets on behalf of the trust and make decisions in relation to such assets. Trustees are bound by certain rules and obligations and are required to act in the interest of beneficiaries. In family trust situations usually both spouses are trustees.

In my view, a professional independent trustee who will assist in the administration of the trust is an advisable addition. Please note that involvement of all trustees in all decisions is a key requirement for maintaining the validity of a trust. There is no use appointing an independent trustee and then not involving them in decisions or having them simply 'rubber stamp' them.

3. **Beneficiaries** – these are the people who benefit from the income and capital of the trust.
4. **Appointors** – these are the people who have the ability to appoint and remove trustees. This is a critical role as the holder of the power of appointorship has ultimate control of the Trust via the ability to control who the trustees are.

What is gifting?

In some countries gift duty applies to gifts of assets with a value of, for example, more than $27,000 in any 12-month period. Where a donor makes gifts in excess of this amount, gift duty is payable at varying rates starting from 5% and ranging up to 25%. Following this, an issue arises where individuals wish to movc large assets such as homes, that may be worth hundreds of thousands of dollars, into the ownership of a trust.

The starting point for moving a home into a trust is to sell it at fair market value. If the transfer of a home into a trust takes place at market value no gift arises. When the sale takes place at market value, the trust recognises a debt to the individuals as consideration for the purchase. Note at this point that while no gift has arisen, because the property was sold at market value, the individuals have not been successful in migrating any wealth into the trust. This is done via the *gifting programme* which sees them forgiving the debt that the trust recognises it owes them at a rate of, for example, $27,000 per annum per person.

The documentation of the debt that the trust recognises it owes the individuals is crucial as until that debt is completely forgiven, it represents an asset in the individuals' hands. This means should the individual be vulnerable to a claim it is possible that pressure could be put on them to call for the trust to repay the debt. Skilful drafting of the Deed of Acknowledgement of Debt can help mitigate risk in these circumstances.

Some trusts and arrangements to avoid

One outmoded trust structure that I still see being utilised from time to time is a so-called 'mirror' trust structure. A mirror trust structure is a hangover from the days when estate duty applied. A typical mirror trust structure involved two trusts being set up for a married couple whereby each spouse was not a beneficiary of the trust that they established. Given that estate duty in many countries, such as New Zealand, was abolished in the 1990s, I consider mirror trusts to be unnecessary. Not only do they involve the extra maintenance and administration of two trusts but the beneficiary structure, which sees each spouse excluded from being a beneficiary of one of the trusts, is also flawed.

Another relatively common practice that should be avoided is the maintenance of life interests in properties when selling them to a trust. In this scenario, the individual who owns the property sells it to the trust subject to a life interest to occupy the property. This is often used as a means of deflating the value of the property upon acquisition by the trust, in order to reduce the length of the gifting programme. While it might be advisable in certain circumstances, in many cases it does not work because it results in a potentially appreciating asset being held in the individual's hands. It is also a difficult and sometimes costly arrangement to unwind, in the event that the trust property is sold.

Basics – what is an estate plan?

Passing assets between generations

Estate planning involves considering how assets are to be passed from one generation to the next. The usual components of an estate plan are wills and memoranda of wishes. A will is a document that deals with an individual's personal estate upon death. A memorandum of wishes is a letter written to trustees of the trust to describe how assets are to be dealt with within the trust.

A common mistake is not to link wills and the establishment of a trust. I often see individuals who have established trusts but have not prepared new wills to reflect this. In this instance, they often have existing wills prepared many years before that pass assets to spouses or children personally upon death. Once a trust is established such a will is flawed for two reasons. First, you do not want assets to pass to surviving spouses or children personally when they can be directed straight into a trust free of gifting restrictions. That is, it is important to note that any bequests under a will are not subject to gift duty. Second, given that a trust has been established and the individual is seeking to minimise their personal estate, their will has become redundant to a certain extent.

Broadly speaking, the objective of an effective will is to direct assets into the ownership of the trust on death. This will prevent assets from accruing in the hands of the surviving spouse and family members and also prevent gifting programmes from being extended. Having directed all assets into the trust, it is then under the memorandum of wishes where instruction is provided as to how the assets of the trust are to be dealt with.

A memorandum of wishes is not a legally binding document. It is a letter written to the trustees of the trust, describing the settlor's wishes as to how trust assets are to be dealt with. The key to an effective memorandum of wishes is to provide the trustees with instruction to consider the asset-protection requirements of any beneficiaries when making distributions from the trust. For example, if a beneficiary is in a relationship, the trustees should consider the stability of the relationship and the desirability of passing assets through to the beneficiary individually, where they could be subject to a relationship property claim in the event of a separation.

Above I have discussed how your own estate may be managed via a will and how the assets of your trust can be distributed via a memorandum of wishes, but it is also critical to give thought to the receipt of any assets via inheritance. In particular, where appropriate, I recommend that my clients approach their parents and have them direct any inheritance through to trusts, rather than their own hands. The reason for this is as stated above – it prevents the accumulation of assets in personal hands where they then have to be introduced into gifting programmes to be protected in a trust.

Blended families

Another important aspect of estate planning is to consider the impact of blended families when constructing an estate plan. A typical situation that I often see is as follows:

Mr and Mrs Brown are married and it is the second marriage for both parties. Mr Brown has three children from a prior relationship and Mrs Brown has one. Together they have had another child and all five children live with them. Mr and Mrs Brown have been married for 10 years and consider all of their assets to be joint assets from a relationship property perspective. However, Mr Brown would like his share of the joint relationship assets to be passed through to his children, being the three children from the prior relationship, plus the one child from the current marriage and Mrs Brown would like the same.

In this case a single trust with a memorandum of wishes is not likely to be sufficient to give the clients comfort that their wishes will be carried out following their death. Instead, the estate plan will likely involve the use of two family trusts with separate memoranda of wishes and appropriate beneficiary streams. Each family trust will hold any separate assets, but together they will hold the joint assets in partnership. Properly set up, this structure can allow each party's share of the relationship property assets to pass through to their children as they wish.

Finally, note that in this situation one of the exceptions to the rule discussed above in respect of life interests emerges. Although I have said that I do not generally condone the retention of a life interest when selling a property into a trust, a life interest can be useful in this situation to ensure that the surviving spouse has use and enjoyment of the joint family home when control of half of it has passed to the deceased spouse's children.

The basics – tax

A useful starting point here is to confirm the current tax rates for individuals, trusts and companies.

Individuals

Australia	
Income	**Tax rate**
$0 – $6000	Nil
$6001 – $25,000	15c for each $1 over $6000
$25,001 – $75,000	$2,850 plus 30c for each $1 over $25,000
$75,001 – $150,000	$17,850 plus 40c for each $1 over $75,000
Over $150,000	$47,850 plus 45c for each $1 over $150,000

New Zealand	
Income	**Tax rate**
$0 – $38,000	19.5%
$38,001 – $60,000	33%
Income from $60,001 plus	39%

Companies and trusts

Companies and trusts are subject to the tax rates in the table below irrespective of the level of income.

Companies
Australia 30%
New Zealand 33%

However, there are a couple of provisos to this. The first is that trusts have the ability to split income to beneficiaries before tax is paid such that the beneficiary bears the tax liability at their marginal tax rate.

What is taxable income?

Taxable income is the product of a calculation that starts by firstly determining the amount of gross income. From this, all allowable deductions are subtracted, to arrive at an amount of taxable income before losses. Any allowable tax losses either from prior years or from other sources are then deducted to produce the amount of taxable income. Taxable income is then multiplied by the tax rate to arrive at the amount of tax to be paid.

In the case of rental investments, the taxable income from a rental investment property is calculated by firstly determining the gross rental income and then subtracting from that all allowable deductions. Allowable deductions include all expenses incurred in producing that rental income, such as interest on money borrowed to purchase the rental property, expenditure on repairs and maintenance, management fees paid to property managers, insurance, rates etc. Deductions are also allowed for depreciation, which I will discuss in greater detail below. Having subtracted the allowable deductions from the gross rental income, the rental property either produces a profit or a loss. If it is a profit, this is taxable income and tax is paid on this amount. If it is a loss, it may be able to be offset against other income, thereby reducing tax paid elsewhere.

In the case of individual investors, if the property is owned personally and runs at a loss, this loss can be offset against other personal income. Further, if the property is held by a loss attributing qualifying company (LAQC) and the shares in the LAQC are owned by an individual, the loss can also be utilised by the individual by being offset against other income to reduce tax paid on that. This begs the question – what is an LAQC?

What is a loss attributing qualifying company (LAQC)?

An LAQC (available only in New Zealand) is a company incorporated under the Companies Act 1993 and registered with the Companies Office as an ordinary company, but where the shareholders and directors of the company have made an election for the company to enter the LAQC regime.

The LAQC regime is a tax-specific regime. The rationale for the regime is to provide smaller-scale business owners with a structure that is a hybrid of a company and a partnership. Like a company, an LAQC provides shareholders with the protection of limited liability. Like a partnership, an LAQC provides shareholders with the ability to personally utilise losses produced via the business activity and, also like a partnership, capital gains can be freely passed from an LAQC to shareholders. It is these latter two characteristics that make the LAQC an attractive proposition for rental investors.

Given that many rental investments run at a tax loss and produce capital gains if held for a long period of time, an LAQC that will pass tax losses through to individual shareholders and allow individual shareholders to draw capital gains from the company is an appropriate structure for such investments. Some other points to note about the LAQC regime include:

- Shareholders have to be either natural people, other qualifying companies or trusts that meet certain conditions.
- There have to be five or fewer shareholders.
- There can only be one class of shares.
- Shareholders guarantee the income tax liability of the company.
- In the event that shareholding changes take place, new shareholders usually have to sign LAQC elections within 63 days of the shareholding change in order to maintain the company's LAQC status.

Depreciation

Depreciation is an allowance for the diminution in value of buildings and chattels over time due to wear and tear etc. The exact application of depreciation to rental property varies from country to country and we recommend you take specific advice from a qualified accountant. The Taxation Department publishes a booklet that provides the depreciation rates for various assets.

Depreciation deductions form an important part of the tax benefits of investment in rental properties and it is worth noting the following points in relation to depreciation:

- The depreciation can normally be claimed in two ways, either on the diminishing-value basis or the straight-line method. I recommend that investors employ the diminishing-value basis as this gives a greater weighting of deductions early in the life of an investment.
- Separately identifiable chattels can often be depreciated at higher rates. Hence the value of having a chattels valuation performed on a rental investment after acquisition. A chattels valuation provides you with a split of the purchase price on a rental investment between the land, buildings and chattels components.
- Depreciation is based on the cost of assets, as opposed to market value. For example, if a property is purchased for $250,000 but has a value of $300,000, the depreciation claimable will be based on the cost of $250,000. However, given that most sale and purchase agreements do not split the $250,000 between land, buildings and chattels it is then that the value of a chattels valuer emerges. A chattels valuer is able to provide you with a split of the global purchase price, such that part of

the cost is attributed to the chattels. Obviously the higher the amount that is attributed to the chattels, the more generous your depreciation claims will be.

- When a depreciable asset is sold a calculation must be performed to determine if there is any depreciation to be recovered. Depreciation recovery is equivalent to the difference between the sale price of a depreciable asset and its book value, with a proviso that the amount of depreciation recovery cannot exceed the amount of depreciation claimed over the life of the asset.

For example, take a property purchased for $250,000 and assume that the land component of this was $110,000 and the buildings and chattels component $140,000. The property is then held and rented for a period of three years and during that time $20,000 of depreciation is claimed on the buildings and chattels such that there is a book value of $120,000. The property is then sold for $300,000. Here the presumed sale price of the building and chattels will be at least the original cost of $140,000. Thus, the total amount of depreciation claimed to date is recovered, being $20,000. This amount has to be returned as income by the seller.

I often see potential investors who are put off from claiming depreciation on the basis that it is likely to be recovered when the property is sold. However, I strongly disagree with this practice on the basis that it is not a given that depreciation will be recovered and furthermore, at worst, it simply results in the investor repaying to the Taxation Department the tax benefits derived during the life of the investment property. Thus, at worst, depreciation is an interest-free loan.

Finance

Interest on funds borrowed to purchase a rental investment can be claimed as a deductible expense for tax purposes. While this is a relatively straightforward premise, note that this issue can be complicated if the entity purchasing the investment does not undertake the borrowing.

For example, individuals often have a revolving-credit facility in their own names, secured against their home, that they then draw down on to purchase a rental property. If the rental property is ultimately settled into a company, which then borrows the remainder of the funds required to purchase the property, the interest on the revolving-credit facility is in fact incurred by the individual and not the company that purchased the property.

The obvious solution to this issue is to ensure that all funds borrowed to purchase a rental investment are borrowed by the entity that is going to own it. I do note that it would be possible in my example above for the company to reimburse the individual for the interest incurred, but there are complications and risks in taking such an approach. For example, depending on the quantum of interest paid by the company to the individual, tax may have to be deducted and remitted to the Taxation Department. Although this will not result in any additional tax payable overall, as the individual can often qualify to get a refund of the tax deducted, it does tie up your funds.

Besides deductibility of interest, the other key aspect to consider when borrowing funds is the security provided to secure such funding. If you are required to utilise your home as security for funding the purchase of rental properties, your objective should be to limit the exposure of your home to the risk of the investment debt. This is often best achieved by obtaining funding from more than one bank. In general, you should aim to diversify your financial risk by splitting your borrowing between different banks. This can allow you to have your home held as security by one bank and the rental investment portfolio held as security by a second.

When do you pay income tax on the sale of land?

Australia has a capital gains tax but New Zealand does not! However, in New Zealand there are a number of provisions in the Income Tax Act which provide for the payment of income tax on the sale of land. In particular, the sale of land is taxable in the following circumstances:

1. Where the land is bought with the intention of resale. It is important to note here that the intention of resale does not have to be the only purpose or even the dominant purpose. It simply has to be a purpose, although it is noted that almost any purchase of land is completed with the expectation that one day it may be sold. This is not enough of an intention to give rise to the application of this provision.
2. Where you are in the business of dealing in or developing land or in the business of erecting buildings, the purchase and sale of land in the course of that business is taxable.

3. Where you are in the business of dealing in or developing land or in the business of erecting buildings and buy land other than as part of that business, but sell it within 10 years, the sale is also generally taxable. Note that this provision applies slightly differently to builders in that it requires improvements to be made on the property and the 10-year period runs from the time of completion of the improvements.
4. Where you are associated with a dealer, developer or builder and sell land within 10 years. This is commonly known as 'tainting'. Once again, the tainting provision in relation to builders is slightly different in that it requires improvements to be made and the 10-year period runs from the time of completion of the improvements. The key to establishing tainting is that there has to be an association between the person or entity purchasing the property that is potentially tainted and the dealer/developer or builder.
5. Where property is purchased and subdivided within 10 years of acquisition. The subdivision has to involve work of more than a minor nature, but it should be noted that this provision is interpreted relatively narrowly in that few subdivisions qualify as being minor.
6. Where a major subdivision is carried out on the land at any time. This provision is directed at major commercial, residential or industrial divisions or developments, but is also known as something of a catch-all provision in that it does not have any time limits.
7. Where land is sold within 10 years and 20% of any gain is attributable to a change in zoning or grant of consent or some other similar factor.

Following the above, note that there is a wide variety of instances where income tax may apply to gains made on the sale of land. However, I do hasten to point out that there are exemptions available to the provisions above. For example, a residential home is exempt from many of the provisions if the taxpayer acquires and occupies the land as a residence. One further point worth noting in relation to the exemptions is that some of them are only capable of being utilised by individuals. For example, the residential exemption which applies to taxpayers who acquire and occupy a property as a residence in some instances does not apply to trusts, because a trust is incapable of occupying a house as a residence (that is, it is the beneficiaries that occupy the house).

Perhaps the provisions that I get questioned on the most are the tainting provisions.

What is tainting and how do you avoid it?

Tainting describes the acquisition of land at a time when the purchaser is associated with another person or entity in the business of dealing in or developing land. It also applies to the improvement of land at a time when there is association with a person or entity in the business of erecting buildings.

The avoidance of tainting is especially important in New Zealand so as to maintain the most tax-efficient structure for investors.

For example, where there is association at these times, the land in question is tainted. This means that the land is likely to be subject to income tax on any gain on sale if sold within either 10 years of acquisition or 10 years of completing improvements. I often see keen property investors who want to dabble in both long-term property investment and dealing and developing. One of the biggest challenges these types of investors face is ensuring that the dealing or developing business does not taint properties purchased for long-term investment purposes.

As already noted, tainting arises where there is association between the person or entity purchasing the land for investment purposes and the person or entity conducting the business of dealing or development. Thus, in order to avoid the potential application of tainting, you need to ensure that no such association exists.

Association is a term defined in the Income Tax Act and can apply between companies, individuals and trusts. No generic structure can be said to prevent tainting as each investor has different priorities and needs. For example, a company may be appropriate for holding property investments required by one investor, but a trust may be appropriate for another. Given this is the case, each has different association provisions to consider when trying to build an entity for dealing or development purposes that is not associated with the entity acquiring the rental properties. Having said that, I note that the utilisation of trading trust structures for property dealing or development purposes is usually a useful way of preventing association from applying.

In summary, note the following important points in regard to tainting:

- Tainting is only an issue where someone is in the *business* of dealing in or developing land or erecting buildings.
- If such a business exists, there then has to be association between the person or entity in the business of dealing, developing or building and the person or entity buying the property for investment purposes.
- Tainting does not apply retrospectively in that properties acquired or improved before the period of association cannot retrospectively be tainted by the commencement of a dealing, developing or building business.
- There is a time limit on tainting in that if properties are held longer than the relevant 10-year period, they are no longer subject to income tax.
- There are exemptions to the tainting provisions. For example, there is a residential exemption.
- Association can be prevented via the utilisation of appropriate structures. While there is no generic answer to this, often the employment of a trading trust structure for the dealing, developing or building business is an appropriate means of preventing tainting.

Issues for Australian tax residents investing in New Zealand

The first comment I have to make to Australian tax residents looking to invest in property in New Zealand is an obvious one – if you do this, you will be operating in two tax jurisdictions. As Australian tax residents, you will generally be subject to tax in Australia on your worldwide income regardless of the source. Given that the income from investment in property in New Zealand will also be sourced in New Zealand, you will be subject to tax in New Zealand.

When considering an appropriate structure as an Australian tax resident, it is the Australian tax rules and the rest of your Australian structure that should drive how you invest in New Zealand. For this reason it is critical that you get Australian tax advice first and then dovetail that advice into a structure that works from a New Zealand perspective.

Below is discussion of the key issues that an Australian investor will be faced with when investing in New Zealand:

- **Same tax rules:** As an Australian investor investing in New Zealand, the same rules that apply to New Zealand investors apply to you. That is, when you invest in New Zealand, you are taxed in New Zealand on your New Zealand-sourced income under the New Zealand income tax rules. The tax rates are the same, whether you are a resident or non-resident and the rules in terms of assessability of income and deductibility of expenses are the same.

If we apply this to an Australian investor investing in a rental property here, the rent will be assessable income; deductions can be claimed for interest incurred on the funds borrowed to purchase the property, as well as other expenses such as rates, repairs and maintenance and depreciation. This means that Australian investors are just as likely to incur tax losses as New Zealand investors. Thus, overall, there will be no New Zealand tax to pay.

- **Tax credits:** In the event that there is a tax liability in New Zealand, tax will be paid here at the applicable New Zealand tax rates. Companies and trusts are taxed at a flat rate of 33% and individuals at the relevant personal marginal tax rate, depending on the level of New Zealand income. This means that an Australian investor who is producing tax profits in New Zealand would be taxed at 19.5% personally on up to $38,000 worth of

New Zealand-sourced income. In the event that the Australian tax investor does have to pay tax in New Zealand, they will be entitled to a tax credit in Australia for the tax paid in New Zealand. This reduces their tax liability in Australia and prevents them paying double tax on the same income in New Zealand and Australia.

- **Don't use LAQCs:** The LAQC regime is specific to New Zealand only and is not recognised in Australia. While an Australian tax resident could establish an LAQC and, for New Zealand purposes, any tax losses would then be attributed to the investor personally, this structure is not likely to work from an Australian perspective, as the LAQC regime is ignored there. From an Australian perspective, the investor is utilising an ordinary company structure, which is not likely to be the best answer.

The only example where an LAQC might be an appropriate vehicle for an Australian investor would be if they were considering moving to New Zealand in the near future. In this case, in the long term, an LAQC structure may be an appropriate investment vehicle. In the interim period, when they have the LAQC, any losses that are attributed to them personally will be carried forward, and available to them, when they arrive in New Zealand. Note that there are some hooks in operating an LAQC outside of New Zealand. In particular, the rules state that LAQCs cannot be classed as what are called 'foreign companies'. In general, a foreign company is a company that is not resident in New Zealand under either New Zealand domestic tax law or through the application of a double tax agreement. New Zealand has a double tax agreement with Australia that states that companies that are resident in both countries are ultimately resident in the country where management is exercised. This means that LAQCs that are incorporated in New Zealand can end up being non-resident in New Zealand for tax purposes, due to management being exercised in Australia. This is an important point to be monitored if you are setting up an LAQC from Australia (which of course you will only do if you are moving to New Zealand in the near future).

- **Personal or trust ownership:** Personal or trust ownership is likely to be the best answer for an Australian investor who is going to remain an Australian tax resident. This is on the basis that company structures can be inefficient from a tax perspective and there are discounts available in Australia in relation to capital gains tax for individuals and trusts that do not apply to companies. Thus, in general, Australian tax residents should invest in New Zealand either in their personal name or through a trust structure. As already noted above, it is crucial that specialist Australian tax advice is obtained to ensure that the right choice of investment vehicle is made in this regard.

- **Tax on capital gains in New Zealand:** Australian tax residents will only be taxed on capital gains in New Zealand if they fall within the land tax provisions, as described above. As already noted, the tax rules that apply to resident or non-resident investors are the same. Thus, Australian tax residents will be liable for tax on capital gains in New Zealand only if the property is bought with the intention of resale, if they are in the business of dealing/development etc. If this is the case, the tax rate is as per the ordinary tax rates for individuals, companies, and trusts, as outlined above.

Issues for New Zealand tax resident investors investing in Australia

As a New Zealand tax resident investing in Australia, it is important to note that your investment income will be taxable in both Australia, as the income is sourced there, and New Zealand, as you are resident here and liable for tax in New Zealand on your worldwide income. Included in the income that will be subject to tax in Australia are potential capital gains. Also note that stamp duty is an issue that should be considered when investing in Australia. The following is a summary of the key issues that need to be considered for a New Zealand tax resident investing in Australia:

- **Don't use LAQCs:** In general, LAQCs should not be used by New Zealand tax residents investing in Australia. This is because there is a restriction on the amount of foreign income that an LAQC can derive and still remain within the LAQC regime. If the gross rent of an Australian investment exceeds NZ$10,000 per annum, this threshold is breached and the LAQC will lose LAQC status.
- **Calculation of taxable profit/loss:** Where a New Zealand tax resident invests in Australia, the amount of tax profit/loss that the New Zealand resident has to return in New Zealand is calculated using New Zealand income tax rules. This means that you have two calculations to perform when preparing your tax returns – one for the Australian tax return using Australian rules and one for the New Zealand tax return using New Zealand rules. In general, the two calculations will be exactly the same although different depreciation rates and rules apply. Where the Australian investment produces a tax loss, this loss will be available to be offset against other income derived by the investor. For this reason, it is often necessary for a New Zealand tax resident to invest in Australia in their own name, in order to get access to the tax losses personally (as noted above, an LAQC often does not work). An LAQC does not provide suitable asset protection, thus trusts are often used as the Australian investment vehicle, as they offer the required asset-protection benefit. However, it should be noted that if the investment produces a tax loss, the loss will be locked in that trust and the effective utilisation of the tax losses is dependant on the trust producing some income.

- **Non-resident withholding tax (NRWT) on interest:** If a New Zealand investor borrows funds and pays interest to a non-resident lender, there may be an obligation for the New Zealand investor to deduct NRWT from the interest paid to the non-resident lender. In terms of interest paid to Australian lenders, NRWT applies at a rate of 10%. There are two exemptions to NRWT. The first is where the interest is paid to an Australian bank that has a branch registered in New Zealand. This includes the likes of Westpac, ANZ, HSBC etc. The second exemption is if the New Zealand investor registers under the approved issuer regime. This is something that cannot be done retrospectively, but if the New Zealand investor registers as an approved issuer, the deduction of NRWT at 10% is not required. Instead the New Zealand investor pays a 2% approved issuer levy to the Iland Revenue Department annually.

Note that there can be tax implications on the foreign exchange movement, where the loan is denominated in Australian dollars. This can mean the investor has either a foreign exchange gain or loss to include in their return. The foreign exchange fluctuation is either returned on an annual basis in the tax return, or for individuals with borrowings below a certain threshold, only when the loan is eventually repaid.

- **Capital gains tax in Australia:** Besides the rental income being taxable in Australia, it is also likely that any capital gain will be taxed under the Australian capital gains tax regime. Generally speaking, trusts or individuals qualify for a discount on capital gains tax, which again is an incentive to invest in Australia either in personal names or utilising trust structures. It is essential that you seek Australian tax advice, prior to settling on the appropriate structure.

SUMMARY

In summary, in employing an appropriate asset ownership structure you can:

- Protect your assets.
- Implement an effective estate plan to pass on assets to future generations.
- Minimise your tax.
- Protect assets from relationship property claims.

In order to achieve a holistic, well-rounded structure you need to engage holistic, well-rounded advisors. Many accountants and lawyers focus exclusively on their areas of expertise, to the detriment of providing a well-rounded solution for their clients.

Gilligan Rowe and Associates have tax expertise and legal experience that enable them to provide their clients with a holistic solution to their structure issues. They can be contacted through the Recommended Suppliers section of Richmastery's website. They offer half-price initial consultations to Richmastery clients and would be more than happy to see you to discuss the application of the issues raised in this chapter to your situation.

Chapter 9

Getting ready

CREATING A TEAM OF EXPERTS AND PREARRANGING FINANCE

'Surround yourself with a team of professionals who know more than you about their area of expertise.'
— David Leon

Start with the correct structure

As discussed in the previous chapter, setting up the correct asset-planning structure for tax is crucial before you begin buying property. If you do not do this correctly from the start it can be hugely expensive to remedy later, especially if you have to sell or gift your properties into the correct entity. However, if you already own property it is well worth going through this process, despite the expense, to make sure your properties are in the correct entity. Get professional advice as soon as possible on how to achieve this. Once you know what your structure is going to be you need to get help setting it up.

Creating a team of experts

You will be much more successful if you have an outstanding team of people working with you. You do not need to know how to do everything yourself; you just need to employ the right people to do it for you.

Your team should be made up of experts who are knowledgeable and reliable. You must be able to trust them to do what they say they are going to do in the time frame they promise. Be aware of how organised they are, ask questions about their experience and knowledge. Make sure you get recommendations from other investors and references, as this advice will be invaluable.

Step 1: Find a good accountant

It is very important to have an accountant who specialises in real estate investing. They will be an invaluable asset for your business for years to come. We recommend that you look for an accountant who invests in real estate themselves. This is because they will be able to better understand your goals. They will be aware of the issues and needs of real estate investors and will have looked to maximise returns for their own portfolios. You can benefit from their first-hand knowledge and expertise in this area.

You should feel comfortable when talking to your accountant. Different accountants will operate within different risk profiles. Some accountants are well known for pushing the envelope and if you are a conservative real estate investor you will run into conflict. Similarly, if you want to push the envelope and your accountant is very conservative the relationship is also doomed to failure.

Step 2: Find a good solicitor

Your solicitor should specialise in real estate investing and not just general law. Word of mouth is a good way to source a good solicitor. Do not go on price only, because in most cases cheap will end up being more expensive in the long run. Ask as many fellow real estate investors as possible who they use so that you can come up with the best solicitor for your strategy.

Your solicitor should always be in touch with your accountant so that they can find the right balance between tax minimisation and asset protection. After you find a solicitor who you are comfortable with and you feel is likely to get this balance right, get them to set up your structures.

Step 3: Find a good mortgage broker

As discussed earlier when looking for a mortgage broker, interview several. Talk to other investors about which mortgage brokers they use and why they keep using them. Make sure that your mortgage broker is a real estate investor.

Other team members

Other members of your team will include:

- property managers
- tradespeople
- building inspectors
- registered valuers
- chattels valuers
- real estate agents who put you on to good deals.

When you find someone who fits your team treat them with respect, look after them well and always pay them immediately. Remember that if you build a good rapport with your team you will get preferential treatment, which will be hugely valuable to your business. Check out www.richmastery.com for recommended suppliers.

Take your team to dinner

It can be a great idea to invite all the members of your team to a dinner at least once a year where you can talk and they can get to know each other better. This will make your team and your business just that little more solid and you will find that they always come up with great ideas by bouncing off each other. We do this and recommend you do the same once your team is up and running.

Mortgage pre-approval

A mortgage pre-approval means that the lender has decided that they are, in principle, willing to lend you a specific amount of money for the purposes of purchasing a property. You can still renegotiate all the terms of the pre-approval of finance before you receive the final mortgage offer.

It is best to get your mortgage broker to prearrange finance before you view any properties. This way you will know where you stand and the maximum value of real estate you will be able to purchase. This is also important because, depending on the structure you are going to be using to purchase property, your mortgage broker and your solicitor will have to structure the loan through different processes. For example, if you are buying an investment property under a trading trust, the borrowing will be organised in a very different fashion than if you were just purchasing the property under your own name. This is why it's so important to set up your structures before you prearrange any finance.

Another advantage of having your structures and finance ready is that you will have more leverage when negotiating a deal. Most buyers are time wasters and you do not want to be perceived as a time waster. If you are pre-approved for finance you will be ready to buy. Real estate agents will love you and will take you much more seriously. They are also more likely to tell you about hot deals first.

Be prepared and know your goals

Reading this book will give you the knowledge you need prior to meeting any of the above-mentioned professionals. When you meet with them show them your ideas and strategies and have a clear goal of what you want to achieve through real estate investing. Be prepared and have a list of questions or suggestions as this way you get the best out of your time with them. If you are clear about what you need from them they will think more highly of you and you will therefore get the best-quality advice possible.

SUMMARY

It is important to build a strong team of experts around you who will bring their expertise to your real estate business. Choosing these professionals well can be the difference between success and failure. A great team will turbo-charge your profits and minimise your risks. Get your mortgage broker to prearrange finance before you start buying real estate to add more leverage to your negotiations. This will also help you to work out how much and what type of real estate you want to be purchasing before you start viewing properties. Start building your team of experts today from the Recommended Suppliers at www.richmastery.com

Chapter 10

Analysing areas

LOCATION, LOCATION, LOCATION

'Become the local expert in the areas that fit your strategy.'

— Kevin Green, Welsh multi-millionaire investor

Having clear goals

Choosing a target area to invest in is an important step to successful real estate investment. Some people make the mistake of jumping into buying a property because they've heard that someone made money in that area or because a friend advised them to. This is not recommended. What works for someone else won't necessarily work for you. Others find themselves over-analysing an area and end up not buying or buying too late.

Earlier, we stressed that the first thing you need to do is to write down your goals. Different goals require different strategies, which will lead you to different areas where you will be able to find properties that fit your strategy. So make sure you have clear goals about what type of investment strategy you want to follow. Then, begin looking for your target area. The best way to go about analysing whether an area will fit your strategy is to follow the simple steps below.

Healthy growth markets

The first question you need to ask about an area is how healthy the first-time buyer market is in a particular place. To work out how healthy a first-time buyer market is in any given area you can use the ratio calculation below and look at the interest rates. (We will assume that first-time buyers earn an average salary.)

Growth potential ratio = Purchase price ÷ Average annual salary

Let's look at a specific area, such as Palmerston North. Here the average salary is around $35,000 and the average starter property can be bought at around $200,000. This gives us the ratio of 5.7 (i.e. $200,000 ÷ $35,000), which is extremely healthy. (The lower the ratio the better.)

In our experience anything above a ratio of 10 could potentially indicate that there will be a limited amount of capital growth in the next few years. This is especially the case if in combination with interest rates of 8% or above – meaning that this particular area is not likely to be a good investment.

You can be as specific or as general with this calculation as you want to be. You could evaluate neighbourhoods or the health of an entire country's real estate market. The only thing you need to add for different scenarios is the right averages and you will be able to calculate the right ratio.

Future development areas

Check with the council

The second factor you need to identify are future development areas. Go to the city council in the area where you are buying. Ask them about any new developments that are planned, such as new motorways, bypasses or roads, supermarkets, shopping centres or residential housing projects. Your aim is to work out where future capital growth will occur. You will be amazed at just how much information you can get from your local city or regional council about upcoming developments. You may also be surprised how many investors don't bother taking this important step.

Follow the big stores

Some real estate investors like to follow big corporate names, such as McDonald's, Starbucks or K Mart. These companies have research teams that analyse all areas to see where they expect a bigger growth and they build their stores or franchises there. Do you think the property prices are likely to go up in that area? If these companies have a newsletter, subscribe to them, or make sure you read the newspaper regularly to keep up with planned developments. In this way, you will know where they are planning to establish new outlets before anyone else does. Then you can start buying property in these areas and benefit from the growth that is likely to follow.

It's worth asking an interesting question at this point: What kind of business do you think McDonald's is in? If you said the hamburger business you would be wrong. In fact they are in the real estate business. McDonald's makes more money out of the appreciation on their buildings in prime locations around the world than from the cashflow that they produce from selling fast food. So you can assume from this that they will have done their research thoroughly on different growth areas before setting up new stores.

Remember – research, research! Location, location, location!

Measuring average asking to sell price ratio

The third factor you need to measure is the percentage of the asking price that the properties in a particular area are selling for on average. The reason you should calculate this percentage is that anything with a percentage below 90% of the asking price is a slow market, 90–95% is a steady market, and above 95% is a booming market.

You can get lists of actual recent sales along with the original asking prices from real estate agents in your target area. Once you have these, divide the purchase price by the asking price and multiply this number by 100 and you will obtain the percentage.

Percentage asking price = (Purchase price ÷ Asking price) x 100

This doesn't necessarily mean you shouldn't invest in areas where the percentage is under 90%. However, if you do you will need to make sure that you negotiate well to buy below value in these areas. This will be easier as there will be more motivated sellers who will take low offers, and this is great for educated real estate investors looking for hot deals.

Remember that you make your money when you buy not when you sell. Treat real estate investing as a business or you will be bound to fail.

Other factors

More diverse and stable economies

In general there is a steadier capital growth in places with a more diverse and stable economy. For this reason purchasing in larger towns or cities is better than remote and small country towns where the health of the economy may be dependent on a single industry.

Areas you know well

It is better to invest in areas that you know well and, if possible, are near to where you live. This way you can keep an eye on the market more easily, and once you buy you will be closer to your investment. However, that said, the growth of real estate sales on the Internet is now making it much easier to get acquainted with markets in diverse locations not so close to home. You can easily hire property managers to look after your investment for you, so utilise the Internet in your target market search.

Lower-priced areas for a higher yield

In general, lower-priced areas will make it easier to get a higher yield. Also there will be a larger pool of tenants who will be able to afford the lower rents. Higher yields can be achieved in high capital-growth areas if you buy properties that have more than one income stream, such as home-and-income properties or units.

SUMMARY

When analysing an area to see if it is likely to grow in value, you need to look at three main indicators: whether the particular area has a healthy growth market; whether it is near a future development zone; and whether it has a high or low ratio of selling to asking price. Once you have analysed these factors you will be able to get a good idea of whether it is a good market to invest in and which strategy you should use. However, make sure you don't over-analyse before deciding where to invest, as you may miss the boat.

Chapter 11

Making offers

LEARN HOW TO SAVE THOUSANDS

'Time is your most valuable asset, learn to leverage it.'

— Brad Sugars

If the numbers work, make an offer

Even when you know what you are looking for, making offers can be an emotional experience, especially when you are starting out. If you are not 100% sure about a property, get some advice from someone who knows, such as your mentor or an experienced property investor. You must take care not to let your emotions get the better of you – even if it is the most gorgeous house you've ever seen in the most beautiful location you've ever laid eyes on. If the numbers don't stack up you must not buy it – an investment property is only a good investment if it makes money, not if it costs you money!

Once you find an investment property that fits your strategy, jump on it and make a formal offer. To make offers and protect yourself while you do so you will need to become a master at reading and writing sale and purchase agreements. You will need all the clauses you can get your hands on so that you can negotiate any deal at any time.

Types of clauses you need to use

The types of clauses you need to include in your sale and purchase agreement are designed to protect your interests and to give you a period of time to ascertain if it is a deal worth settling on. You will use clauses that will allow you to pull out of the deal if the property turns out to be a lemon. At the same time they should still give you the sole option to purchase it before anyone else.

It would be infrequently that you present an unconditional cash offer. You will need to be 110% sure that the deal will work and that you have your finance set and ready to go before you do this. You will also need to be an experienced investor who knows their target area very well before making unconditional cash offers.

In general, the fewer clauses the better as far as sale and purchase agreements go. A myriad of clauses will make an agreement look too complicated and can scare off the vendor. However, we recommend that you include at least one in case the property doesn't pass inspection so you can cancel the contract. You don't want to be forced to buy a dud!

Remember that clauses must be genuine. You must not insert them willy-nilly into a sale and purchase agreement just to give you a way out if you change your mind. Buying property is not about mucking people around!

Subject to due diligence

The best clause to use is the due diligence clause, as this covers a multitude of things. This states that you are able to perform any due diligence necessary on the property during a fixed time frame and can, before that time is up, pull out of the deal if you are not happy with anything. You can set the time frame – aim for as long as you can get, e.g. up to 21 working days. However, at a minimum try to get seven days, or five working days that go before and after a weekend so you have an effective seven days.

All conditions contained within clauses will have a time limit on them. Make sure that you state 'business days' rather than just 'days' for the length of time they apply. This will give you some extra time (the weekend days) to get the information or approvals you need.

Your due diligence clause gives you time to confirm finance, carry out property inspections, valuations, building inspections, check the council file and to get quotes to verify any renovations or repairs you may need to do to the property.

There is a due diligence clause in the RevIQ software and also an 18 Point Due Diligence Checklist in the downloads page for this book which outlines all the steps you should take to carry out due diligence on a property before you make the decision about whether to go unconditional on the deal.

Without a due diligence clause you would need to include many clauses, so due diligence is the way to go.

However, you may come across real estate agents who don't like due diligence clauses. They may think vendors don't understand what the clauses mean and are apt to think it is just a way for you to wriggle out of an agreement because you are not really serious. (You would think the agent would explain to a vendor what a due diligence clause is, but it seems some of them are reluctant to do so.) Explain why you have used such a clause, and if you still meet with resistance, you may have to put in all the separate clauses instead.

Alternatives to due diligence

If you can't use due diligence, some of the other clauses that may be useful include the following.

- Subject to valuation.
- Subject to building inspection.
- Subject to finance. You would be well advised to include this if you are waiting for approval on your finance – you don't want to be in for the nasty surprise of losing your deposit if you can't get it. While an agreement will be more attractive without a subject-to-finance clause, including and then removing it as a negotiating tool can be an excellent strategy (as long as you are very sure your finance will be approved). You will also need to include a finance clause if you have applied for a construction loan for major renovations or developments. Sometimes these may not be approved until the last minute, and you don't want to be in the awful position of having to pay for a property you will not have the money to improve.
- Subject to solicitor's approval.
- Subject to spouse's approval.
- Subject to business partner's approval. (A good alternative to the due diligence clause.)
- Subject to engineer's report.

- Subject to carrying out a feasibility study.
- Subject to body corporate search.
- Subject to pest inspection.
- Subject to soil test – this is particularly important when you are buying bare land you intend to build on in case it is not suitable.
- Subject to survey – use this clause if you are intending to develop the property.
- Subject to an asbestos check.
- Subject to an environmental report – this is important if the property is on a toxic site such as an old petrol station, as it can be very expensive to excavate and refill in order for it to be safe to build on.
- Subject to investigating flood risk.
- Subject to investigating fire-safety issues – especially if the property is in a high fire-risk area, or if it is going to be used for something that requires fire codes to be complied with (e.g. a boarding house).

Please note that full versions of these clauses are included free as part of the RevIQ software, which we highly recommend all investors use. For more information go to: www.reviq.com.

Subject to access

The other clauses particularly suitable for properties you are going to renovate are those that give you access to the property before you take possession. The best one is 'subject to access and the right to perform maintenance during the settlement period'. This works very well if you have a long settlement period – your renovations may be complete, or nearly, by the time you take possession.

If the vendor is not too keen on this idea, you can change the clause to something like 'The vendor grants the buyer permission to arrange external maintenance repairs upon this agreement becoming unconditional.' This way you will be able to get the external painting, landscaping and fencing out of the way before you take possession. Failing this, a clause giving you access to organise quotes during the settlement period will at least give you a head start on your planning.

If you just want access to organise quotes, you can include an agreement to give the occupants at least 48 hours' notice and to limit your access to a maximum of three times in order to make a resistant vendor more receptive to the idea.

If the vendor is totally baulking at the idea of giving you any access at all, you could offer to pay for a licence to access the property to start your renovations. Although it will cost you something, it will be less than the holding costs (made up mainly of mortgage payments) you would incur if you had to wait until after settlement to start your renovations.

Subject to builder supplying costs

If you are buying a brand-new property in an area where you are able to claim capital allowance (depreciation of the building itself), make your contract subject to the builder supplying you with the costs of all claimable items. This will save you having to pay for a quantity surveyor to do the same thing.

The offer and the real estate agent

Clauses

Do not let agents push you around when you try to insert clauses, such as due diligence and access upon going unconditional. Real estate agents will tell you all sort of things about these great clauses. They may try to say that they are not legal. Once you tell them that your solicitor will call them personally to offer them some insight they often change their story to 'The vendor will never go for it'. Real estate agents who are against these clauses may influence vendors not to accept your clauses so make sure that you have a professional agent presenting this kind of offer.

Ask the agent if you can explain the offer and the clause yourself to the vendor. If this is not enough you could suggest that they call your solicitor to check that the clauses are legal and there will be no risk for them to accept them. Having a great real estate agent and great tools will help you become a master negotiator. Richmastery's real estate negotiation book also provides a battery of resources to help you attain success.

Negotiation and price

Remember that bargains are found in the negotiation. When you are looking for property, don't tell the real estate agent you want to buy a property that has high returns for a whopping great discount – they'll tell you it's not possible. It is through your negotiation skills that you will get a bargain (we cover this in more depth in Chapter 13). Remember, you will very rarely find a bargain at the asking price and must make your offers well below market value.

Ask the agent what the selling range for the property is. As a rule, real estate agents will not tell you what a vendor's bottom price is if directly asked. However, if you ask them what the selling range is you will get a pretty good idea.

Let the agent know you are serious about purchasing the property. If they know that you are serious about your offer on a property, they are more likely to assist you in wearing the vendor down because it is to their advantage to make a sale as well.

Be careful not to tell the agent too much. The vendor or the agent selling a property does not need to know what you intend to do with it – and you must not tell them. (Heavens knows, they might decide it is such a good idea they'll do it themselves!) They especially don't need to know what your top dollar is. If you tell them that, you are going to have a very hard time paying anything less!

Beware agents' tactics

Make sure you don't fall for agents' tactics. They will often tell you there is another offer on the table in order to get you to put your price up. Beware of this trick (nasty and slightly underhand in our opinion). Unless an agent insists that you fill out a Multiple Offer or Best Offer declaration, there is probably no other offer at all. (However, even this can be a trick – some agents have even been known to get purchasers to sign multiple offer forms when there are no other offers.)

Some real estate agents have been known to get someone they know to put in a very low offer on a property just so they can tell the other buyer they are now in a multiple-offer situation. Remember: even if there are other offers they may be lower than yours but you cannot allow this to influence you and you must not become emotional.

Get your offer presented quickly

Once you have decided to make an offer, make sure it is presented immediately. Don't let the real estate agent muck you around with delaying tactics, as they may be waiting for another offer to pitch against yours and you may miss out on the deal. Even if the agent tells you your offer is too low, insist that they present it. Tell them you are waiting by the phone, and if they don't get back to you, call them. If an agent point-blank refuses to present your offer, politely remind them that they are legally bound to do so. If this still doesn't elicit the cooperation you are looking for, tell them you will approach the vendor directly. This will probably get the agent a little more motivated!

Multiple offer situations

When there is more than one offer, you will usually enter a sealed-bid offer situation. This means that all the bidders will put forward their best offer and the seller will pick one of them if any are to their liking. They do not always pick the highest one, but the one they like the most in terms of conditions and timing.

Tenders

In a tender situation all the buyers are supposed to place their best offer before a given date. Then the seller will review all the offers that the property received and pick the one they like the most.

The best you can do is to make sure you are clear about what the property is worth to you and put your best offer forward. Do not let real estate agents push you around and tell you that your offer will never be accepted; only the vendor can determine that.

Keep asking and remember this: If You Don't Ask You Don't Get.

Making successful offers

Step 1: Research

Always do you homework! This means doing as much research about a property and the vendor as you can before you make your offer. You will carry out more thorough due diligence once your offer is accepted, and you can use this to negotiate the price down even further. But you need to have as much information as possible so your first offer is realistic. It really pays to find out how much a vendor's mortgage is, for example. If you discover a vendor has a small mortgage and a lot of equity in a property, you will know that they will be in a better position to accept a lower offer. You also should know how much they bought the property for in the first place and what it is worth now, as this is another indication of how flexible they might be. (You can get this information from the property file at council, or using the RevIQ software; see www.reviq.com.)

Step 2: Work out your maximum purchase price

From your research work out what your maximum purchase price is before you enter into negotiations. This is very important. Work out what the maximum price is that you can pay and still make a profit before you make an offer. Do not go one cent over this price. Be prepared to walk away, and never let your emotions get the better of you. Make this a rule, and never, ever break it!

Step 3: Find out why the vendor wants to sell

Find out what is motivating the vendor to sell, as this can often give you good bargaining power. If you can, speak directly to them rather than through an agent. You can also talk to the agent and the neighbours to gain some insight as to their motivation. If you discover they are desperate or in a hurry, you will be in a much better position to buy the property for a discount than if they are just testing the waters and can wait for the next 10 years.

Never make an offer until you know what the seller wants. For example, they may want a long or short settlement period, they may need to get a certain price to keep the bank off their backs, they may be sick and tired of dealing with bad tenants, or they may just want to get rid of a property they have been lumbered with (as can happen with a deceased estate). Use this information to your advantage – if you can help the vendor out in some way by solving their concerns and giving them some of the things they want, you will be in a better position to bargain down the price. You will just be stabbing in the dark if you don't know what it is they want.

Step 4: Make the agreement appealing

Make the sales and purchase agreement appealing to the vendor. Don't use a company name on your offer, use your own name coupled with the 'and or nominee' option when you are making an offer, rather than a company name. This way you can change it later. (In Australia DO NOT use 'and/or nominee'; you must specify your buying entity). But, if you use a company name the vendor may be given the impression that you are an investor and may be inclined to think that you have a bottomless chequebook.

Step 5: Offer and conditions

The first offer you make should be your dream offer in terms of price, settlement, deposit and conditions/clauses. Prepare a new set of demands to trade for any concessions you have to make. If you have to give in one area, take in another! One of your dream conditions on your offer should be a long settlement period. A long settlement period is a good idea from a renovations point of view if you are able to gain access.

You can also reduce a long settlement period as an excellent way of negotiating. You could always name a date and say 'or earlier by mutual agreement' so you can negotiate without conceding on price. (If you want the right to settle early, you must add a special condition like this into the agreement).

It is also an excellent idea to make sure that the settlement date you agree on is at the beginning of the week. That way you can begin your renovations as soon as you take possession.

Avoid offering with rounded figures. If you offer with a strange figure, it will appear to the vendor that you have done all your calculations meticulously and that is the last penny you can squeeze out. Rounded figures just seem to invite more countersigning. (More on this in the next chapter.)

Step 6: Increase offers in small steps

Don't meet half way when you are countersigning. The idea is to get the property for the best price possible, so if you have to increase your offer, do it by small amounts and try not to move more than the vendor! Countersigning half way will probably mean you have moved more than was necessary. (More on this in the next chapter.)

Other tactics

Two offers at once

Presenting two offers at once can be a good way to get the vendor thinking along your lines. Make one offer a very low price for cash (as long as your finance is assured) and the other for a slightly higher price but with vendor financing or some other clause that really works in your favour (like the access to do renovations one, which is worth its weight in gold).

Include a cheque

Including a cheque with the agreement is another way to make your offer seem very attractive to the vendor without you having to compromise on price. Put a time limit on your offer, for example a time limit of 48 hours. This will create a sense of urgency. This is a good way to give the vendor the hurry-along, as they may be concerned they will miss out altogether if they don't at least countersign.

SUMMARY

To become successful at making offers you must completely understand the sale and purchase agreement. Learn how to use different clauses to protect yourself and to give you time to check that the property fits with your strategy before you have to commit to completing the purchase. Do not allow emotions to interfere when you are making offers, be clear about your numbers and your maximum price and stick to it. Do not let real estate agents push you around or pressure you. Know how much you are willing to pay so that it will fit with your strategy. If you're not sure, don't go ahead – another better deal will be just around the corner.

One of the best ways to improve your negotiation skills is to attend the Richmastery Negotiating Real Estate Deals one-day course. See www.richmastery.com.

Chapter 12

Viewing properties

SIMPLE STEPS TO MEET YOUR CRITERIA

'View 100 properties, make 10 offers and purchase only 1 of them.'

— Dolf De Roos

Know what you want

There is no such thing as a magical number of properties you have to view before finding the 'perfect' property. You just need to be very specific about what you want. If you think you have found a red-hot deal it's a good idea to get it under contract even before you view it or at least be ready to move on it quickly.

Do your figures first

If there is one money-making piece of advice we could give you it is to analyse the potentially great deal to make sure it meets your criteria before you actually go and view it. Time is your most valuable and profitable asset and you should be very careful about how you spend it. You can always make more money, but you will never be able to make more time. So if you think a deal looks good, do the numbers, negotiate the deal, get it under contract and only then view it. Then negotiate even further.

This way you will save time, lock up deals before other buyers can get to them and turbo-charge your way to real estate success, making more money than you dreamed possible.

Building inspections

Listen and learn

The best way to learn how to evaluate properties quickly is to first use a specialised building inspector when you are viewing a property. Make sure you take notes or even record on tape what the inspector says and what they look for during the inspection. This way you will know exactly what to investigate. With experience you may find you won't need a building inspector to help you work out if the property is sound enough to purchase.

Obviously, you will not be looking for the same characteristics across all property types. You will not be investigating the same things with a 1960s flat as with a brand-new house, so you will need to take the building inspector to several types of property to become a real expert yourself.

If you do not want to view a property yourself, always arrange for a building inspector to inspect it and write a report before you make a decision on whether you will complete the purchase.

Remember to ask the building inspector roughly how much it will cost to repair any faults. This way you can guesstimate how much it would cost you to bring each property up to standard. In turn, this will help you do your figures and decide whether you want to purchase it.

If you encounter a new problem or repair later that you did not get a costing on, or if you just forget the price, your building inspector will be only a phone call away and you will be able to make decisions quickly.

Giving you the edge

Having this knowledge of building inspections will give you an edge in three different ways.

- Agents and private sellers will take you as a serious, professional property investor who will not waste their time.
- Most importantly, this knowledge will give you an incredible amount of leverage when you are negotiating your deals. As soon as you can, work out what needs to be repaired immediately on a property you are looking to buy and what could be repaired but isn't essential. You will be able to use this knowledge to influence real estate agents and vendors to take a lower offer and achieve your preferred outcome when negotiating.

- You will also know how much the repairs that require immediate attention will cost; which improvements will give you a higher rent; and which ones will create more equity. You will be armed and dangerous!

Get familiar

View sufficient properties in your target area so that you become an expert in the particular neighbourhood. Check the demand for renting and buying in your target area, talk to real estate agents and let them know what you are looking for. Ask them to contact you first if any deals that meet your criteria come on the market.

Remember that demand will change depending on what type of property you are interested in. The kind of property you are interested in will differ according to your strategy and target customer. For example, if you are aiming at properties to buy and hold and intend to rent to specific types of tenants, such as nurses or students, you will be looking at different areas and different properties than if you were aiming at properties to subdivide and trade.

SUMMARY

Do your figures using the RevIQ software before you view a property so you do not waste time viewing properties that do not meet your criteria. Always use a building inspector to ensure the quality of the property until you have seen enough properties to know what you are looking for. Become an expert in your target area so you know a hot deal when you find one and get to know real estate agents so they bring deals to you. Following these simple steps will massively increase your profits, boosting your portfolio to a whole new level.

Chapter 13

Negotiating deals

MAKE MONEY WHEN YOU BUY

'Risk is essential. There is no growth in staying within what's safe and comfortable.'
— Anonymous

Let the process begin...

The negotiating process starts from the time that you know about the property and decide that you are going to pursue it. You will be negotiating when you make an offer and when you view the property.

The tactics offered in this chapter will add to the knowledge that you have already acquired in the last two chapters on viewing properties and making offers, as they are all part of the negotiating process.

The four personality types

Your negotiating strategy will change with every personality type you encounter. Let's divide people into four main personality types:

- driver
- analyser
- socialiser
- amiable.

Depending on which category the vendor falls into you will want to deal with them in a different manner. Let's first describe the main characteristics of each type. Try thinking of someone you know that fits each of these four categories.

Once you associate a face and a name with the personality type, you will always remember these descriptions.

Drivers

Drivers are usually high-powered individuals who live their lives by this sentence: 'I want to WIN.'

They love competition and they love beating people. They hate wasting time and dislike people who cannot decide quickly. They are usually business owners or hold positions with levels of responsibility. They want things done yesterday.

Is this description starting to sound like someone you know? Maybe someone who is holding this book right now? If you are a driver, we can assure you that you will win the property-investing game by reading this book.

Analysers

Analysers are usually obsessed with numbers and accumulating information. Their favourite sentence is: 'Do the NUMBERS and DATA work?'

They usually enjoy justifying their decisions logically more than they enjoy the result of the decision itself. They usually work as accountants, data analysts, researchers, scientists, IT specialists, mortgage brokers, financial advisors, solicitors, and the like. They are highly organised and love to keep everything they have in order. All their belongings will be colour coded and alphabetised. They spend hours on the Internet looking for facts and materials.

Decision-making is not an important process for analysers; they are only interested in how you get to the decision-making stage. The longer they can drag out this preparation stage the more fun they will have.

Do you have a good idea now of who we are talking about?

Socialisers

Socialisers are the easiest group to relate to. They live their lives thinking: 'How can I have FUN?'

They have a great zest for life, and they try to enjoy every second and do not like jobs where they can't talk and relate to others. They usually work as real estate agents, receptionists, in PR, as event organisers, and the like.

They will only do something if they can see the fun side of it. If they don't see the social rewards, they will become completely uninterested and unmotivated and will quickly give up. They have lots of friends and acquaintances, and their mobile phone bill is usually massive. Their need to be around people sometimes translates into sadness and even depression when they are by themselves. Success and money are just tools to get them to the next party. Probably you know quite a few socialisers; they will have made themselves well known around your social group.

Amiables

Amiable people are driven by love. There life is a constant question: 'Am I LOVED?'

Amiable personality types need to belong in order to be happy. They need to feel part of a group where they will get their craving for love satisfied. If something goes wrong, though, they will make a great fuss about it. In this way other people will want to console them and then they get the love dosage that they so desperately need.

Amiables usually work as personal assistants, actors, nurses, charity workers, and the like – in any field where they can feel appreciated. They will literally do anything to feel they belong. Their feelings are easily bruised because they mull over what every single act, thought or word means. They tend to be moody since their emotional states rock back and forth within minutes from depression to ecstasy, depending on whether they feel lonely or loved.

Where an investor should fit

Where do you think you fit in the four personality types? (See the chart on the next page.)

As a real estate investor you need to fit right in the middle of the chart. Your personality should be able to adapt to the situation and the person you are dealing with.

We have met lots of real estate investors who fit so strongly into one of these four personality types that they find it practically impossible to deal with the other three types of people. This limits their chances of success by a massive 75%. It does not matter even if you believe strongly that you belong to one of these groups. When you are investing in real estate you must put your neutral personality-type hat on. Next, quickly identify which kind of personality you are communicating with and adjust your style accordingly.

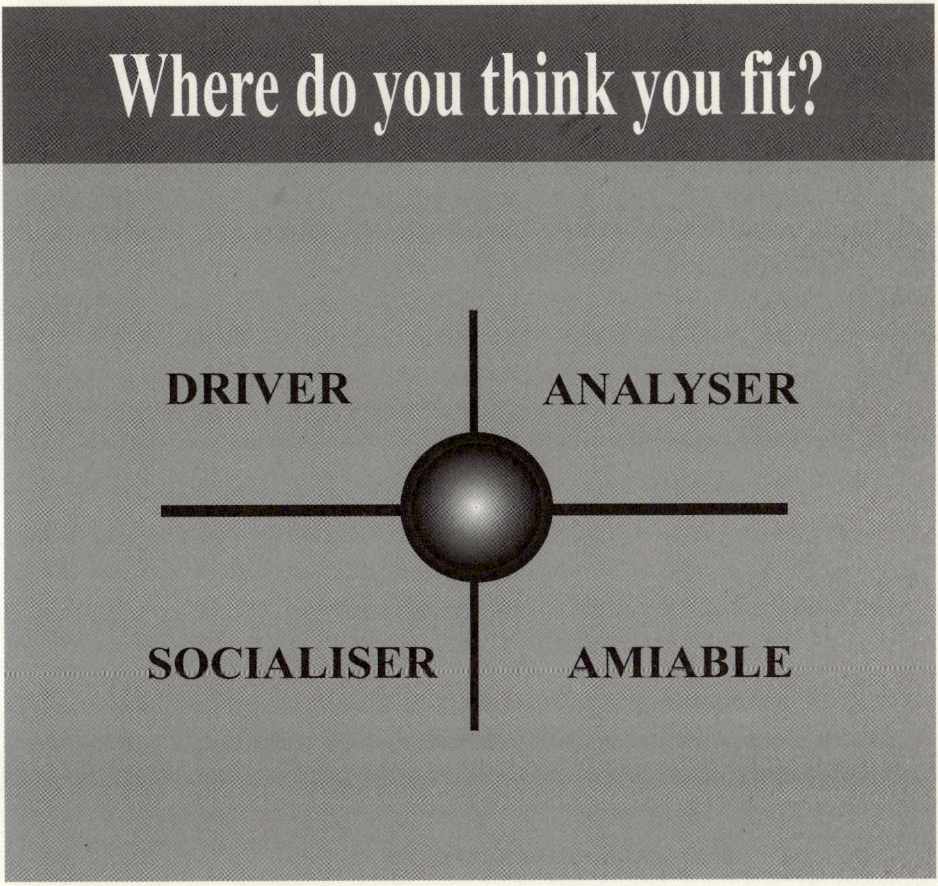

Using the vendor's personality type

Identifying their type

If you are able to, it is best to negotiate with the vendor directly. When you meet with them you need to have some good questions ready and be attentive to the way they answer them. One of the tactics you can use is to arrive around five minutes late, and make sure you look upset about something. Then complain about the traffic and how horrible it was to get here. Then stop, and see how they react or respond to the comment.

- A driver would respond something like this: 'Let's not waste any more time and put this deal together because I am very busy and need to get going.'
- An analyser would ask: 'What road did you take to get here? If you had taken Road 66 to the intersection at Quick Road then you would have made it with three extra minutes to spare. I can also see that you drive the old 98 model Porsche Boxster without the improved variable timing valves and only a 2.5-litre engine. If you upgraded to the newer model you would have also saved another two minutes and it is even more efficient in gas consumption...'
- A socialiser would say: 'That is OK. I am not meeting my friends for the new Tom Cruise movie until three o'clock so I am not in a hurry. Have you watched the movie yet? A friend called me to say it was excellent, but please do come in and we can have a drink and a chat before we look at the property...'
- An amiable would right away explain: 'Oh dear, it is not your fault. I shouldn't have made you come here at this time of the day. I feel horrible about it, please come in and I will get you a cup of tea and some biscuits...'

You can be as creative as you want with your situation; the real trick comes down to listening for key words and actions that will show into which category they are more likely to fit.

Speaking the vendor's language

Once you determine their personality type, start speaking in their language.

- Show drivers immediately and without a pause how they are going to benefit or win by putting together this deal.
- Go back to your car and show analysers a lot of data and articles on other property for sale in the region and why their property is actually worth 20% less than what they expect to get.
- Show socialisers how much fun you are and they will automatically want to deal with you.
- Give amiables the time they need to feel comfortable with you and the

deal is sure to follow. There are lots of cases where property is sold not to the highest bidder but to the person that the seller liked the most.

You will be amazed at how many more deals you will put together when you master this simple practical strategy.

Negotiating strategies

There are several strategies that you as a successful real estate investor should be aware of and think about utilising to negotiate great deals.

Increase your offer only by small increments

Most people make an offer, receive a counter-offer and usually meet in the middle. This method is nothing more than poor negotiating skills. You should always let the buyer know that you are getting very close to your limit, and that it may be the last offer they will ever see from you. Here's an example of a good negotiation:

A property is advertised at $165,000. You know that you can pay a maximum of $148,000 so that it would fit your portfolio. You offer $145,500 for it. The vendor counter-offers right away just in the middle at $155,000. This is a good sign. You then counter-offer at $146,250. The vendors then go down to $150,000 and you make a final offer of $146,750. The vendors accept it and the deal is done.

Let's look closely at the numbers. You went up $1250 from your first offer. The vendor went down $18,250. In an ordinary negotiation, an amateur negotiator and a seller would have met at $155,000, paying an extra $8250 that could have been used for renovations or as a part of a deposit on your next deal.

Why do we suggest you first offer $145,500 and not just $145,000 or $146,000? With this offer you indicate that you are close to your maximum offer. Remember, round numbers usually indicate that there is more money still in the piggy bank. That is also the reason why you would make your second offer $146,250 and your third offer $146,750.

This strategy of using small increments will save you a small fortune during your investing career – use it and profit!

Good cop, bad cop

Most of you will be familiar with this strategy, but few of you probably use it. This will work really well if you have a life partner or business partner. In this strategy one of you will be interested in buying a property while the other person (the bad cop) will keep reminding you that the deal is too expensive and risky and that you can't afford it. If the vendor is present you can even take your argument to a high level where you start shouting (being the good and bad cop) and the seller will be pushed to restore the peace by lowering his selling price.

The bad cop does actually have to be present in the negotiation. You could use your mobile phone to contact them. When the seller makes a counter-offer just tell them that you need to consult your partner. You can then go on to arguing over the phone about the deal and make your low final offer. It is amazing how well such a simple strategy really works. Use it and stand in awe at the results you will obtain.

Conditioning the vendor on a low offer

This strategy is very useful for 'conditioning' sellers. Not many people know about it and even fewer use it, which leaves lots of potential for you, the professional real estate investor. You go into a property with a clipboard and a property inspection checklist that has a large box on it labelled PURCHASE PRICE OFFER. You then go on to inspect the property and write down in the purchase price offer box what your initial LOW offer will be. Even justify it by writing down that a vendor one street over is willing to take the same amount for a similar property.

Next ask the vendor you are with if you could possibly use the bathroom. They will point you in the right direction and you will leave the clipboard in a highly visible spot near the vendor. Curiosity is a big driver and most vendors will read the contents of your clipboard and inspection sheet. This will condition them to start accepting that their property may not be worth as much as they thought it was. Be creative and include as much information as you may think necessary in the folder. Remember to make the information you want the seller to focus on as big and bold as possible. Underline the important points you want them to read.

Carry a torch and a damp detector

A torch is a great tool with which to indicate problems with a property to the sellers without opening your mouth – even if it is just a stain on the wall. Just remember to always write something down in your inspection report when you point the torch at something. (Even if you write 'must remember to stop by the supermarket to get some bread and milk'.)

Always carry around a damp detector (you can purchase these at hardware stores) to all your inspections. The best are the ones that scream when they get any unusual reading whatsoever. It is really impressive for the seller to hear that horrible sound. Do not say anything about it, just make a worried HMMM sound.

Always point out what is wrong with the property and never seem too eager to purchase. Leverage is very important in the negotiating game: the less you want or need a property, the higher the chances of getting it at a good price. Always remember that another deal is just around the corner, and the deal of the century comes once a week.

Negotiating tactics

Negotiate price and conditions via fax first

Educated real estate investors often negotiate the property price and conditions via fax before ever setting foot on the property itself. If the numbers work, only then will they make the effort to look at the property. This method of negotiating deals will save you a lot of time, and you will be able to quickly identify who the motivated vendors truly are.

Start with your end-price in mind

When you are negotiating deals, always start with the end in mind. This means that you need to start off knowing the maximum price that you would be willing to pay.

While you need to buy at a price that works for you, you also need to be fair. This is not about screwing a vendor down to the last penny so that they feel ripped off, when the deal would have worked really well for you a few thousand dollars ago. You must not worry about paying an extra $10,000 if you are going to make $100,000 in profit. Remember the big picture!

Many 'investors' never end up owning more than one or two properties because when they look at a deal they want to get every single cent out of every property they are interested in purchasing. This creates a problem for them, since other investors or buyers will offer a slightly higher amount and end up getting the deal instead. If you follow the 'getting the last cent' philosophy on property investing, you will have a very hard, long and unproductive career.

Aim for win-win results

Always leave something on the table for the next party or parties. This way of thinking will take your portfolio to completely new heights. When people do a deal with you and they feel like they have also won, they will want to do more deals with you and recommend you to their friends. This is what property investing is all about. There are two 'Ps' in 'ProPerty'. The first P stands for Preparation and the second P stands for People. People skills are necessary for a successful and fun-loaded career.

You will probably be asking yourself, how do you work out how much money you need to leave on the table for the other party? The answer to this question is simple: It depends. Your goals and buying rules will determine what the maximum price is that you can offer for a property. Then you will start with a negotiating strategy that will take you to that goal.

Negotiate face to face, in a neutral place

Whenever possible, meet the vendor face to face when you are negotiating. It is well worth doing as it is much easier to crank the price down if the seller is sitting across the table from you than if you are negotiating through an agent, who may not be telling the whole truth to either of you. You can include a clause in your agreement that you are to be present when the offer is presented. The agent might squeak about this a bit, but be insistent – it could cut the whole negotiating time down significantly as well as making it a lot easier. It is far better to negotiate when the vendor is feeling relaxed. For this reason it is preferable to negotiate when they are at home rather than at work where they are likely to be busy and distracted.

Always negotiate in a neutral place. If it is at the property, go to the kitchen, as all parties will feel comfortable there. People usually mingle in the kitchen and you should use it to your advantage.

Condition the vendor

Condition the vendor by chatting to them first to find out why they are selling. When negotiating, if you know the vendor's soft points you can tell them what they want to hear. For example, if the house is a neglected mess, sympathise with them and say you know how hard it is to maintain property these days. If they have lousy tenants, blame the tenants or the property manager. You can even blame bad luck, but never blame the vendor.

Point out all the things that need to be done to the property and explain that they will cost a lot of money to do. Remind them how expensive renovations are, that the property obviously needs work and you will have to bear these costs over and above what you pay for the property. Tell them it will cost the same to get the property up to scratch no matter who makes the improvements, and if they will accept a fair price for it they will avoid the not insignificant hassle of having to renovate themselves. (Just in case they are starting to think that this renovations thing is a good idea!)

Highlight potential problems

Highlight potential problems with the property – point them all out (again without in any way blaming the vendor), even if the problems don't concern you. For example, you might highlight the fact that the section will be very tricky and expensive to subdivide, even if you have no intention of subdividing it now or in the future.

Be aware of body language when you are negotiating. Take note of the vendor's body language, as this will help you in your negotiations. Reflect the feeling and energy of the vendor to make them feel comfortable. Be a good listener and empathise with the issues they have. If they are leaning forward and looking excited it could be a good time to start closing the deal. Keep asking the vendor questions. Whoever asks the last question controls the negotiation – so make sure it's you! It is perfectly acceptable to follow a question with another question, especially if it's a negative one (such as 'How long has that rot been there?' or 'Aren't you worried that the stairs are so dangerous they might cause an accident?' or 'Do you realise how hard it is to get rid of cockroaches?').

Use your research

You can use the research you have done on a property to negotiate, and use figures from your feasibility study to back you up. Never show a vendor or agent your entire feasibility study, however, or they just might decide you have such excellent plans that they will carry them out themselves. The fact that they know you have done your research diligently will often be enough to stop them mucking about anyway.

A property that is being sold specifically as an investment will often come with some sort of rental guarantee. If it doesn't, you could use its absence to bargain the price down.

Show you have other opportunities

Don't put all your eggs in one basket – keep looking for other properties even while you negotiate. This will not only mean you are one step ahead in finding the next deal if this one falls over, you are also sending a clear message to the agent and the vendor that you may cancel at any time because you have found a better opportunity.

Continuing on our theme of the previous tip, let both the vendor and the real estate agent know that you are still actively looking for properties, by accidentally pulling other agents' cards out of your pocket. This may well encourage the agent to get a wriggle on and persuade the vendor to seal the deal, as they will be worried that you will buy something else instead and they will not get their commission. Showing these cards will also motivate the vendor if they know that you are happy to walk away because you have other options up your sleeve.

Leave the price until last

Negotiate on all the other things first and leave the price for last. For example, you could negotiate the settlement date, chattels (e.g. appliances) and rubbish removal first. Ask the vendor what their price is. Often the price of a property is not advertised, and even if it is, we all know it is not what the vendor really expects to get. Ask the vendor to tell you what their realistic asking price is, so that you know whether you can make a deal with them.

Tell them you don't want to waste their time or yours, and if they will tell you what they really want for the property you will know if it is a possibility worth pursuing. Ask them if they think that telling you what their price is, so you know if you can do business, is fair (which of course it is!).

Ask how the vendor arrived at the price

As part of your negotiations, ask the vendor how they arrived at the price they are asking. If they do not have a good reason, but have just grabbed the first figure that came to them, your facts and figures about what needs to be done to the property will have a much better chance of persuading them that their price is too high.

Ask the cash price

Ask the vendor what they would accept if you were to pay cash. Be silent when they give their answer. If you don't say anything they may well feel compelled to fill the silence with an even lower price. Then ask them if that is the best they can do.

Always tell the vendor that you will pay cash for their property, which means that you can move in quickly – not that you actually have the cash in your bank account. You will not be lying because you will be paying cash since all transactions are basically cash transactions.

The vendor's response to an offer

If a seller countersigns your offer, you will know that, at least to some extent, they are motivated. If a vendor counter-offers with a big drop from their asking price you will know that they are anxious to sell and the deal is very worth pursuing. If they don't budge, or only very slightly, you could well have a hard, if not impossible, road ahead to persuade them to sell at your price. Anxious vendors are the ones we like best – not to take advantage of them, but to create a win-win situation where you buy the property for the price that works for you, and they get out of a sticky or unpleasant situation.

If you know the vendor is desperate to sell because they are in financial difficulty, ask if they will sell the property for what they owe on it. This is a particularly good question to ask people who are just about to be foreclosed on by the bank.

Negotiating payments and vendor finance

If you have had to move in other areas to get the deal to work, you can negotiate to pay the purchase price in instalments. A motivated vendor may be receptive to this idea if they really want to close the deal.

You can also negotiate vendor finance. You may be prepared to raise your price a little if the vendor will provide finance. This can be a great way to make a deal work for both parties, especially if the vendor is not desperate to receive the full amount immediately. They will be earning interest on the money they leave in the property, and you will be getting finance.

Renegotiate at the last minute

If you are having trouble clinching the deal, raise your offer and include a due diligence clause or property-inspection clause. Then you can use the problems you find during your inspection to renegotiate before settlement. If you are going to do this it is best to leave it to the last minute to renegotiate, as the vendor will have been feeling fairly certain the sale will go through, and they may be alarmed enough to be receptive to your lower offer.

You can also use a finance clause or subject-to-valuation clause to renegotiate at the last minute. For example, you could say that the valuation was not high enough for the bank and they will only give you finance if the vendor will agree to lower the price. As with all your dealings, only do this if there is at least some truth to it!

If your offer isn't accepted

If your offer is rejected because the vendor has been presented with, and accepted, a higher one, submit yours as a back-up offer. Include a clause stating that if the first purchase falls over, the property will be sold to you.

SUMMARY

If possible meet with the vendor face to face when negotiating. Your strategy will change depending on the personality type of the vendor or agent you are negotiating with. So first you need to work out what this is and then adjust your approach to build rapport with the vendor or agent. Only use the strategies and tips that you feel comfortable with. It's not about using them all; it's about using the right ones to achieve your desired outcome. Dip into this negotiating toolbox and see your profits soar. Also read Richmastery's book on Negotiations – it's packed full of hundreds of fantastic tactics you can use to master the negotiation process.

14

Sealing the deal

Going unconditional and completing the purchase

'Failure is easier to live with than regret.'
— Tony Robbins

Going unconditional

Going unconditional basically means that the property is now yours since it has met all your conditions and you have not decided to pull out of the sale and purchase agreement but instead will complete on the deal. Now you are just awaiting a specific date to transfer the balance of the money owed minus the deposit you would have already paid to the seller on acceptance of the agreement.

Paying a deposit

Make a low deposit – or none at all

It is usual for a deposit to be paid on signing the sale and purchase agreement, or within a specified period after doing so. Make your deposit as low as possible – i.e. keep the amount of cash you hand over to an absolute minimum. It is perfectly OK to pay a deposit of $100 even if the agent is asking for 10%. You may even be able to get away with paying no deposit at all if you agree to settle promptly. An agent may push you to pay at least 4% as they will want it to get their commission immediately (usually about 4% of the purchase price) but you are under no obligation to pay this much.

Always get a receipt from the real estate agent (or from the vendor if it is a private sale) for your deposit. And always pay your deposit to a real estate agent's or solicitor's trust account – NEVER to the vendor's bank account.

Solve a problem instead of paying a deposit

You may even be able to solve a problem for a vendor in exchange for not having to pay a deposit. For example, you may agree to solve their bad tenant problem in the period before settlement. Or you may make urgent repairs in that time so they can keep the tenants they have and get rent during the settlement period. This is a great way to make your purchase a 'no-money-down' deal.

In order to seal a deal, you could offer to pay the vendor's conveyancing costs. This will be very attractive to a vendor for whom money is tight, and the costs involved will probably be small compared to the profit you will make if the deal goes ahead.

Get access if agreed

If there are lots of repairs to be done and you have negotiated early access, expect to get the keys when the agreement has gone unconditional. Hopefully you will have extended the settlement date as far as you can, so that you can finish the repairs and show the property to possible tenants or buyers.

Legal fees

Ask your agents not to send any contracts to your solicitor before you declare it unconditional. Otherwise you will be up for paying a lot of unwanted and usually expensive legal fees.

Building insurance

Make sure that the property has building insurance during the period from going unconditional through to completion of the purchase. It is a bit of a grey area whose responsibility it is to insure the property during this period. It should be the vendors', but just to make sure, always get insurance from the date you go unconditional. Don't take the seller's word about having building insurance and then find out that the property you've just bought burned down on the night prior to settlement.

Settlement of the purchase

Settlement day is when the purchaser takes possession of the property. When the sale and purchase agreement becomes unconditional, the solicitors will get the conveyancing process under way so that both parties will be ready by settlement day. Always check the property on the day of settlement to make sure that it is in the condition that you expected it to be in. If it is not, you can always choose not to settle and hold back the funds until you are happy with the condition the property is in. You really do not want to be buying a big pile of ashes on a section.

SUMMARY

Pay a low deposit, or none at all if you can arrange it. You may be able to fix a problem for the vendor in exchange for not making a deposit. Make sure the property is insured once the settlement has gone unconditional. Settlement day has no real secrets; it's just a mere formality. Congratulations! You have just bought an investment property. Make sure you inspect the property on the day of settlement.

Part Three

22 top real estate strategies

Introduction

INVESTMENT STRATEGIES TO INCREASE YOUR PROFITS

'Invest in yourself first, before you invest in anything else.'
— David Leon

By now you are familiar with some of the key concepts of investing in real estate, understand the buying process step by step and the need to set up the correct structures for tax and asset planning. You are ready to learn about some exciting investment strategies you can use to massively increase your profits.

You do not have to use all the strategies we cover, but you can be aware of them and understand how they work so that you have them as part of your investing toolbox. You can use them when you find a deal that will work well with a particular type of strategy.

The aim of this book is to be a reference that you can always refer to when bringing deals together. Each of the strategies outlined can be utilised to accelerate the growth of your portfolio, depending on the type of deal you find, how much equity or cash you have to invest and which part of the cycle the real estate market is in.

Also remember that new strategies develop on a regular basis so keep learning, networking and educating yourself constantly so that you can keep reaping the benefits of new ways to invest in and profit from real estate.

The strategies explained in this part of the book are not in a specific order. We have started with the simplest strategies and followed with the slightly more difficult ones so that you build your knowledge and understanding.

If you are not clear why you are getting into real estate investing you should read Chapter 37 on goal setting before you start learning about these powerful strategies. The strategies outlined here are like a loaded gun: you will decide when and if to use them and if you proceed when you are not supposed to the results could potentially be ugly. On the other hand, once you finish reading this book (including the goal setting chapter) you will be armed and dangerous and ready to make some exceptional financial returns.

Let's get started by building up your credit history so that you will be able to borrow money and create true leverage and success!

Chapter 15

Building a credit history

GETTING IN GOOD SHAPE TO BORROW

'Problem + Solution = Profit.'
— Steve McKnight

Having a good credit history is crucial to being able to borrow money and thus to being able to build a successful and profitable real estate investment portfolio.

There are national agencies that are in charge of keeping records of all your borrowings and credit history. This means any finance applications, missed bill payments or even mobile phone contracts under your name will be recorded. All lending institutions will have access to this information and this information is known as a person's credit history or credit rating.

Why is a credit rating so important?

A credit rating is used by lenders to determine what the risk is in lending money to a particular person or entity. A big part of their final decision on whether they will lend money is based on this credit rating, which means it is very important that yours is in good shape.

The first thing you should do is get a copy of your full credit history to determine where you currently stand.

How do I access my credit information?

The law guarantees that you are generally able to have access to your own file kept by a credit reporting agency or to a credit report kept by a credit provider. Under the law, a credit provider must notify you if it has refused to grant you credit on the basis of a credit report obtained from a credit reporting agency.

If you wish to obtain a copy of your credit information file, you should write to the relevant credit reporting agency requesting a copy. Give your full name and current residential address and any other permitted information which the agency requests for the purposes of identifying you; for example, your previous residential address if you have moved in the past three years, date of birth and driver's licence number. The credit reporting agency must provide a copy of your file within 10 working days of having received your written request.

The two main credit reporting agencies in Australia are:

- **Baycorp** (for residents of mainland Australia) www.creditadvantage.com.au
- **Tasmanian Collection Service** (for Tasmanian residents) www.tascol.com.au

In New Zealand the main credit reporting agency is:

- **Baycorp** www.baycorpadvantage.com

The agency may provide your credit information to a person who has been authorised, in writing, by you to act on your behalf.

You can also write to a credit provider for a copy of the specific credit report that the credit provider used in the assessment of your application for credit. If the credit provider no longer has the report, it will advise you to contact the credit reporting agency that issued the credit report.

Check your credit report

Check for errors

Once you get a copy of your credit report, make sure it does not contain any factual errors. Around 40% of all credit files kept by these agencies have at least one error in them. This could be something as minor as the misspelling of your last name and this mistake could be affecting your credit rating hugely because you are being judged on someone else's debts.

There have been cases where people have impersonated others to obtain credit without them being aware, resulting in a dramatically impaired credit rating for the victim of the impersonation. One poor investor constantly has to go to court to clear his credit history because there is another gentleman with the same name who resides in the same city and keeps getting into trouble by not making payments on debts. Debtors register this lack of payment with the credit reporting company and the agency then shows that this poor investor has a bad credit rating, even though it is the other gentleman who is causing the problem.

Attend to debts

If there are any past debts that you have not attended to that are affecting your credit rating you need to take action immediately. If you haven't yet paid the debt, contact the company and offer to pay this straight away. This can often be enough to get them to go back to the credit agency and eliminate the record. If you have already paid the debt a friendly phone call or letter can help get the bad debt taken off your record.

If you do not think it was fair that the debt has been lodged with a debt collection agency you can challenge the decision with the company who lodged the bad debt. To do this get in touch with the company directly and see if they will write a letter to the credit agency on your behalf to get this removed. If all of this fails approach the credit reporting agency directly and explain the situation to them. They are obliged by law to help you and remove any mistaken or unfair information.

How to build on a minimal credit history

Having no credit history or a very minimal one is almost as bad as having a bad credit rating. Lenders will look at your credit history and won't be able to make up their mind on whether to approve your loan as no one else has lent you any money previously.

The more you borrow from an institution the more likely it is that you will be able to obtain credit from them at a later date. Having a record as being a good borrower helps when borrowing money.

Ask for loans from different banks

An exercise that can help build a credit history is to ask for loans from different banks. One course of action you can take is to start by asking for loans with no redemption penalties and then place the amount that you borrow into a savings account for one month. After the month is up, repay the entire loan and all you will lose is the difference between the interest paid for the loan and the interest gained on the savings. This is a very small price to pay to be considered a good customer by several banks and you should repeat this process as many times as you can.

Asking for loans example

Here is an example to illustrate in a clear time-lined way just how powerful this strategy can be if you need to build a loan history.

- **Step 1:** Start by obtaining a small amount of funds. Let's make it $1000 for the sake of making the numbers in this exercise simple to calculate.
- **Step 2:** Open a savings account with 'Bank 1' (a bank that you do not already have a relationship with) and deposit the $1000 that you had to start with.
- **Step 3:** Ask 'Bank 1' for a loan of $1000. Because they do not already have a relationship with you they will ask for some kind of security. Offer them the $1000 savings as a security for the loan. They should then be able to lock the money until you repay the loan. Ask for a loan with no penalties for early full repayment; if you don't do so you will pay the consequences in the form of high penalty fees.
- **Step 4:** Take the $1000 from the 'Bank 1' loan to another bank you also do not have a relationship with – we will call this 'Bank 2'. Open another savings account with the $1000 from the 'Bank 1' loan.
- **Step 5:** Ask 'Bank 2' for a loan of $1000. Because they do not already have a relationship with you they will ask for some kind of security. Offer them the $1000 savings that you now have in their bank as a security for the loan. They should then be able to lock the money until you repay the loan. Remember about asking for no penalty fees for early repayment of the loan.
- **Step 6:** Repeat steps 2 and 3 in another two banks.

- **Step 7:** You will end up with $1000 in your pocket from the last bank you requested a loan from. Pay off the first complete 'Bank 1' loan of $1000 with the $1000 that you have in your pocket.
- **Step 8:** They will now release the money from your 'Bank 1' savings account that you will use to pay off the 'Bank 2' loan.
- **Step 9:** Repeat steps 7 and 8 with the other two banks.

Result: You will end up with the $1000 you originally had minus the interest that you have paid for the loans and plus the interest you have earned on your savings accounts.

While this exercise seems time-consuming, the exciting part comes now that you have built relationships with four new banks within a short amount of time. You can now probably borrow the same amount of cash from these four banks without any security. That means you can have $4000 at any time by making four phone calls. If you need more money, add another zero and play this game as hard as you want – it works.

Try it with credit cards

You can also do this exercise with credit cards instead of loans. The only difference is that you will be doing balance transfers to establish relationships with different credit card lenders. Ultimately the outcome will be the same – increased borrowing capacity and improvement of credit rating.

SUMMARY

Building a good credit history is essential for any investor to be able to successfully raise finance and thus to build a profitable real estate business. You don't want to miss out on a deal just because you do not have the deposit for it. Research your credit rating with your local agency: check that there are no mistakes; if you have bad debts lodged against your name work to get these struck off and sorted out with the company who lodged them or with the credit agency directly. If you have a bad credit rating or have a minimal credit history, follow the exercise above to build one up.

Summary of steps

1. Obtain your current credit history.
2. Fix any errors you find on your file.
3. Challenge any small debts that should never have been lodged with the credit agency.
4. If you have a minimal credit history or bad credit rating establish relationships with different lenders by borrowing money as shown in Steps 1–9 above to build a new and positive credit history.

Chapter 16

Quick cash deals

FLIPPING PROPERTY FOR PROFIT

'Some people make it happen, some people watch it happen, and some people just sit around and wonder what happened. Which one are you?'

— Anonymous

Buying real estate and selling it again within a short time frame for profit is known as trading. Other names for this strategy include flipping property or doing 'quick cash deals'.

If you are in need of some quick cash or are just starting out in real estate investment and wanting to build up some capital, this strategy can be a fantastic way to make money fast.

Maximise your profits

The best way to maximise your profits with quick cash deals is to buy a property at a discount, add value through renovations and then on-sell the property quickly.

Using a 'quick cash' strategy is especially good in countries such as New Zealand where there is no capital gains tax. However, you can still make some huge profits from following this strategy in Australia, just as long as you factor stamp duty and capital gains tax into your figures when you calculate what your profit will be on the deal. The RevIQ software makes this easy.

There is only a limited number of people practising this strategy, leaving plenty of opportunity for serious and educated investors, like you, to make a lot of money from it.

Purchase your quick cash deals with the right entity

When you are buying to sell ensure that you do so within the correct structure. As discussed in Chapter 8 it is very important that you get your structure right before you start. Take advice from your asset planning expert, accountant and solicitor BEFORE you purchase any properties that you want to trade. Your situation may be more complex and different types of structures may be more appropriate in different circumstances.

You will need to pay tax on the profit you make with these deals, and this should be built into your budget before you commit to purchasing the property. Remember you only pay taxes when you make a profit. So don't be scared about having to pay tax, factor it into your pre-purchase analysis, make money on the deal, pay tax, and move on to the next deal.

What type of properties make good quick cash deals?

The hardest part of making this strategy work is finding the right discounted property to do a profitable quick cash deal with. Below are some techniques we recommend you can use to find the right property for a quick cash deal.

Only buy quick cash deals at a discount

To profit from this strategy you need to purchase the property below market value.

One way to purchase property at a discount is to buy properties that need simple, cosmetic renovations that will put off many buyers. Look for properties that are basically sound but have things like old cars in the front yard, graffiti on the fence and rubbish out the back – nothing that a bit of simple landscaping and general tidying up can't fix. There might be some peeling paint inside and the place might need recarpeting and some simple modernisation such as new kitchen units or bathroom fittings, new light fittings and door handles. These sorts of improvements are relatively cheap, easy and quick to do. You can add a lot of value in a very short time.

Avoid purchasing properties which require major structural renovations or which have a lot of maintenance issues as they will require a huge cash injection and a lot more time to bring them up to scratch.

Identify motivated vendors

Another fantastic way to find properties at a discount is by finding a motivated vendor.

The six Ds is always a good place to start when looking for motivated vendors.

The Richmastery Six Ds

- Divorce – are the vendors selling up because they are divorcing?
- Death – is the property being sold as a deceased estate?
- D'bank – is it a mortgagee sale, or are they behind in their loan repayments?
- Deadlines – does the vendor have to move or to sell by a certain date?
- Developers – does a developer need to sell some property fast to reach a pre-sales target or clear out unsold units in a development?
- Dummies – is the vendor unaware of what the property is worth because he/she is living in a different area to where the property is being sold?

If you are dealing with a real estate agent, keep asking them questions about why the vendor is selling to make sure you get the real reason.

As discussed in Chapter 13, if you can meet with the vendor face to face it will always be easier to find out how motivated they are. When dealing with the vendor directly you will be able to identify a motivated vendor by a few telltale signs. They will always listen carefully, they will seem anxious about the deal and they may be receptive to new ideas.

As soon as you find a motivated vendor you know you are on the right track to making a profit as they are much easier to negotiate with because they have a reason to sell.

Place classified ads to check demand and find motivated vendors

One of the most effective tools for finding some red-hot deals below market value and to identify motivated vendors is the classified ad. It is a simple and easy-to-use tool that is accessible to anyone.

The first step is to find out which newspapers and magazines people read in your target area when they are looking to purchase or rent a property. Also look into which websites they go to, as the Internet is fast becoming the method of choice for many prospective buyers and tenants.

Once you have worked out which publications or websites are the most popular for your target area you can start the process described as follows.

Research the best type of properties for your target area

Before you decide which type of 'quick cash' property to buy it's a good idea to research what the majority of people in your target area want to buy or rent. Are they predominantly families who want three-bedroom family homes with a good size section and garage? Retired people looking for two-bedroom, easily maintained units? Groups of students wanting large multi-room properties?

You can often find out this information simply by talking to locals and real estate agents about what demand there is for different types of properties from buyers and tenants looking to buy or rent in the area.

The next step is to check if the market is ready for the quick cash strategy by placing advertisements in the publications or websites you have identified.

By placing ads before you purchase you can double check the demand for the type of property you are advertising (and looking to purchase). Confirming the demand in the market through this method decreases your risks.

Tips in writing classified advertisements

Always specify the type of property, area and price when you are writing an advertisement.

Always use female names on the ads because experience has shown us that people feel less intimidated calling and talking to a female. We have tested this and can guarantee that by changing a male name to a female one you will almost certainly increase your number of leads by about 25%.

Always give a mobile number that is not your personal or business one. You never know who will be getting hold of your number and it will be highly inconvenient to be forced to change phone numbers because of one lunatic caller who is making your life impossible. We call this extra mobile number the 'psycho line'. The cheapest and simplest option to get a second number is to buy another phone with a prepaid card. Then if someone starts really bothering you with unwanted phone calls, you can always disregard the number without too much inconvenience or expense.

Example 1: Classified Ads to Test Demand in the Market

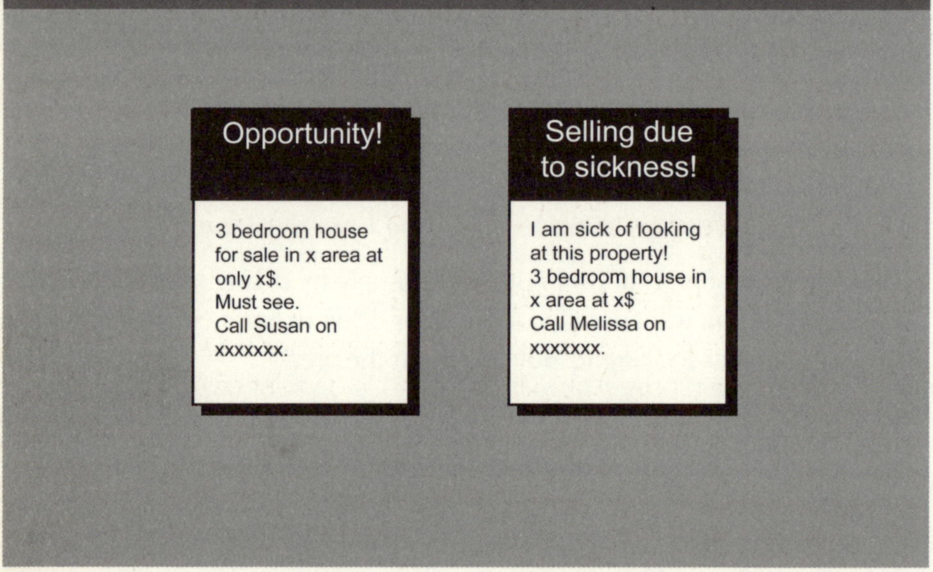

Checking demand

Remember that at this stage you are only trying to check if there is any demand for a specific kind of property by counting the number of phone calls you receive per ad placed.

If you receive more than 20 calls on the first day after you place an ad specifying the area and the type of property you have to let or for sale, you will know that there is demand for that kind of property.

Usually selling is a bit more unpredictable, but if you get 20 or more calls it is very likely that you will be able to sell the property reasonably quickly. However, if you don't get any calls then perhaps the demand for this type of property is just not there and you may need to find something different.

Remember that you are assessing the market. However, there is one other benefit to this process – you are simultaneously building a database of possible purchasers or tenants.

Building your database of possible purchasers/tenants

In order to build a database of possible purchasers or tenants you will need to take certain details from the callers who reply to your ads.

When they call to enquire about the property you have advertised tell them: 'I'm so sorry! The property advertised is unavailable, but we'll be getting another property in the area shortly. Can I take down your name and number and we will contact you and give you priority when we put the next one on the market.'

Each call you receive not only gives you a clearer evaluation of the target area you are focusing on but also represents a possible future customer.

Ads to source red hot deals

Once you have tested demand, you will be ready to place your second classified ad (see example next page). It is this ad that you will use to find great deals.

Both these ads give very good results; the only difference between them is that the second one is a bit less aggressive and you will come across as a first-time buyer rather than an investor with big pockets. Test them both and see which one gets you the best results.

How to identify motivated vendors from ads

After placing these ads you will then start receiving phone calls and the first question you need to ask is: *'Why are you selling the property?'*

The reason for asking this question is to identify motivated vendors. Depending on their answer you should be able to tell whether they are serious about selling so you can work out if it's likely you can negotiate with them to purchase the property under market value.

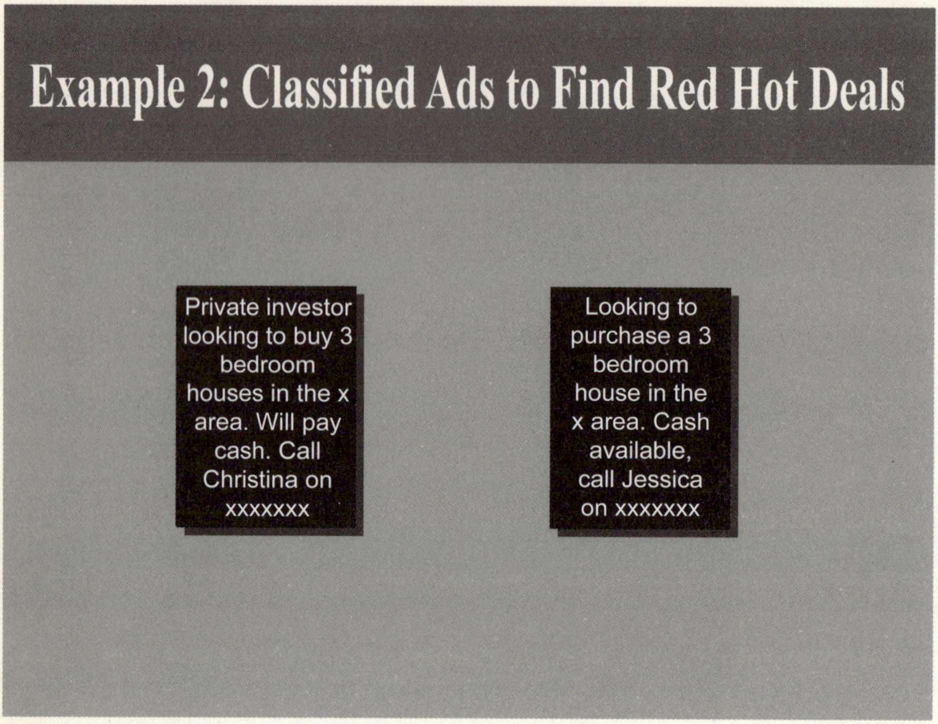

Always look for the win-win result

Let's clarify something before we go any further. You are not trying to rip anyone off! You should always aim to make the deal a win-win for all parties involved. Look to create solutions for the seller of the property.

By advertising yourself as a serious buyer you will be providing people with a service. If they sell their property to you they will not have to pay any real estate agency fees, they won't have to sign any complicated exclusivity contracts and won't have to suffer having time wasters and unwanted visitors viewing their property. Besides this, you can also be flexible in terms of the timing of any sale and this can prove valuable for vendors. All these factors combined make up the discount on the market price that you need to achieve when you purchase property. In this way the deal will produce enough profit to make it worthwhile for you.

As discussed in Chapter 13: Negotiating Deals, your aim is to get to know as much as you can about the vendor so that you will be able to offer them several alternatives on the sale of their property.

This concept will become clearer when you read the next few strategies. All the strategies explained in this book will provide you with a set of tools that you can take out to tackle any deal you may encounter. Each time you will be looking to provide solutions to different problems that different vendors will be experiencing.

Build a rapport with the vendor

Always ask vendors what their time frame is, what they are expecting and what they know about the buy-sell process and offer them some advice and help.

Your aim is for them enjoy dealing with you. One simple technique you can use to have a better chance of establishing an instant rapport with the vendor is to imitate the tone of their voice and their cadence of speech. Don't worry about being too obvious when you try to emulate their tone, you will not be obvious in 99% of the cases. People like people who are like themselves, and that's why it is a great technique to apply this tip when dealing with vendors or real estate agents.

Follow up your hot leads quickly

Of all the phone calls you get, only a small percentage will be good leads. You have to be able to identify the good leads quickly and arrange to meet with the person as soon as possible. Take action immediately or it will be too late.

The more you get used to receiving these phone calls, the better you will become at getting information and being able to sort them out to produce the outcome you are after.

Never lose focus of your outcome with a quick cash deal – which is to create income by purchasing a property under market value, doing cosmetic renovations and selling it for a profit after tax and expenses.

Should you sell with or without a real estate agent?

There are benefits for and against selling the property yourself or using a real estate agent.

Selling the property privately

If you decide to on-sell the property yourself you can use classified ads to sell your property quickly or contact your database of interested buyers and fellow investors to see if they are interested in purchasing it.

The ads can be the same style that you used when you were testing the market in Example 1 above.

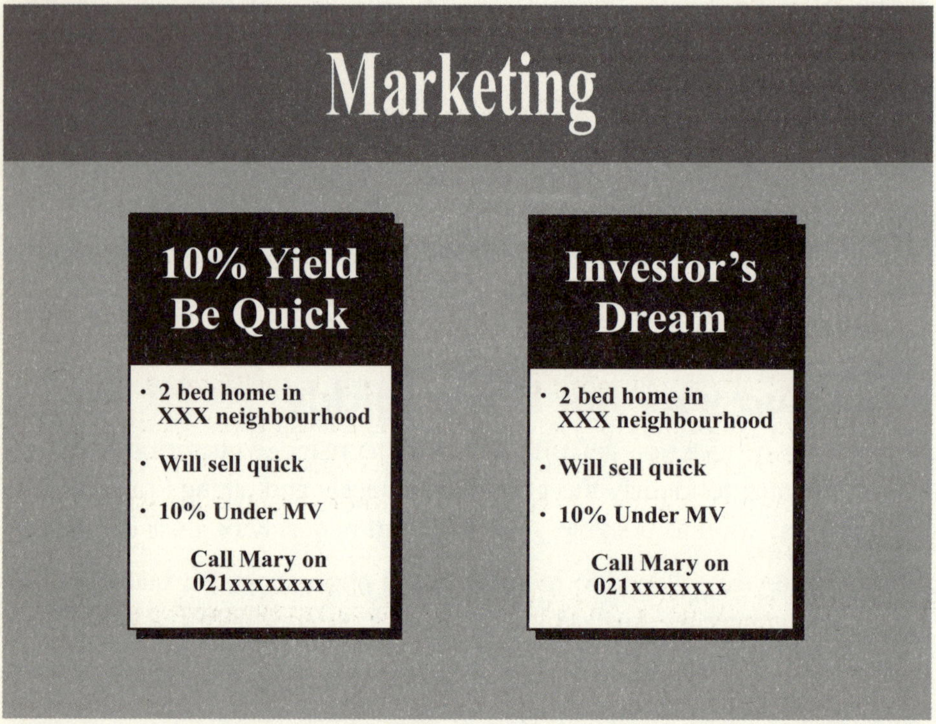

The main benefit of advertising deals yourself is that you can save on real estate agent fees and this will help you to be in a better position to offer your buyers a good deal.

Remember with quick cash deals not to focus on always getting the highest price for your property. It is much better to get a slightly lower one and to keep rolling your money quickly so you do not increase holding costs and you can move on to the next deal.

Selling the property through a real estate agent

If you decide to sell the property through a real estate agent you must be able to build the real estate agent's fees into your costs and still make a profit. (Use the RevIQ software to do this.)

Real estate agents can be a very useful part of your team. If you get the right agent, they will have a rich database of prospective buyers, and this can minimise the time it takes to sell your property and thus help you to maximise your profits. A good real estate agent can often be the difference between great and average profits with this strategy.

If you choose to use a real estate agent always get the top real estate agent in the area to on-sell the property for you.

Keep your money moving

Rotating your money and not waiting for the last dollar is a very important point. Remember that there are other deals around that will make you even more money, so fast turnover is crucial. It means you will be able to leap on the good deals when they come along. This is an extremely important concept in any business endeavour you will be undertaking. When you adopt this strategy you become a professional property trader, not just a home buyer. Rotate your money quickly and keep creating more profit. In this game, speed equals success.

Use the buying process to your advantage

You can use the real estate buying process discussed in Part Two to your advantage when doing quick cash deals.

Gain early access

As you know after reading Part Two: The Buying Process Step by Step, there is a period of time between going unconditional and settlement day on any purchase. This period is one that varies depending on the length of time the buyer negotiates with the vendor. As a professional investor you can use this period to increase your profits.

When you make the offer you will want to negotiate to delay the final settlement date as long as possible if you need to do repairs and renovations to the property.

As outlined in Part Two, to arrange early access you need to get the vendor to agree to including an early-access clause in the sale and purchase agreement. This will allow you access to the property from the time you go unconditional (rather than on the settlement date).

If you complete this simple process you can do all the repairs, or at least most of them, before you even start paying for the mortgage. Also remember that you pay the mortgage in arrears (usually a full month in arrears), which gives you extra time to complete the repairs before you start making mortgage payments. It means the property will be ready to on-sell sooner and thus you will have to make fewer mortgage repayments before you on-sell it – all of which will help your profit margin.

Not all vendors will be willing to go for an early access clause, but as outlined in Chapter 13: Negotiating Deals, if you can negotiate directly with the vendor, they will usually understand the situation. Remember to try to avoid intermediaries such as real estate agents as much as possible when you are negotiating. They have the ability to make you lose strength when you negotiate. It is like playing Chinese whispers. Real estate agents will be reluctant to let you speak to the vendor directly when they do not know you because they will be scared of losing their commission. You will have to assure them that you would never do that because you are a professional who wants to make more deals through them.

The more deals you do, the stronger the relationship will be with your agents. This is one of the reasons why you should always keep your word; people will be willing to do business with you and will pass you better deals if they know they can trust you. This process is outlined in more depth in Chapter 13.

Getting agents or others to source good deals

Finding good real estate agents or sourcing agents who can bring you good deals is an important technique to utilise when looking for quick cash deals. This is because good agents will know their target area inside out and are involved in their local real estate market on a daily basis.

They will know which properties are about to come up for sale. Thus if they are aware of the type of property you are looking for, they can tell you about good deals even before they hit the market. Remember this:

The best deals are usually the ones that are not for sale yet.

When properties go on a real estate agency's books it is often already too late. Most great deals will already be long gone as they would have been snapped up by savvy investors who have good relationships with the real estate agents selling the deal.

You need to interview real estate agents and find ones who understand what you want to achieve and are willing to help you reach your goal, build a rapport with them and nurture the relationship. They will work really hard for you because they can see that you are a serious investor. The relationship becomes symbiotic because they can earn good commission from your deals.

Be clear with your requirements

When you meet with real estate agents be very specific about what you are looking for. Make it clear to them that you are only interested in viewing properties that meet your criteria and that your time is precious. Make sure they know you do not want to waste your time with pointless viewings of properties that do not match your criteria. It is important to be clear and concise with real estate agents or they may try to sell you inappropriate properties – wasting your precious time.

Sweetening the deal

One thing to always keep in mind when dealing with real estate agents is: it is the vendor who pays their commission, their bills and feeds their kids, not you.

See the business card example on the next page. (Note: Headrush.co.nz produces business cards for many investors – see them first.) Hand out a card like this with the $1000 side face up at the beginning of the conversation with the real estate agent or sourcing agent (who might be another investor). In our experience they will always ask: 'What does the $1000 mean?' Say: 'If you find me a hot deal I will pay you up to this amount of money depending on the value of the deal.'

It is amazing how people react to this technique – they will start 'remembering' properties that didn't exist just a few seconds before. This card will also get you lots of phone calls from people you do not know anything about, so use your alternative mobile number (or 'psycho' line) on this card.

Working out your budget

Usually it is less risky to trade in properties that are around the median price than in the higher price bracket. Currently this would mean houses that are priced between $150k and $450k. Properties in this price bracket will appeal to a much higher percentage of the purchasing public, including first-home buyers and investors and will be much easier to on-sell quickly – which is part of your goal with a quick cash deal.

Also if you have trouble selling your quick cash deal and have to hold and rent the property for a while, properties in this price bracket will have a higher rental yield. Thus you have an exit strategy in that you can hold them and rent them while you try to on-sell them.

Example budget for a trade

$200k purchase price (at a discount)

$20k to spend on renovations

$10k on the real estate agent's fees

$5k on incidentals (interest of $2k per month, plus legal fees)

$20k profit for you

It owes $255k

Put it on the market at $265k and sell it for $255k in order to leave $10k in the deal for the next person so they are also getting a good deal.

(Note: see the sales projection table on the next page. Use the RevIQ software to do this detailed analysis on your deals.)

Adding value to your properties

You must only embark on renovations that will increase the final dollar value of the property. You should be able to increase the final sales price by at least $2 for every $1 you spend on it. If you cannot achieve a minimum of this two-for-one outcome, the renovation is probably not effective.

Look at simple solutions that increase value: landscaping, adding a carport or garage, replacing carpet, painting and decorating, etc... Read Richmastery's *1324 Ways to Get Massive Profits in Real Estate through Adding Value and Renovations.* It's the definitive renovations resource. Keep it simple. Set yourself a deadline for the renovations. Arrange all the tradespeople in advance so as soon as you have access they are doing the work. If you don't want to source contractors and organise the work, specialised companies can arrange contractors on your behalf.

Sales Projection: Property to Trade

PROPERTY DATA	INPUT	TOTAL
GST Applied to Sale		
Private Sale		
Real Estate Agent Base Fee	$400	
Real Estate Agent Commission Rate	3%	
Tax Option	Income based	
Tax Rate		
Weeks Vacant	8	
PROFIT ON SALE		
Sale Price	$255,000	$255,000
Purchase Price	$200,000	$200,000
Renovation Costs	$20,000	$20,000
GROSS PROFIT (BEFORE SALES COSTS)		$55,000
Costs of Vacancy (Loan Interest)		$2,308
Real Estate Agent Commission	$9,056	$9,056
Sale and Improvement Costs		$3,000
Solicitor's Conveyancing Costs	$1,000	
Other Sales Costs	$2,000	
TOTAL SALES COSTS		$34,364
GROSS PROFIT (AFTER SALES COSTS)		$20,636
Total GST payable		$0
Depreciation Loss Claimed on Property	$0	$0
Percentage of Profit Subject to Tax	100%	100%
Total Profit Subject to Tax		$20,636
Tax on Profit		$4,024
NET PROFIT (AFTER TAX)		$16,612
ADDITIONAL EQUITY RELEASED		**$0**

SUMMARY

It is essential to keep your goal with quick cash deals always present. This is to purchase a property at a discount, to add value if need be, and to on-sell it as quickly as possible for a profit after your expenses. There are different tools you can use to source discounted properties that have the right attributes of a quick cash deal. Follow the tips on how best to on-sell the property quickly whether you choose to sell privately or through a real estate agent. Remember to always leave something in the deal for the next person so you can keep your money moving. Speed equals success.

Summary of steps

1. Research the type of properties that are in demand in your target area.
2. Use different strategies to find and identify motivated vendors.
3. Work to find good real estate agents or sourcing agents to find good deals for you.
4. Purchase a discounted property that you can add value to.
5. Add an access clause to your sale and purchase agreement.
6. Arrange for low-cost renovations that will add value and get the renovations completed within a deadline.
7. Sell the property for a profit.

Chapter 17

Property assignment

Pass it on to boost your income

'There are two Ps in property, the first one stands for Preparation and second one stands for People. Know your strategy and build relationships – only then will you be successful.'
— David Leon

In this strategy your goal is to find and negotiate a property deal, get it under contract and then pass it on to another real estate investor for a fee. The better the deal, the easier it will be to find an investor who is interested in it. This is a great way of getting started in real estate investing when you do not have much equity or cash, and if applied properly it is a very low risk strategy.

The best thing about using this technique is that it will help you to build a network of other real estate investors. This is priceless because surrounding yourself with other investors will give you access to knowledge and you will hear about even more property deals. In real estate investing, success is reliant not just on what you know, but also on who you know. Having a great network is very important.

How do you assign a property deal?

When you assign a property you have effectively not bought a property at all. We will outline the process in the following steps:

- **Step 1:** Test the market in your target area. Use the techniques outlined in Chapter 16: Quick Cash Deals to test the demand for certain types of properties in your target area to find out what is in demand.
- **Step 2:** Find the deal. Use the techniques outlined in Chapter 16 to source

good deals at a discount on types of properties that are in demand in your target area. These include researching target areas, placing ads and getting sourcing agents or real estate agents to bring deals to you by telling them what you are after and giving them the $1000 business card.

- **Step 3:** Negotiate the deal using the strategies covered in Chapter 13: Negotiating Deals.
- **Step 4:** Sign a sale and purchase agreement. Add '*and or assigned to*' or '*and or nominee*' after your name when you sign this and include a Due Diligence clause. Go for the longest 'Due Diligence' period you can get – try for 21 working days. See Chapter 11: Making Offers for more in-depth instructions on these clauses. Note: in Australia, rather than using a sale and purchase agreement, use an option agreement and get this checked by your solicitor.
- **Step 5:** Find a buyer. This is the person that you will assign the deal to. Ask them to fill in a Deed of Assignment.
- **Step 6:** Sell the contract or option (*not the property*) to your buyer. To do this you need to get them to fill out a Deed of Assignment. In this deed you will specify your sourcing fee.
- **Step 7:** Charge a researcher's or option fee for finding the property deal for the buyer. It is best to charge between 1% and 2% of the purchase price. Note that you could charge much more than this if you find a great deal.
- **Step 8:** Go back to the vendor just before you give them the deposit and go unconditional. Now, because your name is still on the sale and purchase agreement you need to eliminate the risk should anything go wrong at the time of sale. To do this, you and the vendor need to fill in a Deed of Novation. This is a contract between you and vendor of the property that tells the vendor they cannot sue you if your buyer (i.e. the other person you assigned the property to) doesn't complete the settlement. Some vendors may be reluctant or refuse to sign a Deed of Novation.

Richmastery Property Deals

Property assignment is one way that Richmastery has sourced property deals for its customers. Richmastery in this case employs or contracts property researchers who source hot deals for investors. These deals are then advertised on the Richmastery website and then assigned to buyers. The buyers pay a researcher's fee for this service. These property deals are required to comply with tight investment criteria and strict purchasing rules, which in turn make them good investment properties. This service saves busy investors a huge amount of time that otherwise would be spent sourcing and negotiating deals themselves.

You can source hot property deals at www.richmastery.com

Example: assignment deal

Here is an example of a great assignment deal done by an investor. The yield fitted within the investor's strategy and the ground rules for his portfolio so he did not mind paying a fee to the finder.

He paid a finder's fee of $700 for an $88,000 property that was about $10,000 under current market value. The only thing that he had to do to buy this property was to make a couple of phone calls.

The first call was the one he received from a sourcing agent whom he had given a $1000 business card to and who had been keeping an eye out for good deals. The sourcing agent told him about the deal and asked him if he was interested in purchasing it. After agreeing to buy the deal, the investor then made two further phone calls, one to his mortgage broker and the second to his solicitor. The sale and purchase agreement was then signed by both parties and the deal was done.

He never set foot on the property. There was no real need to do so. He trusted his property finder as she was a fellow investor. She lived in a different town. He had asked her to source deals for him for a fee because he knew that she was an expert in the area and could find better deals than he could ever manage to from out of town.

The property finder benefited from the deal. It was good timing for her as she had just bought about four properties and could not afford to buy any more herself. She already had the relationships with the real estate agents in the area and was given a phone call by one of them offering her the deal. She only had to negotiate the sale and purchase agreement and give the investor a call and assigned the deal. This took a total of 30 minutes of her time. For this she made $700. That is $1400 an hour.

Advantages of assigning deals

There are several advantages for all parties involved in assigning deals.

For the buyer:

- It is not time-consuming as you don't have to find the deals yourself.
- You can access expert knowledge (as sourcing agents who find deals to assign to you are local experts).
- It is good leverage of your time.
- You can buy anywhere (and are not limited to your regional area).
- The decision is based on numbers not emotions. (You do not even have to view the property before you purchase if you don't want to.)
- These purchases offer immediate equity, good yields and good add-value potential.

For the vendor

- They access a broader number of prospective buyers.
- There is less hassle with viewings (buyers will tend to be investors who will purchase on figures and will not always have to view the property).
- They deal with decision makers not time wasters.

For the sourcing agent who assigns the deal

- You make money and boost your income.
- Higher income equals more borrowing capacity.
- There is very small risk (use a Deed of Novation to minimise it).
- There is no need to get mortgages.
- You can assign as many deals as you want.

Think of the return not the cost

As professional investors you should always follow this principle:

Don't look at the price of the shovel when you are digging for gold. You should not mind paying thousands if it will make you tens of thousands.

Always create a win-win solution with any deal and think of the return on your investment not just your initial outlay. Lots of investors don't make money because they don't like leaving money on the table for any other party. In fact, the secret is to leave some fat in the deal for the next investor.

SUMMARY

Remember, property assignment is a great strategy for people who are getting started, want to get their feet wet and do not have much money or equity to start buying big from day one.

We recommend you do this through the Richmastery website: www.richmastery.com Decide which side you want to play on – do you want to find deals and assign them to other people for a fee or have people find deals for you?

This strategy is really useful when you find properties that you cannot afford to buy or that don't fit the ground rules for your portfolio. You can on-sell them to someone who is looking for just this type of property and make a profit from doing so.

Summary of steps

1. Find a property to source.
2. Negotiate the deal (with an assignable sale and purchase agreement).
3. Find your buyer.
4. Complete a 'Deed of Assignment' or 'Option Agreement'.
5. Complete a 'Deed of Novation'.
6. Get paid.
7. Do as many deals as you want.

Chapter 18

Contemporaneous settlements

Buy and sell in a day

'Property investors are just money jugglers. Learn the power of moving money around.'
— Rohan Weerasinghe, real estate investor

A contemporaneous (or back-to-back) settlement is a property transaction in which you buy and sell a property in one day. This is a great no-money-down strategy. If you apply this strategy correctly, you can make some fantastic profits without even needing to raise a mortgage.

How does it work?

In a contemporaneous settlement you buy and sell the property in what could be classified as a double transaction.

What you are doing is finding a 'very good' deal and offering another investor a 'good deal' so that you keep the 'very' part of the deal.

This means that in a good contemporaneous settlement deal there should be enough for each of the three parties that will be involved: the vendor, the first investor (yourself), and the final party or second investor/buyer.

The way to make a contemporaneous settlement deal work is to follow these steps.

- **Step 1:** Work on creating a good network of investors (buyers). These investors (buyers) will be essential to your strategy since they will become the final purchaser of 'your deal'.
- **Step 2:** Find a good deal at a discount, using the strategies outlined previously in Chapters 16 and 17.
- **Step 3:** Sign a sale and purchase agreement with the vendor in which you will have an exit clause. A due diligence clause is recommended.
- **Step 4:** Approach your network of investors to offer them the exciting deal and find a second investor who is willing to purchase the deal from you within the due diligence period.
- **Step 5:** Once you have found a buyer (second investor) you will go unconditional on the deal and pay the deposit to the vendor. At the same time you will receive (at least) the same deposit from the second investor. This way you will cover yourself and will know that the second investor is serious about the deal.
- **Step 6:** You settle on the deal with the vendor and the second investor on the same day. So the money comes from the second investor's account into yours and then flows into the vendor's account – so the double transaction is completed.

Where you make your profit is in the difference between what you paid for the property and what you on-sell it for. There should be a substantial difference between what you pay for the property and what the second investor pays for the property. Negotiating a deal well below valuation is the key to this type of deal. You must also always make sure you leave something in it for the next investor to make it worthwhile for them too.

Example: contemporaneous settlement

Following is an example of an extremely profitable contemporaneous deal that was done by one very successful investor, who does a lot of contemporaneous settlement deals.

He was offered the deal by a solicitor with whom he had built a rapport, someone who knew he was a real estate investor and who had become part of his network.

The property was a tidy four-bedroom, two-storey, brick home. The vendor had had a failed business venture, gone broke and then did a runner out of the country. The solicitor took over the sale of the house for the receivers.

The solicitor then offered to sell the property to the investor. He managed to secure the property on a conditional contract for 20 days for a price of $385k.

The investor then commissioned a market valuation – the valuation came back at $455k. He then approached a real estate agent whom he knew. He listed the property for sale and advised the agent of his short conditional/marketing period, telling the agent he would need to work fairly quickly. He also armed the real agent with his new market valuation of $455k to use as leverage when trying to get the best possible price for the house.

The real estate agent worked his database of clients who were looking for a home that fitted these criteria. Within a week of listing the property he had presented the investor with two offers. One was cash unconditional. Once the investor accepted the unconditional offer he confirmed his original contract to purchase the property and went unconditional on the deal.

From there the lawyers for all the parties worked together to complete a contemporaneous settlement.

The investor's contract price was $385k

The market valuation he commissioned was $455k

Sale price (via real estate agent) was $445k

Profit after costs was $46,650

The real estate agent charged the investor 3% commission on the sale price ($13,350). So after paying this fee plus the lawyer's settlement costs the investor had made an amazing profit of $46,650, in just one week.

His only input was to make a few phone calls and to have a couple of meetings at the property to show through the valuer and the real estate agent. All this was done without the need to raise a mortgage and settle on the property himself.

So you can see from this example just how brilliantly contemporaneous settlement deals can work.

Do your figures first

Never go into a contemporaneous settlement deal unless it will make you more than $15k worth of profit. If you calculate the profit at less than $15k, it would be better to opt to just assign the deal for a fee. Property assignment involves much less risk. Remember you can make an assignment fee of between $3k and $5k (more if the deal is excellent).

Make sure you have a good team

Having a good team around you is important when doing these types of deals. In particular, make sure you have a good solicitor on board to close the deal. They will be worth their weight in gold. You will also need a good mortgage broker with good networking with several underwriters.

Possible issues to be aware of

There are also several potential issues to keep in mind when you try to apply this strategy. You will potentially encounter resistance from some solicitors and mortgage brokers or lenders.

Solicitors

Solicitors find problems in deals for a living, so there are no surprises here. Their goal in life is to find faults and 'potential' problems in any deal that is presented to them. It is important to learn to deal with solicitors. Work on finding a solicitor who is open to new ideas and get them to become part of your team. You may also encounter resistance from the vendor's solicitor. However, if your solicitor is on side they will be crucial to tilting the final balance in your favour. Having a solicitor who is creative and hungry for success and who understands what you want to achieve will help you to solve this possible problem.

Lenders

Some lenders or mortgage brokers working for the second or final investor may also have difficulty with contemporaneous settlements. They see that they are offering a mortgage for a property that the vendor (in this case you as the first investor) does not even own. Lenders do not like risk. The best way to get around this problem is for your solicitor to explain to the lender what is going on and guarantee them a win-win final outcome.

Look out for dodgy deals

You also need to beware of deals that are not so good. An investor we know was offered a contemporaneous deal by a 'friend'. The investor did the figures on the deal. It was a big renovation job, and he would have needed around $30k to bring it up to scratch. But the property would have been worth only about $100k once the renovations had been completed. The investor's friend was offering him the deal for $85k. So the purchase price plus the $30k of renovations would result in a considerable amount of wasted time without rental revenue while the renovations were being completed and the investor would get a house for $115k that was only worth $100k. In his books that made no sense and he told his friend he was wasting his time with a bad deal.

The investor questioned his friend a bit further and found out that he had already gone unconditional on the deal and had only three more days to settle and he did not have any funds with which to be able to settle. This meant that he was extremely motivated to offload the deal at any means necessary, even if it meant ripping off a friend.

Be very wary of so-called 'friends' as sometimes the need for money can override friendship. Obviously the investor does not keep in touch with his 'old' friend anymore. He has since heard that he owes a lot of money to several investors and he is getting closer and closer every day to declaring bankruptcy. He took unnecessary risks. Do not follow his lead.

The friend made three fatal mistakes on this deal:

1. He did not offer a win-win-win solution.
2. He went unconditional without a buyer.
3. He damaged his reputation as an investor by offering a bad deal.

Never, ever go unconditional on a deal unless you can afford to buy it. If you can afford to buy it there is no risk for you.

This story of the dodgy deal happens often so be wary of these situations. Do not get caught as a second investor, and definitely do not become a first investor unless you can afford to settle on the property yourself if you have to. Then you have the option of holding it and renting it until you on-sell it.

Factors that make a successful contemporaneous settlement

While this is a very useful no-money-down strategy, to carry it out successfully will require four main components:

1. A good network of investors.
2. A good solicitor.
3. A good mortgage broker.
4. An ability to settle on the deal yourself if you need to.

If you have these parts covered you can potentially make a lot of money in a short time.

Also remember that you should have a considerable margin to take on the risk. As covered in Chapter 8, take independent accounting and legal advice to set up the correct structure before you begin.

And we will leave you with one final thought. Just as Jerry Springer always ends his TV show with 'Take care of yourself, and each other', so always create a win-win-win solution.

SUMMARY

Doing contemporaneous settlement deals is a great no-money-down strategy that can earn you some fantastic profits and also help to build your network of investors. Only go into a contemporaneous settlement if you can actually afford to purchase the deal. This way you will save yourself a lot of sleepless nights. Make sure that solicitors and lenders are clear on what is happening to avoid last-minute hassles. Use the right structure to avoid costly tax bills. In the long run, it is your team of professionals who will make the difference between you becoming a successful or a mediocre investor.

Summary of steps

1. Find a discount property under market value.
2. Negotiate the deal.
3. Always leave something in the deal for the buyer (second investor).
4. Find a buyer (second investor) interested in purchasing a hot deal.
5. Make sure that the solicitors are communicating with each other.
6. Settle on the deal the same day that you sell the deal onwards.

Chapter 19

Buy off the plan

PROFITING FROM DEVELOPERS

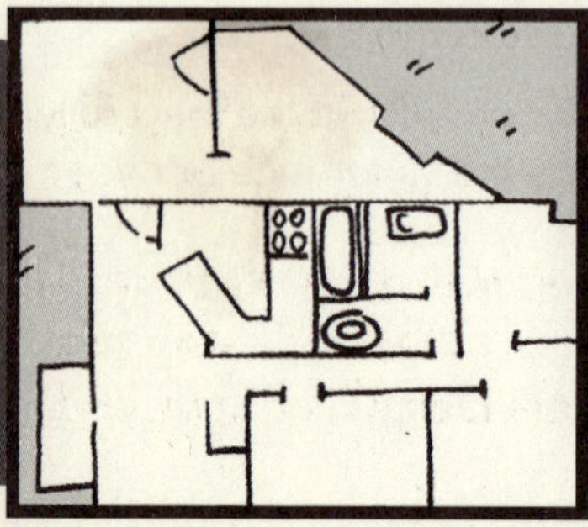

'It seems to be a law of nature, inflexible and inexorable, that those who will not risk cannot win.'

— Paul Jones, Revolutionary War naval hero

A fantastic strategy involving no (or very little) money down is to purchase discounted property from developers off the plan. This means that you purchase the property before it is actually built – so when you buy it is just a planned property.

How does an off-the-plan deal work?

You should be aware of how these transactions work in terms of timing:

- First, you make a small deposit to secure the property (this deposit is fully negotiable).
- Next, upon the property being built and a code of compliance being issued, you settle on the deal.

Why buy off the plan?

Buying at a discount

You are purchasing (or gaining control) of a property at today's prices that will be completed at a set time in the future – often construction will not be completed for two or three years. To make this strategy work you must do research and find sound developments in areas with high potential for capital growth. This way you can gain on the increasing value of the property from the growth in value while construction on the development is completed without having to pay a mortgage or deal with tenants during this delayed settlement period.

In this type of deal you can also save on legal fees and other fees that apply when you actually purchase the property because you will never have legally owned the property until you settle.

You can assign the deal before settlement

You also have the option of assigning the off-the-plan deal to another purchaser before the settlement date, often making a significant profit.

In order to have the option of assigning the deal to someone else before settlement, you need to include the phrase 'and or nominee' in your sale and purchase agreement or use an option contract. This is explained in more depth in Chapter 17: Property Assignment.

Also check with the property developer who you are purchasing the property from that the contract is fully assignable. Most developers will be fine with you assigning the deal, but some would prefer you not to assign. So always check!

Take care here: if the assignee does not settle on the purchase it will revert to you and you will have to settle or quickly find a new buyer.

Terms and timings

To make this strategy more effective, you should always negotiate the terms of the percentages to be paid and the timings of the payments necessary in order to go unconditional. Such payments are usually staggered over the completion period, i.e. you will pay a certain amount as each stage is completed.

The more delayed and the smaller you can make these payments, the better for you. Try to create a win-win solution for both yourself and the developer so that the developer will be happy to do more deals with you in future. If you can make the timings of the payments very favourable, you will have effectively bought time to look for a prospective buyer to assign the deal to if you decide you want to on-sell it.

Which off-the-plan deal should you go for?

There are a few particularly ideal times and situations that you can take advantage of with off-the-plan deals.

Purchase the first property in a development

One good strategy is to buy the first property on sale in a particular development, or at least in stage 1 of the development. The developers will most likely be happy to take a discounted offer on this because they will then be able to advertise that they have already sold some of the properties in the development, which will make the others more desirable.

Purchase the last property in a development

Another strategy is to buy the last property on sale in a particular development. This can be beneficial because you will have more control over fetching a higher price if you wish to on-sell (assign) the deal since there will be no further properties in the development available to buyers. Simple rules of supply and demand apply in this situation.

Buy at the end of the financial year

You can also get great deals at the end of the financial year, especially through the big-name property development companies. They will want to sell some deals to make numbers work, and the sale price is not necessarily the main concern. Remember that taxes are a big deal, and for a developer sometimes selling a property at a discount is actually the smart thing to do.

Buy show homes

If a development has a showroom property this can often be purchased at a discount. You may even be able to lease it back to the promoters of the development for a high rental while they are selling the rest of the properties in the development.

Always beware of developments owned mainly by investors

Do not buy off-the-plan deals in which the majority of the properties have been purchased only by investors and not owner-occupiers. If it is an 'investor-only' development, the rents and property prices will often be much lower than anticipated. In order to take full advantage of the strategy, it is always safer to purchase in developments that have at least a 40% owner-occupier rate and that are being advertised on the open market rather than just to investors.

You can make a lot of money on off-the-plan deals just by finding deals in the appropriate places and at the appropriate times, as explained in the four examples above. Just go out there and start meeting developers today so they know to call you when they have some great deals available.

Always ensure there is builders insurance

When you consider going into any off-the-plan deals make sure that the builder has an insurance policy that will cover him if he goes bankrupt before he finishes the construction of the property. This is an absolute must.

Make sure you pay the right price

Probably the hardest part of buying off the plan is working out the right price to pay for the property. Do not let developers and salespeople convince you the property will be worth x amount in x number of months and that is why you should agree to pay this price today. You only want to pay what the property is worth today and this is fair for the developer and for you. Any growth that you get during the construction process is a bonus to you for choosing the right area and the right development.

Establishing a fair market value

You can use comparables of older properties around the area plus 10% extra for having a new property as a fair market value. Let us show you how this would work with an example:

Let's say that you want to buy a two-bedroom apartment off the plan. Get comparables of existing older two-bedroom apartments around the area and make an average of them. Let's say for the sake of the example that the average is $200k – a new apartment should be worth around $220k maximum. You should never pay any more than this price. In fact your goal is to negotiate to purchase below this price.

Remember that at this stage you are only buying a concept on a piece of paper; you are helping the developer, not the other way around. Do not overpay for these deals. Developers are usually great salespeople and will try every trick in the book to convince you to pay a higher price than what the deal is worth today.

Build relationships with developers

Once you develop relationships with developers, you will be offered the best deals. They will know that you are a professional investor and a serious buyer who is likely to purchase a good deal from them. This will help them in terms of getting sales on the board. So they will start calling you when they know they have the types of deals you are looking for.

If you create win-win solutions they will love you for it. Developers are highly creative individuals, so any deal that you put on the table will be listened to in detail. If it makes sense they will go for it. Developers are always under a lot of stress and tight deadlines. This alone can create a lot of possibilities that you can benefit from.

We have several graduates who are doing very well just investing in off-the-plan deals. They are very common in other parts of the world because this strategy is a great way of minimising capital gains tax. As mentioned earlier, this is a fantastic strategy for investors purchasing Australian developments off the plan as they can avoid a number of the costs.

Off-the-plan example

This is an example of an off-the-plan deal done by a successful investor. He purchased a two-bedroom apartment in a residential development called The Docks. He bought it off the plan three years before the construction was due to be completed. He included 'and or assigned to' on the sale and purchase agreement. He also arranged to pay his deposit using a 'deposit bond', which meant he did not have to give the usual deposit of 10–20% of the purchase price to go unconditional on the deal.

What is a deposit bond and how do they work?

With a deposit bond, a finance company is guaranteeing the developer that the buyer will have the 10–20% deposit needed to purchase the deal. It is pretty much an insurance policy that the developer will accept because it is as good as money.

If you do not have the money available when you have to settle on the deal, the company that gave you the deposit bond will be liable to provide the developer with the deposit amount.

In this case the investor purchased the apartment for $200k. This was 15% below market value at the time. The investor needed 10% of the purchase price or $20k to be able to guarantee the purchase of the apartment.

He did not want to leave $20k stuck in a property that was not going to be built for another three years so he arranged a deposit bond instead. It cost him $2400 to arrange the deposit bond and he did not have to do or pay anything else after that.

The only thing that the investor needed in order to obtain this deposit bond was to show that he had three times the amount of the deposit as unencumbered equity in his portfolio. This meant he needed to show he had $60k of unencumbered equity. Unencumbered equity means that there is no mortgage or other charge against the amount of equity. He could show this.

However, another great thing about this deal was that he could not have used this equity for any other deals because of his high borrowing ratio. By a high borrowing ratio we mean that the lenders did not want to loan any more money based on the equity that he had because he was very highly geared. He was already borrowing over 85% of his whole property portfolio. So the banks would not lend him any more money but he still had enough equity to obtain the deposit bond and guarantee the purchase of the apartment.

How the investor profited from the deal

By using a deposit bond the investor secured the deal for around $2400. The market value of the apartment went up by 15% within the first year. He now owned an apartment that was due to be built within two years and had paid 30% under market value for it.

Because of his high borrowing ratio he decided to assign (sell) the contract to a second investor. He on-sold the deal to the investor at 10% below market value – thus making it a good deal for the next person (the second investor). The second investor paid him $40k to buy the contract.

This meant he made around $37k within one year with a minuscule investment of $2400. Just calculate the cash on cash return on this investment!

SUMMARY

There is a lot of money to be made for the astute and knowledgeable investor buying off the plan. If you do your homework before you buy and purchase the right property in an area of high capital growth, you can make massive profits. Make sure as well that you have your finance ready in case you need to settle on the deal yourself. These kinds of deals are relatively easy to do and are very hassle free. The initial price you decide to pay is the key to profit or loss when using this strategy.

Summary of steps

1. Build relationships with developers.
2. Research and find areas of expected high capital growth.
3. Buy the right apartment(s) at the right time to save thousands of dollars.
4. Negotiate the terms of the agreement (timings and payment percentages, assignability).
5. Decide whether to assign the deal or to keep it.
6. Profit from the capital growth of buying in the right area.

Chapter 20

Delayed settlements

MAKE PROFIT BEFORE YOU PAY

'Only those who risk going too far can possibly find out how far one can go.'
— George Elliot

A delayed-settlement strategy can be utilised to achieve several outcomes. These include purchasing a no-money-down deal, doing a contemporaneous settlement or adding value to a property before you settle and thus not having to pay any mortgage interest payments while you carry out the renovations.

How does a delayed settlement work?

The way it works is very simple. You will state the date of possession and of final settlement on the first page of your sale and purchase agreement. You need to delay the settlement date as long as possible. The more work the property needs, the longer this delay period should be. You will want to get as long as you can and the vendor will try to reduce it to as short as he/she can, so you will just have to reach a compromise that suits both parties.

You will also need to add the following clause or one like it to the conditions in your sale and purchase agreement.

Conditional on access and improvements:

(The Vendor agrees)

- To provide the purchasers (and or its invitees) access to the property as many times as necessary in order to carry out its due diligence investigation.
- Upon this agreement becoming unconditional, the purchaser may do all things necessary in order to carry out cosmetic improvements and/or secure a tenant.

If the vendor agrees to your delayed settlement offer, you will have access to the property from the time your sale and purchase agreement becomes unconditional. This will give you the opportunity to fix it up or show tenants around before you have to settle and begin paying for the property.

Delayed settlement opportunities

Renovate prior to settlement

If you renovate the property prior to settlement you can get a new market valuation once you complete the renovations. Then, before you settle on the property, you can approach the lender and ask if they will give you a loan based on the new market valuation.

On a normal deal they will lend based on the market valuation or the purchase price only, whichever is lower. However, if you have carried out renovations they will usually be prepared to lend to you based on the new market valuation because you have added value to the property. Adding value prior to settlement could easily mean you end up paying little or no deposit for the property, thus making your deal a no-money-down deal or very close to it.

Find a tenant prior to settlement

You could also have enough time to find a tenant if you wanted to hold the property and rent it out. The advantage in this situation is you will not have any vacancy periods when you buy the deal as most inexperienced investors do.

Contemporaneous settlement

Instead of finding a tenant you could also find a buyer and then go into a contemporaneous settlement, making it once again a no-money-down deal. The contemporaneous settlement strategy is explained in depth in Chapter 18.

Example

An investor purchased a property that needed recladding as there had been some problems with the way the windows were fitted and water had been getting into the timber, causing rot. Nobody had been able to raise finance to purchase this property because of this existing problem. Buyers knew that recladding the property would take a reasonably long time. In that period they would have to not only pay for the repairs but also make the mortgage interest payments, as until the work was completed the property could not be tenanted.

The vendor was desperate to sell the property and so was very motivated to do a deal. The investor offered the vendor the opportunity to sell the property with an access clause and an access period of six weeks, in which time the investor could reclad the property, find tenants and get a new market valuation. The investor was able to negotiate not only a discount on the purchase price but also a delayed settlement. This meant that once the recladding work was completed the investor was able to get 100% finance on the purchase price, thus making a good profit from the deal and someone else's problem.

SUMMARY

Delayed settlements have several advantages and can be used to produce fantastic profits. The great bonus with this strategy is that it is very simple to apply. By negotiating the addition of clauses for a delayed settlement period with access to the property into the sale and purchase agreement you will be laughing all the way to the bank. You can create contemporaneous settlements, no-money-down deals, carry out renovations or find tenants before you settle – all just by using this simple strategy. As a sophisticated investor you can negotiate win-win outcomes with vendors just by using these clauses effectively to create wealth where others just see problems.

Summary of steps

1. Delay the settlement date as long as you can by skilful negotiation.
2. Add an access clause to your sale and purchase agreement.
3. Repair the property, find a tenant or find a vendor in your negotiated time period prior to settlement.
4. Profit from this strategy.

Chapter 21

Cash-back contracts

Minimise outlay, maximise return

'The future is not something we enter; the future is something we create.'

— Anonymous

The objective of this strategy is to avoid putting a lot of your own money into property deals so that you can maximise your purchasing power and be in a position to keep buying more properties. This should always be one of your main objectives as an investor to minimise your risk and increase your leverage and return on investment.

How does cash back on settlement work?

This strategy works using the concepts of leverage and infinite returns discussed in Part One. In most cases you will only get cash-backs from developers, in private sales or when you negotiate the asking price down. In this strategy you will be preparing a separate contract over and above the sale and purchase agreement in which the vendor will be giving you a sum of money when the deal settles, usually to 'do some repairs'. Some vendors get creative and may even offer vouchers for a specific shop. The cash back that you receive on settlement can be anything from $500 to 5–10% of the purchase price.

Creative investors could get bridging finance to come up with the 5–10% part of the deposit and pay it back as soon as they settle and get the money from the vendor. The other option is to go unconditional without paying a deposit. If the vendor agrees to it, always go for this option.

Cash-back contracts

You need to get the cash-back contract written by up by your solicitor. They will hold the money from the vendor and will only pass it on to you when the deal settles. This will leave you and the vendor in a position of safety, because you will be entrusting a solicitor to oversee all the parts of the agreement.

You need to know what the current market value of the property is. Then you will know how much you will be getting from the bank at your preferred loan-to-value (LVR) ratio. Once you know this figure you can start playing with cash-backs, gifted deposits and other tools that will take care of the whole deposit or most of it.

> **Important:** note that many lenders do not like cash-back contracts and it is important that all aspects of the transaction are disclosed to them.

Make sure you get a fair market valuation

Make sure you commission a fair market valuation of the property. Do not try to overvalue property and then try to get cash back from the vendor. This is not legal and could be viewed as mortgage fraud, which will not help you buy more properties.

Example: cash-back strategy

Let's look at a real-life example of a cash-back deal in action. An investor found a property that was on the market at $300k. It had been stuck there in a buoyant area for a couple of months. The reason was that an old couple had lived in it and the interior design was very dated – 1960s style. The son of the older couple was selling their house so that he could afford to pay for a new bungalow that he had bought them so they could be close to him.

The house needed an investment of $20k to bring it up to date. Once all the renovations were done, it would be worth around $340k, which left a pretty good margin. The investor offered the vendor $300k with a cash-back contract attached of $30k. The way this worked was that the sale and purchase agreement was for $300k and the cash-back contract stated that the investor would get $30k back once the property deal settled.

In this case the investor obtained a 90% LVR mortgage and usually for this he would have needed to come up with a $30k deposit for the vendor.

However, the cash-back deal covered this deposit so the investor only needed to find money to do the renovations. The investor employed the services of a company to arrange contractors to carry out all the renovations and they offered an option of deferring the payments for up to one year interest free. This meant he was able to purchase the property with no money down.

Some buyers are not receptive to these kinds of deals because they think that they are illegal. The investor in this case also offered the vendor, as an alternative, a $260k straight offer. The vendor opted to take the cash-back offer of $270k and the deal was done.

SUMMARY

Cash-back deals will minimise your deposit outlay and will maximise your return on investment. Try to get cash back on any deal you make. Always base the deal on a fair market valuation. Never overvalue the property or influence the valuer, as this may be considered mortgage fraud. Just be creative on all your deals and always look at the vendor's motivation to sell and how you can help them out. Remember problem + solution = profit.

Summary of steps

1. Find a discounted deal.
2. Explain what a cash-back contract means.
3. Arrange the dollar amount and the cash-back contract.
4. Go unconditional with no deposit or with bridging finance.
5. Settle on the deal and use the cash back to finance part of it.

Chapter 22

On the cards

PURCHASE AND RENOVATE PROPERTIES USING CREDIT CARDS

'Do it, do it right, do it now and do it right now.'

— Anonymous

In this strategy you will utilise the 0% or low introductory finance periods offered by credit card companies as a way to purchase property.

Zero or low interest rates on credit cards

Low-interest or 0% finance periods have traditionally been offered in New Zealand and Australia on home furnishings and appliances.

You will have seen the BUY NOW AND DON'T PAY ANYTHING UNTIL NEXT CHRISTMAS! INTEREST FREE FOR 12 MONTHS etc. slogans in advertising for these types of products. In many other parts of the world you can get 0% interest promotional periods on new credit cards. The periods they offer commonly range from five to 18 months.

Increasingly in Australia and New Zealand low-interest and even 0% interest periods are now being offered by several credit card companies as an inducement to move debt from one credit card company over to a new credit card company.

Search the Internet for the latest deals on credit card rates and changeover deals.

Why are 0% interest or low-interest periods offered?

You may wonder why anyone would let you defer payments interest free for a whole year. This kind of finance is offered for a very simple reason – a high percentage of the people that need to take this form of financing will still not be able to pay for what they bought at the end of the interest-free period. They will then opt to take the finance that will be offered by the retailer, which usually has an unbelievably high interest rate – it can range from 15% to 30%!

This is how retailers make the big bucks because people do not know how to do any financial planning and just take the easy (and very expensive) way out. Credit card companies are also now taking advantage of this strategy.

Since you are budding investors, we will show you how you can use these deals to your advantage and be able to utilise the interest-free period but not get stuck with the high interest rates.

Example: financing with credit cards

Here is a real-life example of how an investor purchased a property using none of his own money by using 0% interest credit card finance.

The property was for sale at around $75k. The investor negotiated the price down to only $63k.

The house was a typical example of a do-up needing a cosmetic renovation job. It needed new floorboards so urgently that the real estate agent literally put his whole leg through the floor when he first showed the investor the property. It also needed gas heating, double glazing, paint and a couple of other minor fix-ups.

The investor arranged for the renovations to be done by contractors and did not do any of the work himself. The renovation costs came to around $15k. That plus the $63k purchase price meant the property had cost a total of $78k.

The way the investor financed the total amount of this purchase is as follows:

- **Step 1:** Some credit cards offer a high credit limit, and you can arrange to have the limit increased. The investor borrowed $78k using several of his credit cards, which we will call credit cards A, and transferred this amount to his bank account. This created an outstanding balance on his credit cards of $78k.

- **Step 2:** He applied for two new credit cards that had 0% balance transfer introduction periods.
- **Step 3:** He transferred the outstanding balance from credit cards A onto his two new credit cards. He now had a nine-month interest-free loan to fund the purchase price plus the cost of the renovations.
- **Step 4:** After the renovations were completed the investor got a new market valuation for the property of $105k.
- **Step 5:** He then refinanced the property at 80% of its new market value with a traditional lender and paid back the credit card loan. That meant he now had a mortgage of $84k on a property valued at $105k.

He had paid only $78k, which meant that **he got paid $6000 to purchase this house.**

SUMMARY

The property market is a like a living organism, and new strategies are developed continuously. You, as a professional, will need to make an effort and a firm commitment to keep on top of all these new strategies. Credit cards are just another finance tool and strategy that, as educated investors, you can use to your advantage.

Summary of steps

1. Create a balance in one or several credit cards.
2. Use this balance to pay for renovations, deposits or whole properties.
3. Apply for new credit cards offering low or nil interest transfer periods.
4. Transfer you balance and pay little or nothing for an introductory period.
5. Transfer your balance to another credit card if your introduction period expires.

Chapter 23

Non-traditional lenders

USE THEM TO PUMP UP YOUR PROFITS

'In the long run, we get no more than we have been willing to risk.'

— Sheldon Kopp

As a committed real estate investor it is likely that from time to time you will run out of extra equity or cash to finance a deal. You may find that the traditional lenders will not agree to continue supporting you. They may become uncomfortable with your level of borrowing and refuse to lend you money for the next deal. However, there are alternatives to the traditional banks where you can obtain the finance you need.

In this chapter we will explain the different ways you can source or supplement your borrowing when a traditional lender will not provide the finance you need to do your next deal, due to a lack of cashflow or equity.

Second-tier lenders

One place you can look to raise capital from is second-tier lenders, chiefly finance companies. A good mortgage broker will let you know exactly what is on offer and who has the product to suit your needs.

The problem that you will have with this kind of borrowing is that you will usually have to pay higher than normal interest rates. Typically the rate will be somewhere between 12% and 19% per annum depending on the perceived level of risk and the type of deal. This is a lot higher than the interest rates you will pay with a traditional lender.

Generally, you should try to avoid having to use second-tier lenders. However, if a fantastic deal comes along, the numbers work and you cannot raise finance from anywhere else, do not hesitate to get a loan on these terms.

Private investors

You can look to borrow money from private investors. To find them you could advertise in the paper, approach well-known entrepreneurs who offer finance for business/property ventures or search the Internet for investors looking for investment opportunities.

However, expect to pay high interest rates for this type of money, anything up to 19% per annum.

Contributory mortgages

This is another non-traditional source of finance, useful when bank lending is not available. A contributory mortgage (also sometimes known as a nomineee mortgage) is an investment structure that amalgamates a number of relatively small investment contributions into a larger sum, which is then advanced to a borrower.

Unless otherwise advised, all contributory mortgage advances are secured by registered first mortgages of real estate, the value of such advances usually being 50–60% or less of a valuation of the real estate as assessed by a professional registered valuer. Advances are generally further supported by collateral guarantees. Investors contributing to the pool of funds earn a relatively high yield of 9–14%.

You can obtain a contributory mortgage from specialist brokers, and also from sollicitors who operate this facility from their trust account. There are several statutory requirements in Australia and New Zealand safeguarding investors' interests, and which monitor the management of contributory mortgage companies.

Loans from family and friends

A cheaper alternative may be to arrange a formal loan from friends or family. This may sound like a bad idea to some of you, but if these loans are structured correctly you can minimise risks associated with lending from people you know.

Step 1: Make it clear the agreement is strictly business

Let the person lending you the money know that this is a business transaction and that no emotions should be involved and that you will ask them to sign a document to this effect.

Arrange for them to sign the document before you enter into the agreement. This document will say that they acknowledge that this is strictly a business transaction and that the relationship you have with them will never be brought into it. The fact that you plan to do this should be made clear even before you explain to them anything about the deal. This is very important for two reasons:

1. They will take you seriously – your uncle who used to change your nappies probably still sees you as a kid and this document will get the respect you need in order to proceed.
2. They will know that they will not be able to ask you to change the deal for love or friendship (and this can happen unless you specify against it).

Step 2: Write a formal loan agreement

You then need to write a formal loan agreement where you specify several key points, such as:

- The quantity of the amount borrowed.
- The term of the loan.
- The interest rate.
- The quantity and timing of the payments.
- Any early redemption penalties, guarantees, charges on assets, etc.

Step 3: Get the loan document checked by a solicitor and witnessed by a third party

Get the loan document checked by the solicitor for each party. Also have the signing of this document witnessed by a third party, which will make the deal as legal and formal as possible.

If you follow these steps you will not go wrong, and legally and morally you will always be protected.

What's in it for the family or friend lending you the money?

You may wonder why anyone would lend you money for investing in real estate. The question to ask here is, '*How much interest will they be able to earn from their savings?*'

Usually they will reply with a very small figure, from nothing to about 5%. per annum. So ask them if they would be interested in making 7% interest on their savings. You can make this rate as big or as small as you want – 7% is just an example. They may now be very interested.

Now you can explain to them about the loan agreement you will have drawn up for both parties to sign.

Offer friend and family a cut of the future gains

Another way you can propose a deal to friends and family that you need finance from is to offer them a share of the future gains of the investment. Depending on your strategy, this could be paid as a lump sum to them, or as a part of your cashflow or equity that you will release to them after a predetermined period of time.

The personality profile of the person who might want to lend you money under these terms is very different from that of the person who will be interested in just lending the money to you at a higher interest rate than they can get from the bank. They will be people who are more financially savvy and have a higher risk tolerance. They will be well informed on the great benefits of investing in property.

A possible candidate could be a well-off aunt who works long hours and does not have enough time to find property herself, but is smart enough to have read books on real estate investing and wants a piece of the action.

If you have friends or family members who have capital that you know they would like to invest for future gains, approach them. Remember – if you don't ask you don't get.

There are great advantages in using this form of financing. It can be a great win-win situation for you and your family member or friend to enter this type of agreement together. You get your finance sorted and they will get a higher rate of interest on their savings than they normally would get. Just make sure to follow the basic principles that have been explained in this chapter before you enter into any agreement.

Security for alternative lenders

Alternative lenders will always look for some kind of security before lending you money. Second-tier lenders will take a mortgage out over the property as security for the loan or look to have a general security agreement over other assets such as your business.

Friends and family, and other private investors, may also want some security. This could be anything from security over your big-screen TV, your car, your business or a second mortgage over one of your other properties.

Just remember that you will be responsible for paying all the legal costs associated with adding a second mortgage or having a general security agreement prepared.

Do your figures on these legal costs as they may outweigh the benefits of doing the deal unless the loan is a considerable one.

Equity partnerships

One other way to finance a deal when you don't have the cash or equity is to enter into an equity partnership. An equity partner is usually someone who wants to invest and has money to do so, but lacks the skill and confidence to find and do the deals themselves.

To enter into an equity partnership you would set up an entity together; get accounting advice as to what sort of entity you need to set up. Then you would supply the skill and perhaps the cashflow while your equity partner would supply the security for the deposit on the deal required by the traditional lender.

There is a huge difference between an equity partnership and the other sources of finance we have outlined in this chapter. That difference is control. It is always preferable to be in the driving seat of all your investments. Once you start sharing the control, anything can happen.

This is a risk you should not be willing to take unless you really know the person who you are planning to go into partnership with well and you both have a clear and identical strategy for the future of your investment.

Before entering into any partnership always draw up a watertight contract in which all eventualities are covered. Also make sure you look into the tax implications of the investment and get advice from an expert accountant and solicitor as to which vehicle to use to purchase the property. This is explained in more depth in Chapter 8.

Always have an exit strategy built in so if things don't go to plan you can pull out.

Equity partnerships can work and they can help you overcome serious problems such as lack of funding and lack of time. However, you must enter into them with the right person and make sure you structure them correctly.

Bridging finance

Bridging finance is short-term finance used when you are planning to do renovations to a property that will increase its value substantially or a development project.

Traditional banks are often willing to lend you bridging finance at a high interest rate and second-tier lenders will lend you up to 75% (and often more) of what the market valuation of the property will be once the improvements have been made.

If you purchase a property under market value, cost out your renovations and get a market valuation on what the property will be worth once the renovations are completed. You can then approach lenders for bridging finance for the money you require to do the renovations and if necessary for the deposit on the deal.

Once the renovations are completed you can then look to refinance the property with a traditional lender at standard interest rates at 80% (or sometimes higher) of the new market value.

If you plan ahead and structure the deal well you will be able to recycle most of your deposit money out of the deal (maybe all of it). Then you can move on to the next deal.

Bridging finance is expensive money. You need to pay high arrangement fees and interest rates that are usually about 5% higher than you would pay with traditional lenders. This is finance you should use only temporarily until you can get access to your 'cheaper' money from traditional lenders.

SUMMARY

As you can see there are lots of different ways of raising capital if you run out of cash or equity to finance a deal and get turned down by the traditional lenders.

If you have a fantastic deal, approach second-tier lenders, private investors or share it with friends or family. They might be keen to earn higher interest rates by going into deals with you than they would by keeping their money in long-term savings accounts or other investment vehicles. They may also be too busy to find deals but nevertheless want to invest in real estate and be happy to lend you money as long as they get a share of the profits. Remember that as soon as they start making money out of the deals you offer them, they will start finding more money to lend you! Equity partnerships can be a great source of finance but always make sure you have a watertight agreement with an exit strategy before entering into one and be aware you will have to share control. Bridging finance can be a good way to fund improvements to a property in the short term. Remember – *'If you find a great deal the money will always come to it'.*

Summary of steps

1. Find a profitable deal.
2. If the traditional lenders will not lend you money on it, choose one of the finance options explained in this chapter.
3. Set up watertight loan agreements legally with those who agree to finance the deal.
4. Profit from the deal.
5. If you have borrowed expensive temporary finance, refinance with traditional lenders offering cheaper money as quickly as possible.

Chapter 24

Vendor finance

Put no money down

'Your quality of life is in direct proportion to how much uncertainty you can live with.'
— Tony Robbins

Vendor finance is a similar strategy to the one outlined in Chapter 23. However, the source of the finance is the vendor of the property rather than second-tier lenders, other investors, family and friends or equity partners.

How vendor finance deals work

When you apply this strategy you will effectively be asking the vendor to finance part, or all, of the purchase price of the property they are selling.

You might be thinking that there is no way any vendor would agree to this type of arrangement. However, as in many of the previous strategies outlined, you need to find a particular type of very motivated vendor and offer them a win-win solution to succeed in doing a vendor-finance deal.

To make a successful vendor-finance deal you need to identify vendors who could be interested in this strategy. If they agree to provide vendor finance you need to add a clause into the sale and purchase agreement. This clause will outline how much the vendor agrees to lend you as part of the deal. It will also state on what terms they are doing this, for what period of time, the amount, the interest rate you will pay and other details of the loan.

Make sure the vendor's solicitor and your solicitor are happy with the contract and that the agreement is structured correctly to ensure a win-win outcome.

Who could be open to vendor-finance deals?

Let's look at some profiles of the type of vendor you will need to target to achieve a vendor finance deal. There are many other examples but these three will give you the idea.

Profile 1

An older couple who are planning to downsize their three-bedroom home with a big garden for a cosy bungalow close to their grandchildren may be open to a vendor-finance deal. They may not need all the money from the purchase price to purchase their new, smaller home and may want a quick and easy sale. This could mean they may be open to vendor financing your deposit or even more if you negotiate well.

To get them to agree to this you would need to offer them a higher interest rate on the loan amount than they could get on the same money in a traditional savings account.

Profile 2

A burnt-out professional couple who are tired of the noise and the expensive life of the inner city and who just want to sell their home quickly and buy a house in a smaller town. They may not need all the money from the sale of their inner-city property to buy a new house out of town and they may be happy to make a high rate of interest on the excess money and get a quick sale.

Profile 3

A retiring real estate investor who has decided they just want to live off the interest on their investments may be interested in a vendor-finance deal. They may only need a bit of cash at the time of sale and might be happy to get a higher rate of interest on their money by vendor financing a deal for you. This retiring investor is likely to be more receptive to the idea of vendor finance than anyone else, because they will know more about the real estate business.

Give vendors options on ways to settle

It is always good to give vendors alternative strategies to consider during the negotiation process. Never offer more than three because you will confuse them, but at least two so that they know you want to help them and that you want to reach an agreement. This is a great tip for getting deals to work.

Deferred payment

A deferred payment means that you will not pay the loan back for a specified time.

Balloon payment

A balloon payment is one where you will only make small payments (usually just the interest part of the loan) for a specified period of time and when you reach that milestone you will then repay a big lump sum of the loan back.

We recommend trying to use balloon payments, and also to always ask for deferred payments at the beginning of the loan period. It is rare to get more than three months of deferred payments from a vendor, but every bit will help your cashflow. You can make the deferred period as big or as small as you want to. Obviously the vendor will try to make it very small and your objective will be to increase it as much as you can.

You can see how balloon payments work in the table below. The example has a three-month deferred payment.

Balloon payments table

$100,000 vendor finance, balloon payments interest at only 6% and final big payment of $20,000 every 12 months.

1st Month	$0	7th Month	$500
2nd Month	$0	8th Month	$500
3rd Month	$0	9th Month	$500
4th Month	$500	10th Month	$500
5th Month	$500	11th Month	$500
6th Month	$500	12th Month	$20,000 + $500

If you follow this table annually over five years you could pay the whole of the loan in that short time. The vendor will be quite happy to collect the $500 every month.

It could be a good idea to show the vendor a table like this one so that they can see how much they will be receiving each month over the five years of the loan. Using this technique you could even purchase a property without ever using a lending institution!

Example 1

An investor we know did a vendor-finance deal with a young businessman who was tired of the stress he had to cope with and who decided he would travel the world for a couple of years. He had a luxury apartment that he wanted to sell and was looking for ways to use his money. He wanted to have the money available in all the destinations he would be stopping at. What the investor offered him was to buy his luxury apartment and wire him as much money as he needed when he got to each of his destinations. The investor also agreed to pay the remainder of the purchase price when the vendor returned in two years' time. This solution worked well for both parties.

Example 2

This is an example from one of David's mentors, Russ Whitney. Russ is a well-known and very successful real estate investor and educator in the United States. He used the vendor-finance strategy to purchase a property using none of his own money.

The property was worth $75k and the owner had run into some financial problems and could not afford to make the mortgage payments. Russ approached her when the property was in danger of being repossessed by the bank and taken to mortgagee sale.

He offered to take over her loan and even pay for her moving expenses. At the time he purchased the property she owed the bank $22k. She also owed her parents $14k that they had lent her to pay for the deposit when she first bought the property. Russ was able to get the same bank that was foreclosing on her to lend him the money ($22k that he needed to take over the property).

Russ also agreed to pay her parents the deposit of $14k that they had lent her, but instead of paying it out of his pocket he decided to offer her parents a two-year vendor finance deal.

This meant that the vendor's parents lent a complete stranger $14k so that he could purchase their daughter's home. Does this sound crazy to you? It really isn't. The parents were given a second mortgage on the property, a security that they did not even have when they first lent the money to their daughter. The other big advantage to them was they were helping their daughter to avoid bankruptcy. Going bankrupt would impair her credit history for years to come.

This is the kind of motivation you will need from vendors to be able to put these deals together. Find motivated vendors with a problem you can solve, get to know them and you will find you can structure some amazing deals.

Example 3

Here is another example of a fantastic vendor-finance deal done by a very successful investor who is a student of Richmastery.

The investor was contacted by a local real estate agent with whom he had built a rapport. She said she had an elderly gentleman who was interested in selling his property. It was not yet on the market. He wanted $380k. The government rating valuation at the time was $339k. So the vendor was asking way above the government rating valuation in what was at the time a depressed market. So the investor went with the real estate agent and the vendor to inspect the property, which had five rental units (five income streams). The property was in two titles. It had two one-bedroom places with a three-bedroom house behind them on one property and two two-bedroom flats on the adjacent one. All had roughcast exteriors with iron roofs and were very well kept. They were all fully tenanted with one tenant having been there for 20 years. Total rents were $695 per week.

The investor did the sums on 100% financing while he was at the real estate agent's office – it was $15k positively geared per annum. He needed $70k for the deposit so he asked the real estate agent for a private meeting with just the vendor, which the agent reluctantly agreed to.

The investor asked the vendor what he was going to do with the money when he sold the property. He said he was going to play the stock market and put most of it in the bank. Our investor said he would pay his price, which was well above the government rating valuation, if he would lend him the deposit at 10% interest per annum and he would finance the rest of the deal through the bank. The vendor agreed to this, after considering it overnight. Because he hadn't listed the property the vendor managed to negotiate the real estate agent fee right down so in this case providing vendor finance saved him money too. The property is now worth more than $750k and rents are $750 per week. The investor is slowly paying off the $25k that he owes the vendor while the vendor gets 10% interest on the loan.

This is a great example of an investor who took the opportunity to test different ways of doing a deal where he put no money down. If he had never educated himself about different strategies and thus not asked the vendor what he was going to do with his money he would never have been able to do the deal.

If the vendor had said no to vendor financing the investor would have negotiated him down on the asking price and the vendor would have had to pay higher fees to the real estate agent. This was a win-win deal.

Obviously this type of strategy will not fit every property sale, but it only needs to fit one for you to make a lot of money.

100% vendor-finance deals

Sometimes people who are willing to vendor finance a deal do not need any of the money up front, so they can even finance the total purchase price. They will in this case have a first mortgage on the property and they will be acting like a lending institution. Don't be scared of asking for these kinds of deals. Asking will make you money, so don't be shy.

The vendor-finance clause we use is included free with the RevIQ software.

SUMMARY

Vendor financing is one of the top tools used by real estate investors around the world to expand their portfolio faster. You can play with the conditions of the loan as much as you want, making these types of deals very flexible for you and for the vendor. Having a good solicitor to draw up these contracts is a crucial. Over time you will become more fluent at changing, adding and deleting clauses of your standard loan agreement and your vendor finance deals will become much easier to set up. Work to form good relationships with vendors who finance deals for you so that they can attest to other vendors that you are a serious investor and are safe to do deals with.

Summary of steps

1. Find a motivated vendor.
2. Get them to finance part or the whole of the purchase price.
3. Decide which security and finance terms to offer.
4. Get a good solicitor to check the clauses with all the terms of the vendor-finance agreement that you have added to the sale and purchase agreement.
5. Purchase a hot deal with no money down.

Chapter 25

Averages

THE CERTAIN ROUTE TO WEALTH

'Repetition is the mother of skill.'
— Tony Robbins

This is one of the simplest and most effective strategies that you can ever apply when you are buying property to hold and rent. You will analyse the demand and supply factors and then you will be able to create a simple template indicating which properties to buy and who will tenant them.

How does an averages strategy work?

First you research a target area to ascertain the demand and supply for rental property, plus work out what the rental property will cost to purchase. Then you do some simple calculations to work out if the area will produce positive-cashflow property, or if it will keep your total portfolio neutral or positive.

What is positive-cashflow property?

Positive-cashflow property is property where the rent more than covers the monthly outgoings. These outgoings include the interest payments, rates, insurance, property-management fees, and other ongoing maintenance.

Buying positive-cashflow property is important for investors because you should have several exit strategies for all your investments at all times. Having a positive cashflow allows you to be in control of when you sell your property. This is important because the only people that will lose money in real estate investment are the ones that have to sell. This is the only instance where you will be at the mercy of the market. When you have a positive cashflow in a market with rental demand, you will always have two possibilities – selling or renting.

Always, *always* cover yourself by having at least two exit strategies. Just remember what we talked about at the beginning of the book when you learned about minimising risks.

Average supply and demand step by step

Let's look at an example of how this strategy works using a target area of the central business district (CBD) of a large city.

The numbers we will be using are just an example. Do not get fixated on them; just grasp the main concept so that you can apply it in your investment area.

Step 1: Analyse demand (tenant profile)

You need to analyse demand, which means you must analyse your average tenant profile. This is an essential step because you are running a business and you need to know who your customers are. By doing a lot of research, especially talking to your good friends the property managers and rental agents, you can come up with an average profile of a CBD tenant. To get this data you only need to talk to some property managers in the CBD area you are targeting who will be more than happy to help you especially if you can bring them some future business.

Many CBD tenants are likely be under 35, semi-professional, and relatively new to their job. This kind of tenant usually wants to live in a one-bedroom apartment close to amenities.

As an example of a CBD target area, we took a snapshot of the CBD of Auckland. At the time there were almost 160 one-bedroom apartments to let in this area, at an average of $295 in rent per week. You can get all this information via a data download from RevIQ (www.reviq.com).

Step 2: Research supply of property

Once you have identified who your tenants are, you need to research the supply of property. Research if there are any apartments for sale of the type you have identified as most in demand to rent. Once you have done this, work out on average what they are selling for. In the same period an average one-bedroom apartment in Auckland's CBD was selling for around $230k.

Now you have what is called the *average supply and demand* in the area you are thinking of investing in.

Step 3: Calculate whether you should target the area

You are now ready to calculate whether it is worth your time looking at property in the area. You can do this with a quick calculation as shown below:

Example 1: 'Should you bother?' Calculation for CBD, Auckland, NZ

Property price	**$230k**
Mortgage at 80% LVR	**$184k (Property price x 80%)**
Monthly rent	**$1278 (Weekly rent x 52)/12**
Monthly mortgage @ 7.5% IO	**–$1150 (Mortgage x 7.5%)/12**
Monthly operating expenses	**–$255 (Monthly rent x 20%)**
Total	**–$127 (monthly negative cashflow)**

Monthly operating expenses (MOE) include insurance, rates, regional council rates and repairs. Usually about 20% of the monthly rent should cover the MOE. (Just remember that as soon as you buy a property, you will have MOE costs.)

In the above calculation we have used a mortgage based on 80% loan to value (LVR) with a 7.5% interest rate on an interest-only (IO) basis.

These are the numbers that we use for this strategy but you can add whatever you need so that you will feel comfortable. You can include other expenses in your total outgoings, such as rent-protection insurance, property-management fees, interest on the deposit, etc.

In Example 1 we obtained a negative value for the monthly cashflow which tells us not to bother investing in this area. We have intentionally used a negative cashflow example to show you that not every area will work. The reason some investors lose money is that they do not calculate basic figures like the ones above before they decide to purchase an investment property.

Example 2: 'Should you bother?' Calculation for Feilding, NZ

In Feilding, a medium-sized town in the lower North Island of New Zealand (like many similar towns in Australia), the average tenant is a semi-professional couple between 30 and 40 years old, with one child, and relatively new to their jobs. Their ideal rental is a three-bedroom house with easy access to schools. They are currently paying an average of $240 per week in rent. The average price of a three-bedroom property in Feilding is $140k. With this data we want you to come up with a total as we did for the example in Auckland's CBD above.

Stop reading and start working it out.

Property price	$____	
Mortgage at 80% LVR	$____	(Property price x 80%)
Monthly rent	$____	(Weekly rent x 52)/12
Monthly mortgage @ 7.5% IO	–$____	(Mortgage x 7.5%)/12
Monthly operating expenses	–$____	(Monthly rent x 20%)
Total	$____	

The answer is a positive monthly cashflow of + $52. If you came up with any other number go back and review your calculations.

Coming up with a positive monthly cashflow in your 'Should you bother' calculation will give you an indication that it would be worth doing some further research in the area and that there could be some profits and positive cashflow deals to be done there.

This strategy is very effective because it helps you identify target areas by using the main principle any business should use – demand and supply.

You will be able to do your 'should you bother' calculations in your head in no time. If that's a struggle, use the RevIQ software.

Demand-supply balance

A different way of applying this technique and getting the demand-supply balance right is to do the following. First, go to a real estate agent and obtain photographs and addresses of the properties they have for sale. Then show these properties to property managers or rental agents in the area and ask them two simple questions:

- 'Which of these properties could you rent right away?'
- 'How much rental income could you get from each of them?'

Once you complete this simple process, you will be in a position to start making offers for the properties that are rentable and that you know should be able to produce a positive cashflow.

SUMMARY

Do simple calculations on the figures for averages in certain areas before you decide to target them for positive-cashflow investment property. By purchasing positive-cashflow property you give yourself a built-in exit strategy to your investment because if it is not the right time to sell you can continue to rent out the property without losing money. This will protect your portfolio in the long run. Supply and demand is the key to success. By measuring what the majority of people want you can create a plan of action to provide them with what they want to rent or buy and create profit in the process.

Summary of steps

1. Analyse averages of an area.
2. Determine its viability for your strategy.
3. Target the high-demand properties.
4. Decrease vacancy rates and sale times.

Chapter 26

Negative gearing

Interest-free loans from the government

'You can learn a lot by just watching.'
— Yogi Berra

What is negative gearing?

'Gearing' is another word for 'leverage', a concept we explained in Chapter 2. This is where you use **O**ther **P**eople's **I**nactive **U**nused **M**oney (OPIUM), along with a deposit of your own money, to control any amount of real estate. The more leverage you can achieve the more property you can acquire.

If the rental income a property attracts exceeds all the outgoings (interest payments, and expenses of the property), the financial result is that the property generates a profit. It is *positively* geared. However, if the outgoings exceed the rental income, the financial result is that the property generates a loss. It is *negatively* geared.

Hang on: why own a property if it makes a loss?

There are two reasons to own property that generates a loss. Firstly, property increases in value over time and with the right property this increase in value will offset and hopefully outpace the cash loss you are suffering.

Secondly, in New Zealand and Australia it is possible to offset this loss in your income tax return against other income such as your salary, business profits or other income-producing real estate – thus minimising your overall tax liability. This is the basis on which the negative gearing strategy is formed.

Do not confuse negative gearing with negative cashflow

Cashflow is the life blood of any business, including real estate investment. A negatively geared property is generally accepted as one that has a negative cashflow. However, by understanding the tax implications it is possible to have a *negatively geared* but *positive cashflow* property. Let us explain this.

As an investor in real estate it is important to understand the difference between pre-tax cashflow and after-tax cashflow. One of the best things about real estate investing, particularly in Australia and New Zealand, is that even though a property may deliver a negative cashflow before tax, once you calculate your tax position it is often possible that the investment can deliver a positive cashflow after tax. This is illustrated in the example below:

Cashflow		**$**	
	Annual Rental Income	17,980	
	Rates	–1200	
	Insurance	–400	
	Maintenance	–1000	
	Interest Cost	–16,980	
	Pre-tax Cashflow	–1600	(Pre-tax Cashflow Negative)
Non-Cash Deductions			
	Depreciation	–10,183	
	Net Profit/Loss for Tax	–11,783	(Tax Loss)
Offset Tax Loss against Other Income			
	Tax Refund (offset from other income)	2600	
	After-Tax Cashflow	1000	(After-Tax Cashflow Positive)

As you can see from the table, our pre-tax cashflow of -$1600 when combined with the tax refund of $2600 provides an after-tax cashflow of $1000. This is a negatively geared positive cashflow property after tax.

Adding negatively geared properties to a positive cashflow investment portfolio produces considerable tax relief. There are many investors, often those on high salaries or who own very profitable businesses, who make negatively geared properties with positive after-tax cashflow their only strategy. However, as a general rule negative gearing should not be your main strategy for investing in real estate. Buy property because it is a viable investment and consider any benefits to be a bonus.

Maximising depreciation

New Zealand and Australia have favourable depreciation tax laws for real estate investors. This is not that common internationally. Let us explain depreciation and why it works so very well for real estate investors.

This tax law allows you to offset against your income the non-cash depreciation costs of your properties. Depreciation is calculated as a percentage of the purchase cost of the buildings and chattels that make up the property.

The depreciation allowance for the building is currently 3% in New Zealand and at varying rates between 0 and 2.5% in Australia, depending on when the property was built and other various state regulations. Depreciation rates for chattels vary from 3% to 50%. More about this later. By calculating a few quick numbers, depreciation can mean a lot of money to deduct from your next tax bill. The RevIQ software has a great function that calculates before-tax and after-tax cashflow for your whole portfolio for up to 10 years. We highly recommend it.

If property depreciates is it a liability or an asset?

What is a liability?

A liability is anything that loses value once it is bought and/or does not produce any cashflow. Examples of liabilities are cars, a boat, home stereo or a computer, etc.

What is an asset?

An asset is anything that increases in value once you purchase it and/or provides you with cashflow. Examples of assets could be paintings, stocks, businesses, houses, etc.

Real estate is an asset. Well chosen real estate will appreciate in value over time. At first glance this is completely the opposite of what the depreciation law we are talking about here says. However, the government recognises that we have purchased real estate as a business and that as business assets our buildings and chattels wear out.

Historically, statistics show that real estate usually doubles in price roughly every seven years, which means a rough average of 10% appreciation per year. The government, on the other hand, recognises that the buildings will wear out and they allow us to depreciate their value.

In the real world land goes up in value but often so does the value of the building. However, this only becomes a concern to us if we sell the property.

Chattels depreciation

In any real estate purchase we buy three things: land, buildings, and chattels. The definition of what constitutes the building and what is a chattel is defined by the government and detailed in schedules available from the tax authorities.

Chattels depreciate in both Australia and New Zealand at rates from 3% to over 50% per annum. (Check the current rates with your chattel valuer or accountant.) Unless you are intending to trade the property, obtain a chattel valuation from a professional chattel valuer as soon as you purchase the property; this will maximise your cashflow immediately.

If you are thinking of doing improvements to the property, you must obtain a chattel valuation before you begin. Your accountant can then offset the total value of the items you throw away (e.g. carpets, fittings, stoves, kitchen units, etc), and you will be able to depreciate the new items you install at the appropriate higher rate.

Following these little tips on how to maximise depreciation will be worth big dollars in the long run so pay attention and start implementing them.

Depreciation recovery

It is important to understand that the total amount of depreciation that you claim may be clawed back by the government if you ever sell the property. This can be a hefty amount, so take it into consideration if you are thinking of using negative gearing and then selling the property.

There are ways of reducing the total amount of depreciation recovered. Talk to your trusted accountant or depreciation specialist for details. However, always remember that even if you do have to repay it when you sell, you have benefited from tax refunds that have effectively been interest-free loans from the government for the time you have held the property. This has to be good!

Taking a tax position

The government will presume that you will take advantage of depreciation unless your accountant notifies them that you will not. When you file your first tax return after you purchase the asset you are taking a tax position on depreciation and it is difficult and inadvisable to change this position once you have taken it. It is important to take care when you decide on whether to claim depreciation or not, and at what level, especially if you intend to sell the property in the near future.

Making the most of your tax refund

Lastly, depending on your ownership and tax structures, you may be able to get the benefit of the tax refund (made possible by negative gearing) for tax paid on your wage and salary on a weekly basis instead of once a year. Your accountant just needs to fill in a form and send it to the tax authority to allow you to take advantage of this option. In most cases this option will work really well for you by increasing your weekly cashflow.

SUMMARY

Depending on your income and your real estate portfolio you can use negative gearing and depreciation to get a sizeable refund on the tax you pay through other income. This tax break will boost your cashflow and will mean that you can maximise every dollar you earn. Be sure to use the RevIQ software (which has built in rates for both Australia and New Zealand) to calculate how much you stand to gain. RevIQ will save you a lot of time trying to calculate it yourself.

You need to have a clear idea of your strategy and what you want to achieve with your properties. Remember that you may be liable for depreciation recovered if you sell the property, but in the meantime you will enjoy the benefit of an interest-free loan from the government.

Summary of steps

1. Find a property that fits your strategy.
2. Determine when and if you are likely to sell the property.
3. If you are likely to sell the deal in the near future, maybe depreciation is not for you. Let your accountant deal with the protocol. Discuss with your accountant what your tax position should be for each property you buy.
4. As soon as you purchase a property, and before you carry out any renovations, get a chattel valuation done by a specialist chattel valuer.
5. Your accountant will use the chattel valuation to do all the paperwork to offset the depreciation against your income so you can get fantastic tax results and enjoy your interest-free loan from the government.

Chapter 27

Equity release

CREATE A CASH MACHINE AND BORROW ON EQUITY

'There is no excuse for making the mistake someone else has already made.'
— Donald Trump

This is one of our favourite strategies because it allows you to really see just how quickly you can build substantial wealth through investing in real estate. The main concepts you need to understand to master this strategy are *equity* and *refinancing.*

What is equity?

Equity is the value of your property less what you owe in loans. When a property goes up in value, the difference between what you paid for the property and what the property will sell for in the current market increases your equity.

Work out your equity

If you already own property, stop reading for a while and start doing some numbers. The following calculation will show you how to work out the equity you have sitting in any property you own. Plus it will show you how to work out how much property you could purchase with this built-up equity.

Total Market Value of Property – Total Loans = Equity

This number often scares people because they do not realise the potential they have sitting in their own home, holiday home or rental properties.

Formula to work out the amount of real estate you are able to purchase

Below is a quick formula that you can use to calculate how much property you could purchase using the equity you already have.

First, add up all the equity you have in your own home, any other properties you own plus any cash you have in savings accounts.

Property Able to Buy (PAB) = Total Equity + Cash + Savings ÷ 0.20

We are assuming that with this formula you will get 80% loan-to-value (LVR) mortgages – that is how we come up with the divisor 0.20, which simply represents the 20% deposit you will need to invest to purchase each property.

If you can get, for example, 90% LVR mortgages, you would divide your money by 0.10 instead to come up with the amount of property that you could buy.

Let us show you a couple of numbers so that you can see how much you could be worth soon.

If you had $100k equity:

Property Able to Buy = $100k ÷ 0.20 = $500k

This means you could purchase up to $500k worth of property with your equity. If we assume a 10% capital growth per year (which is not realistic every year but it will help to keep the numbers simple), you could be obtaining $50k per year just in the growth of these properties.

If they have a positive cashflow, the numbers just keep getting better, with both annual equity and cashflow gains.

If you had only \$50k of equity;

PAB = \$50k ÷ 0.20 = \$250,000

If you had \$300k of equity:

PAB = \$300k ÷ 0.20 = \$1.5 million!

The numbers we have calculated above assume that you do not do any creative deals and you do not increase your cashflow while purchasing. If you were to get creative with the deposits and purchase high-cashflow properties your purchasing power would increase dramatically. Also remember that this is just the amount of property you could buy tomorrow; the numbers will increase dramatically with the exponential growth of time.

Refinancing – how it works

You can transform equity into cash by refinancing a property that has gone up in value over time or following renovations which have added value. There are two options you may choose when refinancing:

- You can choose to stay with the same lender and ask for a 'further advance' on the loan against the property.
- You can decide to move the loan to a new lending institution that can offer you a better deal.

The main advantage of staying with the same lender is that you will not have to pay the fees associated with changing mortgages to a new lender. However, it is often possible to negotiate a deal with a new lender where they will cover the fees associated with getting a new mortgage. This has become more common due to competition in the lending market.

If the new lender agrees to cover the fees and will provide you with a better deal on your mortgage, it is definitely worth refinancing with a new lender. If they won't, just do some numbers and calculate how long it would take you to recuperate your fees if you swapped lenders and then make your decision. The RevIQ software has a special calculator to help you with this.

Refinance Loan Calculator

EXISTING LOAN DETAILS

Loan Type:	Interest Only	
Loan Balance:	$148,000.00	
Loan Term:	25	years
Repayment Frequency:	Monthly	
Current Investment Rate:	7.25	
Fixed Term Remaining:	4 years 0	months

NEW LOAN DETAILS

New Interest Rate:	6.95%

RESULTS

Current Repayment Amount:	$894.17	Monthly
New Repayment Amount:	$857.17	Monthly
Total Interest Savings:	$989.93	

If the fee you will be charged to break your fixed interest loan is less than $989.93 then you may wish to consider refinancing this loan at the interest rate (6.95%) that you specified.

How equity becomes tax-free cash

When you refinance the mortgage on the property to 80% of its new market value the difference between your new mortgage and the mortgage you had before refinancing is tax-free cash in your hands.

You may choose to structure this top-up loan as a line of credit with your bank. You can then draw it down when you need to use it, keeping in mind that you will have to pay the interest on any money when you use it.

You can do anything you want with this loaned money, especially if your property has a positive cashflow that includes repayment of the new loaned amount. Remember your tenant is paying the interest on the loan for you.

You may be baffled by the idea of this equity being tax free; in fact, it is better than tax free. It could be tax deductible if you use a smart accountant who structures your affairs to minimise tax.

Decide how to spend the cash

You can then decide how to reinvest this money. You could use it for deposits on further properties. Or perhaps spend part of it on a new car, a great holiday with the kids, or any other activity that takes your fancy.

Reward yourself when you invest – investing is all about the journey and the rewards.

Keep a good balance between rewards and work. If you keep working hard on putting good property deals together and you do not see anything happening in return, you may lose motivation and want to give up. So reward yourself and the people you love when you reach your goals. Rewards lead to high levels of motivation. Motivation leads to unstoppable success!

Purchase more property at a discount

It is important to purchase the right kind of discounted deals with the money you get from refinancing your property. When you reinvest the refinanced money and buy the right discounted property deal, you will soon create even more equity that you can once again use to refinance and do another deal.

Using this strategy the growth of your property portfolio will become exponential since you will be keeping each of the properties in your portfolio. The results you can achieve in three to seven years of applying this strategy will startle you. This is the true secret of building wealth through real estate investment – the knowledgeable use of leverage.

Play it safe

You must realise that lenders are careful in the way they lend money. They do not like risk and neither should you. They do not really like refinancing properties too quickly, so even if you have a great deal, say about 20% under market value, you may not be able to refinance it for up to six months. Banks just like to play it safe and you need to know this so you don't make unrealistic refinancing plans that are virtually unachievable.

You can accelerate the refinancing process by using the cash-recycling strategy described in Chapter 35 or by making improvements to the property. When you renovate the property you forcefully increase its value by adding value. Lenders see this as a safe bet and will be more likely to refinance your property deal more quickly, as long as you provide them with a new registered valuation once the renovations are complete. If the renovations also increase the rent you can get on the property, show this to the bank too. It will help them understand that the property is now worth more than you paid for it.

Growing your portfolio

The most exciting part of this strategy will be seen once your portfolio starts growing. You can then cyclically refinance your properties to supplement your income or even create a new one.

Just have a look at the rapid portfolio growth theory diagram over the page and you will be shocked by the unbelievable results you can achieve.

In the diagram the exponential growth you can expect if you keep refinancing your properties is illustrated. The following assumptions have been made to come up with this diagram:

- 10% capital growth every year.
- Buying 15% under market value on each new property.
- Reinvestment of up to 90% of equity held in the properties six months after purchase.
- Start-up equity of $20k on a property.

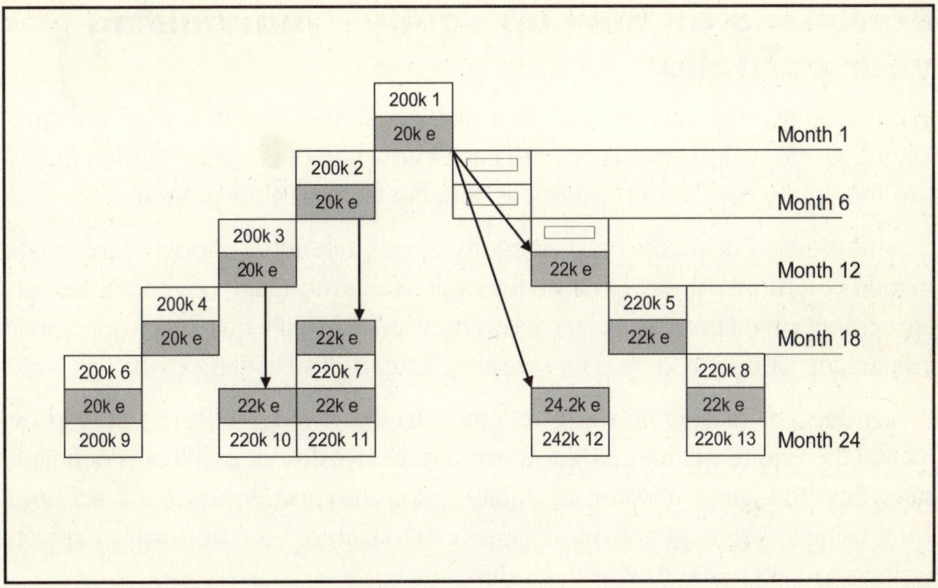

- 90% LVR mortgages.
- No renovations or forced appreciation.

The real estate market does not grow by exactly 10% per year or follow all the other assumptions that we have explained in this perfect pyramid model.

However, the objective of this model is for you to be able to grasp the concept of how quickly and effectively you can use capital growth and the equity you gain from it over time to build your portfolio. You could easily have 13 houses (plus your original one) in two years! If the properties each produce even a tiny cashflow of $100 per month, they will be giving you a total of $1300 a month.

You could make a very good living out of effectively managing these 13 properties and making your portfolio grow even faster. If you keep following the same principles for another six months with the proposed model, you will be able to buy 10 more properties, which will take your portfolio to a staggering 23 properties in two and a half years. Meanwhile, the equity on all the properties in your portfolio will keep compounding too! Just imagine what you will be able to achieve in three years. Your $20k initial investment could have purchased you a portfolio worth around $5 million.

Borrowing on built up equity – maximising your portfolio

In this strategy you use the equity in a slightly different way. Instead of refinancing the property and taking out hard cash into a line of credit account, you just use the equity on your properties as security to buy other properties.

This method of accessing your equity gives the lenders enough confidence to lend you more money because they will have a mortgage or general security agreement on different properties. This method is usually quicker to apply than refinancing since it is only paper money instead of extracting cash.

Lenders will usually be more receptive to this strategy because they know that all the equity will be going towards a new investment and that is definitely safer than the same amount of equity going into someone's bank account. Thus, using this strategy will make it easier to maximise your borrowing capacity or loan-to-value ratio (LVR) with lenders.

Important: we don't recommend using this method of accessing your equity. This is because it will mean that your entire portfolio is cross-collateralised and if you have trouble with one property you may put the whole portfolio at risk.

We recommend that you keep each deal separate by using the first method of refinancing and drawing your equity out as cash into a revolving credit account. A good mortgage broker as recommended on the Richmastery website will assist you with this.

SUMMARY

Working out the numbers and having a clear plan of action will guarantee you a successful investing career. If looking at these numbers doesn't get you excited it's hard to know what will. It is amazing what you can achieve with a clear plan and a strong will. Using equity and capital growth in an effective manner can get you to a massive multi-million-dollar portfolio very quickly. Remember that you must make the money when you buy, and the bigger the discount at purchase the faster you will be able to increase you equity and the number of properties you can own.

Summary of steps

1. Use existing equity as a deposit.
2. Purchase an investment property at a discount (the bigger the discount the quicker the process).
3. Be careful always to keep your portfolio cashflow positive.
4. Use the equity from the first deal as quickly as you can and buy a second investment property (also at a discount).
5. Take advantage of any capital growth that may occur in the market and withdraw equity as it happens.
6. Keep buying properties until your portfolio reaches your goal.

Chapter 28

Option agreements

CONTROL REAL ESTATE AND WIN

'Surround yourself with a group of advisors who are smarter than you. Make sure that they do what they preach.'

— David Leon

What is an option?

An option is a contract – effectively an option-to-purchase agreement. It is a contract between a buyer and a seller that gives the buyer the right, but *not* the obligation, to purchase the property for a set price for a set time. The buyer pays a consideration (fee) to the seller in exchange for them granting this exclusive right.

Benefits of using option agreements

Using option agreements is a very effective strategy for real estate investors who have little or no cash or equity but still want to get started and reap the rewards of investing in the real estate market.

You can apply this strategy in different ways depending on your situation and your goals. These kinds of transactions are very common in the commercial property market and are starting to be used more and more frequently in the residential market.

In an option agreement the property does not change ownership. The purchaser just gets an option to enter into a sale and purchase agreement at a predetermined price for a predetermined amount of time.

The beauty of an option agreement is that there is no transfer of ownership until the buyer decides to exercise the option agreement and enter into a sale and purchase agreement. That's why solicitors like working with option agreements and highly dislike rent-to-own or wrap structures.

What sort of vendors will it attract?

The sort of vendors who will be more interested in entering into an option agreement are those whose property has been on the market for a long time and has not sold. Also, vendors with properties that need a lot of renovations and are in very poor condition.

You will not be able to apply this strategy every time but as you know it is in your investing tool kit you will always be able to use it when the right deal comes along.

How does it work?

When a buyer obtains an option agreement, they have the right to purchase a property for a predetermined time at a predetermined price. In order for this contract to be legitimate, there needs to be some exchange of consideration, which could be monetary or other valuable assets. This is very important in the scenario we are about to explain.

Example

Offering an option-to-buy agreement

You have just found a property that definitely needs some cosmetic updating and this is reflected in you being able to negotiate a price under market value. You can then offer the seller the following:

You will purchase the property within four months and in this time you will pay for all the repairs needed to leave the property in a condition suitable for tenants. Then you will explain to the vendor that in order for this to be legal you need to fill out an *option-to-buy agreement,* which states the costs of the repairs and the time and price of the option to buy the property. Next you will discuss all the possible outcomes under this agreement so that the vendor will feel safe entering into this agreement with you.

Possible outcomes

The possible outcomes are as follows:

1. The most likely outcome is that you will do the repairs and buy the property within the specified period of time.
2. You do the repairs and don't buy the house, in which case the vendor now has a renovated property they can put back on the market at a higher price. This outcome will not benefit you as a purchaser, but you can look at it from a different perspective. If you were to buy a property to renovate and then discover that you need to spend an extra $30k to complete the job, you would be stuck with this bill. However, if you just have an option agreement and you discovered this same problem you could walk away from the deal, saving thousands of dollars. We have seen a lot of people going into renovation deals and discovering costly problems and losing a lot of money in the process. So this strategy can help you avoid this.
3. The vendor decides they don't want to sell the property to you within the agreed period at the agreed price. If this happens, you will have a clause in your option to buy agreement that states that they have to reimburse you with all the projected cost of the repairs, plus a hefty fee for time wasting (make this amount big because your time is worth a lot of money).
4. You could assign the deal to someone else (see Chapter 17).
5. You could go into a contemporaneous settlement (see Chapter 18).

Option agreement compared with delayed settlement

Getting an option agreement is very similar to delaying settlement, but this strategy gives you even more time to do repairs, to obtain the right finance and to get the right tenant without actually entering into a sale and purchase agreement. With a delayed settlement you would have signed the sale and purchase agreement first and thus your risk is much larger.

Access to the property

Once you have the keys to the property, everything does become much easier and smoother. The option agreement contract should always have an access clause included in it so you can get access to the property to do your renovations, show tenants or take advantage of some of the other strategies we cover in the book.

New valuation after renovations

When your repairs are finished, you will approach your mortgage broker so that they can get you a mortgage based on the new valuation of the property after the renovations and not on the purchase price. This way, if you buy at the right price, improve the property and get a fair valuation, you will be able to finance 100% or more of the purchase price. You will then have bought a property using none of your own money, but just with your wits and knowledge.

Ensure your solicitor can deal with vendor's queries

Remember that people will be a bit unsure of these kinds of deals because they won't be very familiar with them. You have to make them feel at ease. Having a good solicitor on your team whom the vendors can call to alleviate any doubts they may have and to confirm that the deal is legitimate is essential. This is the sticky point many investors miss when applying this strategy. Get a good solicitor involved and you will be amazed at just how much more you will achieve.

Understanding the option agreement contract

> **Important:** watch the Lease Options Introduction DVD on the free disc included with this book to understand more about this powerful strategy.

Option agreement terms

Definitions

The first page of the option agreement has all the definitions that you will need to complete the agreement. You will also be completing very important fields like the duration of the option contract, the option consideration and the final purchase price. All these terms are fully negotiable and you should always have enough leverage to create win-win solutions in every deal that you put together.

Note that 'the Grantor' as shown in the contract is the seller, and 'the Holder' is the buyer. 'The Grantor' is also referred to as 'the Optionor' and 'the Holder' is also referred to as 'the Optionee'.

Clauses

Now let's dive into the clauses so you understand how to use one of these agreements. Understanding all of these clauses will be the difference between you making one or one hundred of these deals successfully. You need to 'coach' the optionor or optionee through this agreement so that they will feel confident signing all its terms. Like any other creative strategy that you try to apply, you will find some resistance from different people because they fear the unknown. Your job as a professional property investor is to simplify terms so that the 'unknown' becomes familiar and easy to deal with. As a professional real estate investor you need to create a feeling of confidence and simplicity when dealing with vendors. Below are the common clauses included in an option agreement.

Grant of option clause

This clause explains the terms of the deal. In this case the option is exclusive. You could also have a non-exclusive contract, although it would pretty much destroy what we are trying to achieve here. If you are forced in your negotiations to use a non-exclusive agreement, you should walk away. Win-win outcomes are essential with this strategy.

Exercising the option clause

This clause clarifies the terms on which the optionee will be able to exercise the option agreement and go into a sale and purchase agreement.

This clause will also explain that the agreement is non-renewable. In this strategy it is better to keep it simple and leave it as a non-renewable contract. You could change this very simply by adding renewability terms in the definitions section of the contract and changing the wording to 'The Holder may exercise the option at any time prior to the expiration with the option being renewable under the terms described in the definitions'. Please take independent legal advice when using or amending the option agreement or any contracts, as the law can change and you may not be aware of its implications.

We also let the optionee know that he/she will have the opportunity of entering a standard sale and purchase agreement and we specify the terms of that sale and purchase agreement so that there are no nasty surprises for either party. The negotiable parts of these clauses are:

1. Inclusive or exclusive of GST (currently inclusive)
2. Initial option consideration (currently $0)
3. Late interest rate penalty (currently 10%)
4. Settlement date (currently 30 days)

The entire agreement clause

This lets both parties know that any other agreements they may have entered or talked about entering are completely useless. This option agreement is the 'top dog' and the rest have a lower legal priority.

Assignment clause

This clause is also entirely negotiable. I actually prefer to have a fully assignable contract, especially when working as an optionee. The clause would then read: 'The option holder may assign or transfer this deal and any of its rights or liabilities at any time before the expiration date. The grantor shall not transfer or assign any of its liabilities or rights under this agreement'.

Once again, the final decision is up to you so that you can create a win-win scenario.

No further agreements clause

This clause explains that neither party will be able to enter any dealings in regard to the property before the expiration of the option agreement. You could also add some penalties if either party does so. However, taking someone to court to get that penalty paid will cost you too much time and money and that is why we do not recommend it. When we arrange a lease option downwards agreement, though, you will see that there are heavy penalties for breaching any clause of the contract. This is essential to give you protection.

Costs clause

Every party will pay their own costs (conveyancing, finance, and the like). This is explained clearly in a costs clause.

Property access clause

Important: you need this clause; it is non-negotiable. You need complete access to the property as an optionee to be able to benefit from it. With this clause in the contract you can now show the property to prospective tenants or buyers, let builders start renovating, get quotes, etc. It is essential that you get the keys of the property upon signing this agreement. That is the reason you paid a non-refundable option consideration.

A simple contract

Hopefully you have enjoyed the short travel through the fascinating world of option-to-buy contracts. This is just a short and simple contract. In other lease option strategies such as lease options downwards or upwards we use customised agreements to get the best outcome. That is when it really starts getting fun and exciting. For more information on lease options visit www.richmasteryleaseoptions.com

SUMMARY

Option agreements give you flexibility because you get to control a property without ownership and can make some huge profits. At the end of every option agreement you will have several opportunities to profit from it. There is very little risk and it is very simple to apply, making this strategy a clear winner. Having the right contract and being able to explain all the clauses is essential to get the right kind of vendors.

Summary of steps

1. Find a property which you can add value to.
2. Negotiate a fixed option price for a defined time frame.
3. Sign an option agreement.
4. Pay an initial option consideration.
5. Do the repairs.
6. Choose one of the profit alternatives at the end of every option agreement.

Chapter 29

Lease option downwards

INCREASE YOUR YIELDS BY 50%

'Every failure teaches a man something if only he will learn.'

— Charles Dickens

Lease options

There a number of different ways that you can benefit from a lease option. In the following chapters the lease option strategies we are going to cover are: lease option downwards, lease option upwards, sandwich lease options and investor package lease options.

Any lease option has two separate parts: **an option agreement to buy** and **a lease agreement**.

A lease or tenancy agreement is a contract that transfers the right to control a specific property for a defined period of time. It is a contract between a lessor and a lessee for the use of property subject to stated terms and limitations, for a specified period and at a specified payment.

In a lease option strategy you can use a standard tenancy agreement as a template to create your own lease agreement.

Lease option downwards

This strategy is very useful to help transform high-equity properties into cashflow machines. In a flat or downward-trending market this strategy has the power to make you tons of money, so read carefully.

In lease option downwards, you benefit as the optionor – the person trying to sell the property and offering an option agreement. In this case the option agreement is tied to a lease agreement, making it a lease option agreement.

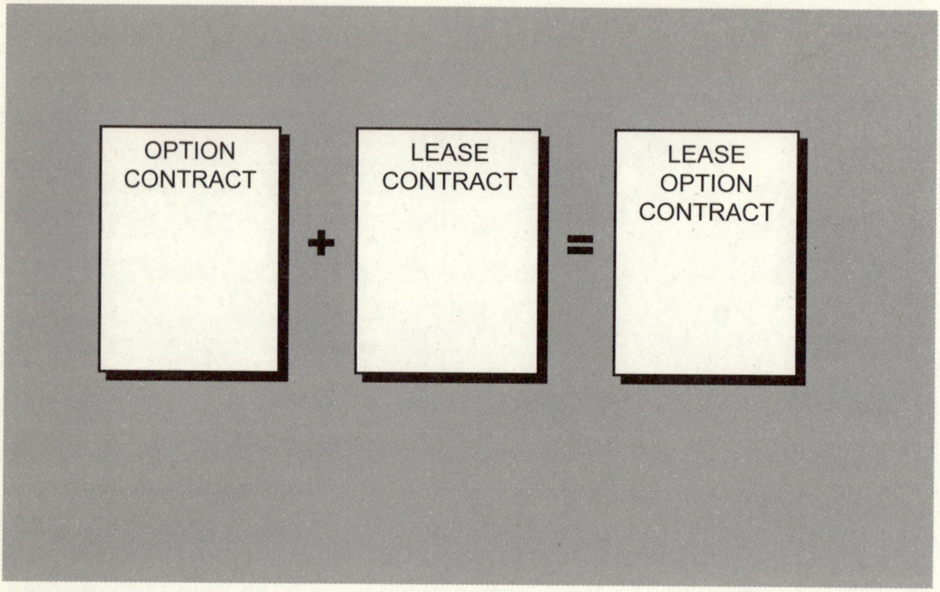

When would the strategy work?

An example of a situation where this strategy would work is if you are tired of having to deal with tenants. Or you may simply not be able to find tenants because you invested in the wrong market and just want out of the property game. At this stage you are looking for a buyer or a tenant quite desperately. You also know that your property is just a little out of reach for the average first-time buyer, but you know that it is the kind of property that will appeal to them.

Tenant buyers

A lease option downwards is the perfect solution for you, because you will be offering that first-time buyer the chance to live in your appealing property right away as a tenant buyer rather than just a tenant. A tenant buyer will feel proud of living in your property because they will feel it is their property. They will take care of your property as if it was already theirs. They will also be accountable to pay for all repairs and maintenance on the property, reducing the amount of money and time usually needed to manage properties under normal tenancy agreements.

Rent payment, and weekly option consideration

You will structure the lease agreement so that they can afford the payments while saving money for the deposit on the property.

The lease payments will be divided in two different pots. The first pot will be just a 'rent payment' based on normal market rent for this type of property. The second pot will be called a 'weekly option consideration'. The 'weekly option consideration' is a non-refundable amount that will be credited towards the final purchase price if the tenant buyer decides to exercise their option agreement and purchase the property.

If they do not exercise the option to purchase all the monies paid as 'weekly option consideration' will be forfeited by them.

Initial option consideration

There is also an initial option consideration, which should be around 3–5% of the total purchase price as specified in the option agreement. This initial option consideration is also non-refundable. However, like the weekly option consideration, it will be credited towards the final purchase price if and when the tenant buyer decides to exercise the option agreement and purchase the property.

This initial option consideration is necessary to make the option agreement contract legally binding. Remember this payment is not meant as rental deposit but it may be credited as part of the payment for the purchase of the house.

It will be clarified as well in the option agreement that all maintenance of the property will be the tenant buyer's responsibility, and if they leave the property, fail to make payments, or decide not to take the option to buy within the specified period, they will lose all the option consideration money that would have been destined for the purchase of the property.

Purchase price

The final purchase price can also be locked in for the tenant buyer. Or you can agree that it will be sold to them at current market value or future market value at the time of purchase, whichever is higher!

Why have a lease option downwards?

Advantages for the tenant buyer

You're thinking why the hell would anyone go into this strategy as a tenant buyer? Well, the benefits are what you must always emphasise when suggesting this type of deal to possible tenant buyers. Advantages for the tenant buyer include:

- They start living in *their own home* right away.
- They are protected by win-win contracts.
- They are not required to buy but have the option to buy.
- They are free to add value to their home.
- They can check whether they enjoy their surroundings.
- They improve their credit history.
- They partake in a compulsory savings plan for the deposit on their home.

Take into consideration that your tenant buyer is not a real estate investor as you are. Their vision of the real estate market, including finance and other factors, will be very limited and you can offer them a solution to their limitations. See the world as they would see it – perhaps it seems impossible to save enough for a deposit on a home and they feel they will be renting forever. Take a third-person perspective on every deal you look at.

Advantages for the vendor

The advantages when you apply this strategy as an optionor or vendor are as follows:

- No real estate agency fees are payable.
- Better tenants (tenant buyers/optionees are good and easy to find).
- No tenant hassles or property-management fees.
- Good selling price.
- Non-refundable deposit. (Go out and buy more property!)
- Keep your equity.
- Tax benefits since you still own the property.

- No maintenance costs as the tenant buyer is in charge of maintaining the property.
- You retain the ownership and the property will still be yours if the tenant buyer does not exercise the option to purchase.
- Only 20% of all tenant buyers actually exercise the option.

Tenant buyers who do not opt to buy

Many tenant buyers do not exercise the option to purchase because they either separate from their partner or are relocated due to employment or other circumstances that are out of their and your control.

There is a major benefit to you if they find they have to leave the property without purchasing it. You keep all the option consideration monies including the weekly option consideration plus the initial option consideration, and you still own a property that probably has increased in value. Plus you can lease it down again to a new tenant buyer, making even more of a profit.

Helping tenant buyers

This profit is the reason why you should choose to help the tenant buyers who do not exercise the option to buy to make their transition as easy as possible. You can offer to pay for moving expenses, or give them a small sum of cash to help them get started in their new venture. This will ensure that even if you are making money you are creating a win-win outcome.

Remember that they have enjoyed a property that they were proud to call their home for the period they were in it. So it's not all bad for them. Plus they had the possibility during that whole period of being able to buy the property outright. Prior to that they did not have enough money to purchase a property on their own.

How do I find a tenant buyer?

There are different tools that you can use to find the right tenant buyers. The tools outlined below are the most useful and powerful ones.

Classified advertising

You can publish any of the following classified ads in the newspaper or online to jumpstart some interest:

Here are some ads that we have used.

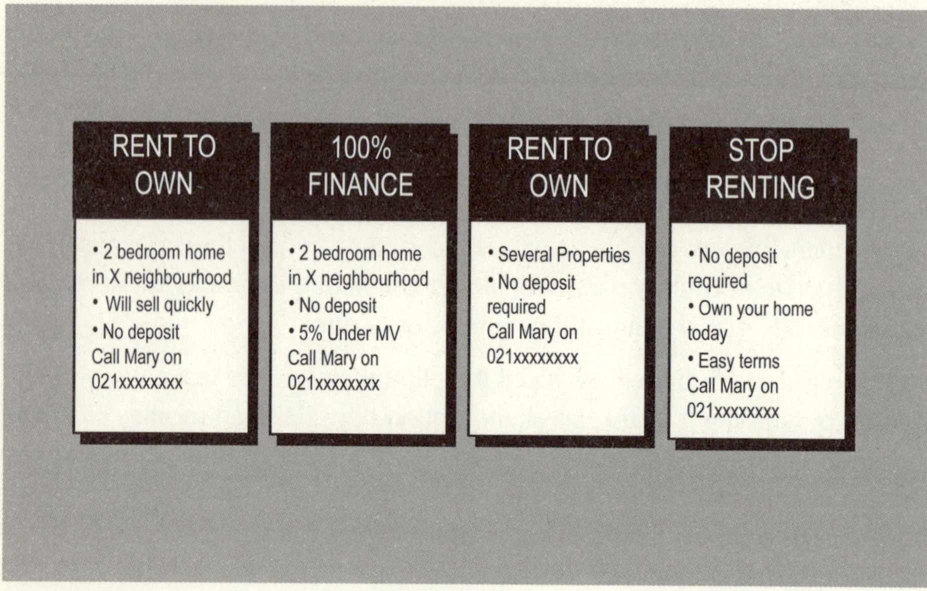

Write a letter to the neighbours

For example:

YOUR DETAILS HERE

Date

Dear Neighbour,

Property Address Here

We have just purchased this property in your neighbourhood and will be completing some renovations. We would like to apologise sincerely for any inconvenience this may cause you. Please call us if you are bothered by anything related to the repairs and we will do our best to assist you.

You are welcome to inspect the property at any time (even during repairs). The property will have three good-sized double bedrooms, a study, conservatory, a new designer kitchen and a landscaped garden.

We will be marketing this property as soon as all repairs are completed, with easy terms for the prospective buyer (vendor finance, rent to buy, etc...). If you know of anyone interested in living in this area please do not hesitate to give them my phone number. It would be great to see if this could be their ideal home. I know how much pride you take in your neighbourhood and I want to offer you the opportunity to choose your own neighbours!

Please do feel free to contact us at any time,

Kindest regards,

SIGNATURE HERE

Use specialised websites to find buyers or tenant-buyers

Websites include:

- www.richmastery.com
- www.trademe.co.nz
- www.youcanbuyproperty.com
- www.realenz.co.nz
- www.plumproperty.com.au

Use open homes

Organising open homes at the property for interested parties will minimise the time invested in finding the right tenant buyer.

The alternative to this is to show the property to each prospective tenant buyer individually. This is much more time consuming and thus more costly than having an open home that they can all attend.

Before the open home you need to make sure you present the property in an appealing manner. Hiring furnishings, or placing desirable furnishings in the property yourself, can be great ways to present the property and thus obtain a higher option price and weekly rentals. It will also attract a better kind of tenant buyer.

Email marketing

Use the databases of companies that could benefit from applying this strategy, such as mortgage brokers and solicitors. These firms can email the people in their databases with your deal or deals, so that in the case of their clients purchasing the property they would also benefit from the email.

Negotiating the lease option downwards

After advertising in any of these ways you will have lots of people calling to see how they can finally jump onto the property ladder. This will be your chance to explain to them how you can help.

You will offer interested parties an option to buy the property within a certain number of years at a specified price. The price that you establish will be based on what you think the property will be worth at the end of the predetermined option-to-purchase time frame.

You can play with the amount of time you give the buyer so that it suits your strategy and hopefully their needs. (We normally start with 12 months and make it renewable.)

Remember to tell them they can move into their new home right away and pay you the equivalent of what they would be paying for rent in a similar place, plus a top-up (in the contract you will always call this a weekly option consideration) that is entirely negotiable and could be credited as part of the final purchase price.

Always include a clause prohibiting the tenant buyer from subletting the property. This clause will save you problems because the person subletting the property will not have the same interest in the property as the tenant buyer will have.

Make sure the tenant buyer pays the initial option consideration when they sign up for the deal.

Example

Let's look at an example in order to make this concept a little clearer:

Property market value today	**$300k**
Rental value today	**$500**
Option to buy in 12 months at	**$310k**
Rent monthly	**$500**
Weekly option consideration	**$200**
Initial option consideration	**$9000**

If you play with these numbers you will come up with the payment that the 'buyer' has made towards the purchase of the house in the 12 months that they are tenants. This payment comes to $19,400, and they would still owe $290,600 if they wanted to take advantage of this option. First-time buyers will be ecstatic when you show them these kinds of numbers since now they will effectively have a substantial deposit to be able to afford to purchase the property. If they need to be pushed to save for the deposit, this is a great way of doing it.

Once you agree on the terms, you will have a tenant who is not really a tenant; they are a buyer who will take care of your house as if they had already bought it. You will not have to bother with property managers because they will be taking care of the little inconveniences and ongoing maintenance that will eventually appear in their new house. Statistically, only around one out of five 'buyers' will opt to buy the property; break ups, work changes and other eventualities will mean tenants will just lose the money they were effectively putting away to buy their home.

So what do you do if they leave you with the property again? Well, that is your call. You have several possibilities: renting it, selling it, renting with an option to buy again.

SUMMARY

If you are following a more traditional buy-and-hold investment strategy, you will usually find suitable high-yield properties in lower socio-economic areas with more difficult tenants. Using a lease option downwards strategy, however, you can get great returns from any kind of property, with great tenant buyers who feel that they are living in their own home. They are better tenants because they have a tendency to stay in a property for a long time. Since they have more at stake they will not tend to move home or change jobs that often and see their rental house as their own home.

Richmastery has developed a comprehensive two-day seminar on lease options. Please visit www.richmasteryleaseoptions.com to attend a seminar near you. Also check out the Lease Options Introduction video on the disc attached to the back of the book.

You can buy or sell your lease option deal through the following websites: www.richmastery.com or www.youcanbuyproperty.com.

Summary of steps

1. Find a property with an average cashflow but high equity, or use one of the properties you already own.
2. Advertise your property as a rent-to-own deal.
3. Draft a strong lease option agreement.
4. Create cashflow in any market.

Chapter 30

Lease option upwards

ADD VALUE AND KEEP THE CASH

'Selling is a trade for the ignorant and a science for the professional.'

— G. Michaelson, best-selling author

This strategy is the perfect solution for the buy-to-sell investor who has run out of borrowing capacity. It can also be a great way for an investor to get into a new property with the potential to increase equity.

It is exactly the same principle that we used in the lease option downwards strategy, but in this case we will benefit from a different perspective. We will benefit as the optionee, not the optionor.

Example

Let's take the example of a property in a waterfront suburb such as Mission Bay, in Auckland. The sale price is $1,250,000. Other properties in the area of similar land size are selling at about $2 to $2.5 million. There is potential for development. There is also potential to subdivide the land and build. The house needs work.

Steps in the strategy

- **Step 1:** Start living in the property and pay market-value rent while you keep an option to purchase.
- **Step 2:** Offer the asking price and ask for a big portion of the rent to be part of the eventual purchase price.

- ◆ Option to purchase at $1.25 million.
- ◆ Rent $350 per week plus $350 (weekly option consideration) total = $700 per week.
- ◆ Initial option consideration is $10 (can be as small as you like; it just makes the deal legally binding).

- **Step 3:** Start renovating or subdividing, or any other work you want on the property.
- **Step 4:** Look for a buyer during the renovations.
- **Step 5:** Contemporaneous settlement on the deal (see Chapter 18).

Why have a lease option upwards?

Advantages for the optionor (the vendor)

Benefits for the vendor include:

- No estate agency fees.
- Better tenants.
- No tenant hassles (no property-management fees).
- Good selling price.
- Keep your equity.
- Tax benefits.
- No maintenance.
- Retain ownership.

Advantages for the tenant buyer

Advantages for the optionee (yourself as tenant buyer) include:

- Start living in *your property* right away.
- You are protected by tenancy regulations.
- Enough time to find a buyer or tenant.
- Free to add value to the property.
- Keep your equity.
- Not required to buy.

This last point deserves expansion. If you were to purchase a property with the objective of renovating and selling for a profit the following scenario could occur. After starting the renovations you could discover that you need an extra $50k because of a problem that wasn't detected during your initial builder's inspection. If your profit bottom line was only $40k you are now $10k down. If the same situation occurred but you applied a lease option upwards strategy, you could always walk away from the deal without losing such a hefty amount of money.

How do I find a vendor?

The marketing campaigns will be geared to find sellers. You need to be very professional and reassure the seller that the deal will work well. Sometimes you will have to nurture these deals, although they all start through good marketing and, in particular, via lead creation.

Classified advertising

Try some advertisements, such as those overleaf, to help generate some good leads.

Send a solicitor's letter

Once you have attracted some interest, a letter from your solicitor talking about lease options will always be well received by a prospective seller. It will reassure them that the contracts are legal and they are fully protected. Offer the seller names of solicitors who would be happy to deal with the contracts.

Negotiating the deal

The first thing you should ensure is that there is sufficient profit for you as an optionee at the end of the option process. The minimum profit margin to work with is 25% of the projected sales price. This means you expect to make 25% on the final purchase price after all the renovations or development work is completed.

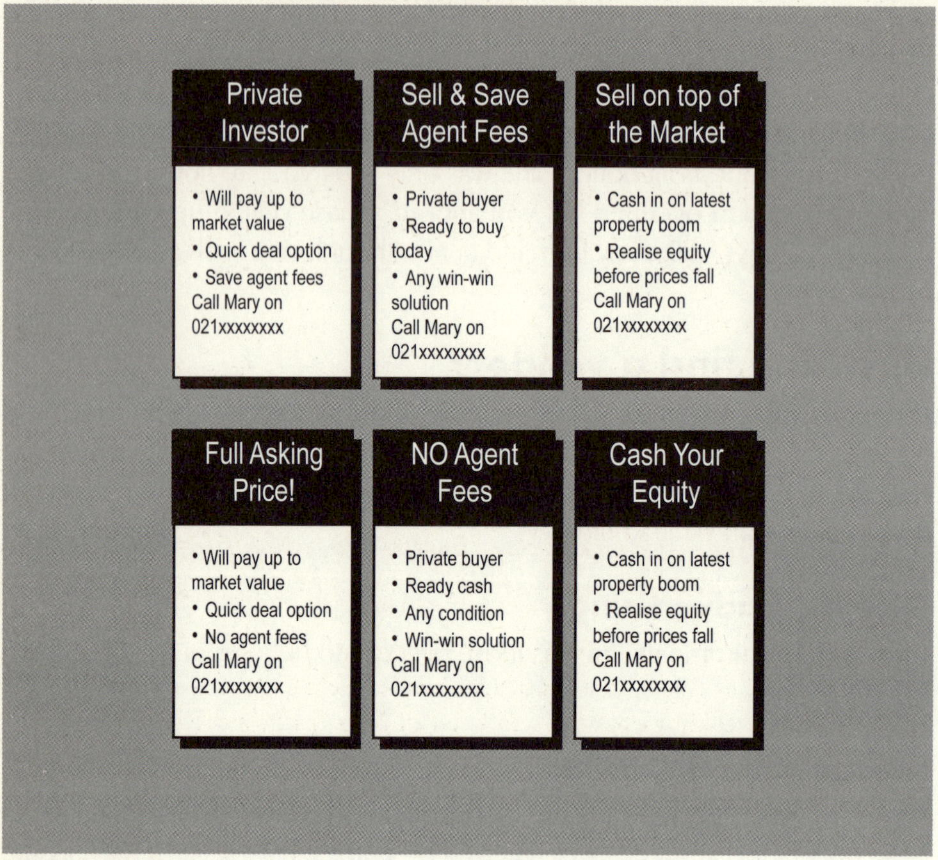

In your option agreement always fix a final purchase price and specify all the components of the sale and purchase agreement.

Have a clause that lets you sublet the property and to enable you to make any improvements without having to ask permission from the optionor.

Have caveats on the property so that the optionor cannot borrow against the property as a security. There should be hefty penalties if the optionor decides not to follow any of the clauses of the agreement.

Remember that you are intending to sell this deal as quickly as possible so leave something on the table for the final purchaser. Investing is all about moving money quickly, not about waiting for the last dollar.

SUMMARY

You can get into property by just using your wits and knowledge. A lease option upwards deal is a perfect example of how this can be done. Making sure you have watertight contracts is essential before you go into this strategy. If you are thinking of moving up in the property ladder and you think you cannot afford to buy, this is a great solution to your problem. It will kick start your investing career.

Summary of steps

1. Do your homework on property prices and average selling times.
2. Negotiate a good purchase price with an opportunity to add value.
3. Sign the option agreement (weekly option consideration to contribute to the final payment if the option is exercised).
4. Put the property up for sale from day one after signing the option agreement.
5. Start work immediately and add value.
6. Work out your profit margin and decide between assignment and contemporaneous settlement (see Chapters 17 and 18).

Chapter 31

Lease option upwards variation

A BUILDER PARTNERSHIP

'Entrepreneurs don't take risks; they simply assess all the facts.'
— **Anonymous**

This is an exciting variation on the strategy explained in the previous chapter. The only difference is that you will have an equity partner in the deal, who will be a builder. Remember that builders usually know how to fix properties but not how to invest in them. This partnership offers a win-win solution for both you as the property investor and the builder.

Builders have extensive knowledge of how to improve properties and will be able to do so at a reduced price because they will not charge for labour. They can also get all the materials at cost price.

How is this agreement different?

A lease option upwards with a builder partnership differs from an ordinary lease option upwards in the following ways.

- The builder will do all the adding-value work and will finance the work and materials.
- You will split the end profit.

Why use this strategy?

Advantages for the builder

Benefits for the builder/partner include:

- Get into property investing with very little risk.
- Get into property investing with very little money.
- Opportunity for a long-term partnership.
- Use your builder/partner knowledge for investing, not just for a job.

Advantages for the investor (optionee)

Benefits for the investor include:

- No property-improvement costs.
- Trade expertise from the builder.
- Improvements only charged at cost price.
- Time leverage.
- Do more deals at the same time because the builder is doing the renovations.
- Opportunity for a long-term partnership.

Who is an ideal builder/partner?

Your perfect builder/partner will meet most of the following criteria.

- Is interested in property investing but has no actual property investment education.
- Trusts your purchasing and selling decisions. Your ownership structure should reflect this point – you should be the sole director and have all responsibility on buying and selling the property. The builder is just an equity partner and you should respect only his building trade expertise. Make sure the builder is aware of and happy with this from day one.
- Believes in the deal and in the power of property investing.
- Has high energy levels.
- Has a proven track record of good workmanship.

- Is motivated to get started.
- Is someone who you have a good gut feeling about.

Marketing

This strategy requires exactly the same marketing that was explained in the lease option upwards strategy. The benefit of having a builder as an equity partner is that they will be out there finding deals and motivated vendors without even wanting to, so the deals will come to you. Remember that the best deals are the ones that are not for sale.

SUMMARY

You can leverage even more of your time and money when applying a lease option upwards strategy by getting a builder as a business partner. If you get the right kind of builder and everyone knows what their roles and responsibilities will be in the deal, this strategy will be highly effective and will work quickly. You can have more than one builder business partner, making your results even more exciting and your profits even greater.

Summary of steps

1. Build a good relationship with a builder who is interested in real estate investing.
2. Do your homework on property prices and average selling times.
3. Negotiate a good purchase price with an opportunity to add value.
4. Draft a strong agreement with your builder.
5. Sign the option agreement (include a big weekly option consideration to contribute to the final purchase price).
6. Put the property up for sale from day one of the option agreement.
7. Let the builder start the work immediately and add value.
8. Work out your profit margin and decide between assignment and contemporaneous settlement (see Chapters 17 and 18).
9. Split the profits with your builder/equity partner.

Chapter 32

Sandwich lease option

INVEST WITHOUT A MORTGAGE

'Nature gave men two ends, one to sit on and one to think with. The man's success or failure has been dependent on the one he used the most.'

— Robert Albert Bloch

There are several ways to implement and make money out of lease options, and one of our favourites is the sandwich lease option. You need absolutely no money to benefit from this technique; you just need your intellect and the knowledge that you will obtain by reading this chapter.

When you do a sandwich lease option you are just an intermediary between the vendor and the buyer. You will create a cashflow machine using absolutely none of your own money and without even needing to raise a mortgage!

How does it work?

Find buyers

To implement this strategy effectively you will first need to find your buyers and then your vendors.

To find buyers you can place classified ads in the newspaper. The ads (see next page) will work as they did for the lease option downwards strategy in Chapter 29.

You will need to create a database with different buyer needs – what kind of property they want and how much they can pay for it. You can then explain to them how this strategy works and how you can help them.

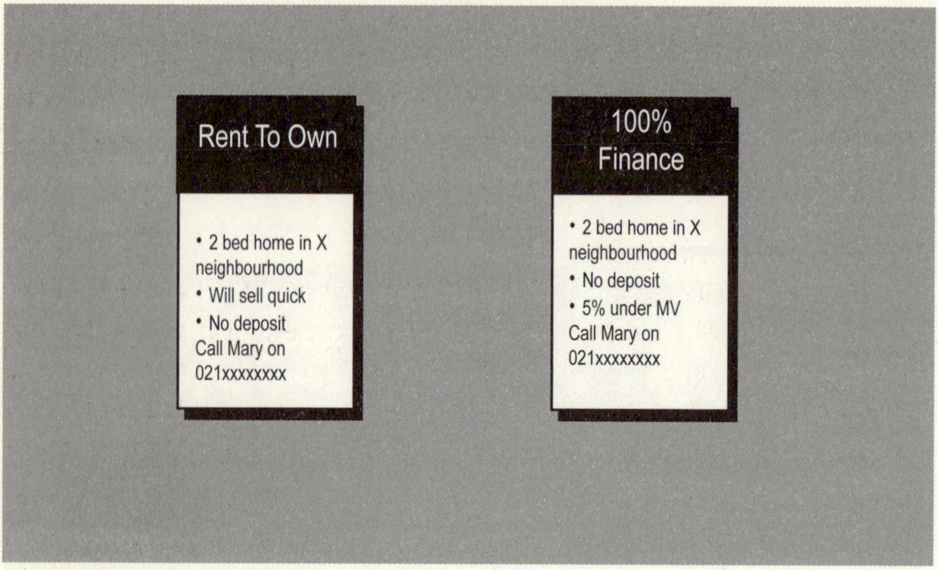

Find vendors

Once you have a strong database of buyers you then need to look at vendors. You can place the following ads to find your vendors in the newspaper of your target area:

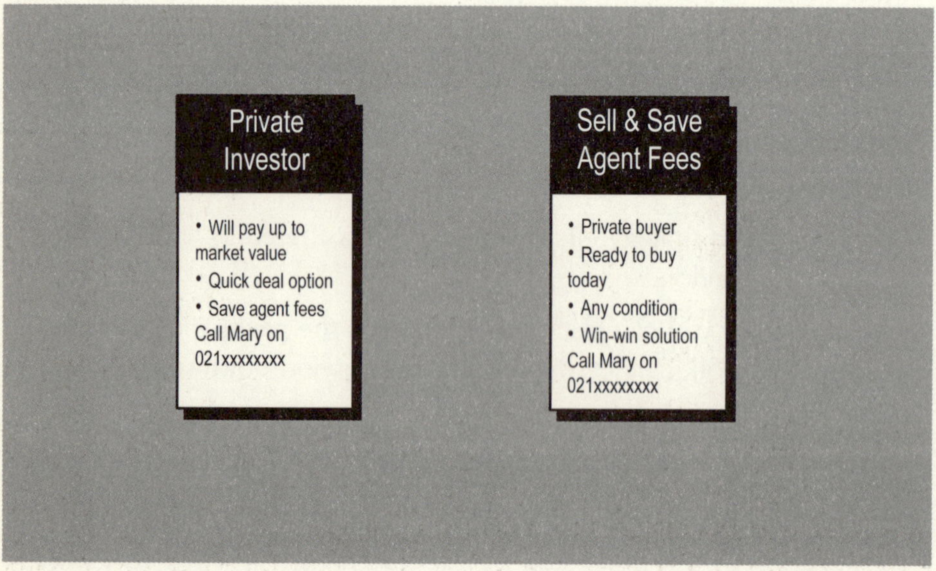

When the vendors call, tell them you can guarantee their rent for up to a certain number of years if you keep an option to purchase the property within a certain period of time. Only then explain that you have a database of serious buyers who will rent the property while they get the deposit to buy it. Not every caller will go for this strategy, but you will receive lots of calls.

Draw up the contract

Now you only need to match up buyers with vendors and customise the contract structure. You'll need to clarify in your contract with the vendor that you can sublet the property. You will prohibit the buyer from subletting the property. You will also need to establish a higher purchase price with the buyer than the one you established with the vendor. Remember to assign the property to yourself 'and/or nominee' (or use an Option Contract in Australia).

Pay the vendor a small initial option consideration. This is necessary to make your option agreement with the vendor legally binding. Also note that the weekly option consideration you pay the vendor will be lower than the one you receive from the buyer. The vendor will be responsible for all major structural damage, and the buyer for minor maintenance. Now that you have created a money-making machine, you can admire it in this simple table.

Lease options	Us with vendor	Buyer with us
Property price	$130k	$140k
Rent	$300	$600
Initial option consideration	$10	$1000
Weekly option considerationt	$300	$100
Subletting	Yes	No

Be sure that the initial option consideration you receive from the tenant buyer is large enough to cover your payments to the vendor for at least two months, in case the buyer decides to leave the property without taking advantage of the option. You then have two months to find another first-time buyer.

What if the buyer leaves?

What happens if the buyer leaves and doesn't buy the property after three years and 364 days? Well, this is the best thing that can happen to you, because:

- You can buy the property if the option-to-purchase price is lower than the market price (and therefore attractive to you).
- You can walk away with the money you've made from the difference between the buyer's option considerations paid to you and the option considerations that you have paid to the vendor.
- You can assign the property to somebody else.
- You can negotiate with the vendor to prolong the option contract etc.

If the buyer leaves half way through the contract period you have two months to find another buyer. You will ask this new buyer to pay more because the market will have moved up, and they'll have a shorter term to buy the property.

SUMMARY

Sandwich lease options are a fantastic no-money-down strategy with which you can create a cashflow machine, bringing you in some serious cash. To be successful in carrying out this strategy make sure you work on getting your marketing right, get a good solicitor to draw you a tight set of contracts, be the master of your contracts, and see the money roll into your bank account.

This strategy will become more and more effective the higher the property prices go because first-time buyers will be desperate to get onto the ladder and amateur investors will not be able to afford mortgages.

Summary of steps

1. Get a database of rent-to-buy candidates.
2. Find a motivated vendor.
3. Sign a lease option upwards agreement with the vendor.
4. Sign a lease option downwards agreement with your buyer.
5. Let the money come in.

Chapter 33

Investor package lease option

CONVERT KNOWLEDGE INTO CASH

'Buy land; they're not making it any more.'
— Mark Twain

Creating an investor package lease option is another great way to profit from lease options by putting together your knowledge on assignment and lease option downwards strategies.

How does it work?

With this strategy you will need to find a tenant buyer for a specific property you already have under contract with a sale and purchase agreement, then you will assign the complete package deal (property plus buyer) to an investor.

You will be applying this strategy to properties that you potentially want to purchase yourself. But instead you will assign it to another party. This enables you to get money out of the deal by applying the wealth of knowledge you have acquired in this book. And help someone else's wealth-creation plan by passing on a great deal to them.

By applying the option strategies you will quickly build a database of vendors and tenant buyers. This database can potentially make you truckloads of money by applying the investor package lease option strategy as detailed here. Effectively in this strategy you are matching up a tenant buyer to an investor who wants to purchase a lease option downwards deal.

The great advantage of applying this strategy is that you don't have any risk and you **do not need any money**.

You will be able to charge more than if you were just assigning a property because you have put together not a good deal with a tenant buyer and a contract associated with it – which makes it an outstanding deal!

Steps in the strategy

Step 1: Find a property

Find a discounted property and get it under contract so you have control over it. The bigger the discount the quicker you will find an investor and a tenant buyer for it. This strategy is all about turning over a lot of properties quickly to make cash for your other property investments.

Step 2: Find a tenant buyer

You will then offer the property to your database of tenant buyers and get a tentative lease option downwards contract with them. Remember: you have built your database of tenant buyers by using classified ads, specialised websites, flyers and any of the other marketing tools that we have given you so far.

Step 3: Find an investor

Once you have this contract ready you can offer the whole package deal to your network of investors. These investors will have confidence in you because of your knowledge of the property market and your mastery of the different types of lease option strategies.

Only deal with investors who will strive to produce win-win solutions for their tenant buyers. You now have an ethical responsibility to the tenant buyer too and you do not want to let them down.

Step 4: Assign the sale and purchase agreement

The last thing you need to do is to assign the sale and purchase agreement through a Deed of Assignment or option agreement to the final investor. This investor will by then also have a lease option downwards agreement with the tenant buyer. You will collect your assignment fee as soon as the transfer of the deal is complete.

Why have an investor package lease option?

The tenant buyer will have the same advantages as any other tenant buyer in the lease option strategies explained in previous chapters.

The vendor will sell the house, which is really what they are after.

There are two investors in this strategy. Investor 1 is the one that finds and assigns the property. Investor 2 is the one that buys the package deal.

Advantages to Investor 1

Benefits for the person who finds and assigns the property include:

- It's no risk and straightforward.
- It creates an income.
- It provides an alternative to sellers who won't accept sandwich deals.
- It maximises your marketing budget.

Advantages to Investor 2

Benefits for the person who buys the package deal include:

- It creates cashflow.
- Provides instant equity.
- No tenant problems.
- Time efficient.
- Increases borrowing capacity.
- Builds a substantial portfolio.

Marketing

You will need to apply the same marketing principles outlined in the previous chapter applying to the sandwich lease option, since you will need to find tenant buyers and vendors. The only difference is that you will not need to enter a lease option upwards agreement with the vendor.

Example

Consider the example we used in Chapter 17: Property Assignment.

Purchase price	$88k
Market value	$98k
Discount	$10k
Weekly rental	$160
Finder's fee	$700

In this example the property finder got $700 for assigning the deal onwards. If she had also found a tenant buyer and put a tentative lease option downwards agreement together she could have charged around $10,000 for the deal. This is because there would have been more money to be made for the investor as the yield would have increased from 9.45% to 12.41% by adding a weekly option consideration of only $50. Think win, win, win!

SUMMARY

Investor package lease options are a great way of creating cashflow and income to get you started into the amazing world of real estate investing. It is also a great alternative to have ready if a vendor does not want to go into a sandwich lease option deal because they need the money as soon as possible.

Get to know your vendors' motivation and what you want to get out of real estate investing and apply this strategy accordingly.

Summary of steps

1. Find a property owner who is thinking of selling.
2. Find a tenant buyer interested in the property.
3. Arrange a sale and purchase agreement with the vendor.
4. Arrange a lease down contract with the tenant buyer (leave optionor name blank).
5. Find a time-conscious investor.
6. Assign the sale and purchase agreement to the investor.

Chapter 34

Apartments

OPPORTUNITIES DISGUISED AS PROBLEMS

'Knowledge is potential power. Action makes it powerful.'

— **David Leon**

To apply this strategy best you will first need to do some research and find a location where there is an oversupply of apartments. In this scenario the apartment market will be achieving lower yields than it would normally. This is due to supply and demand. If there are a lot of apartments to let, rents generally will soften and so will their yield.

This can make investors want to exit the market and sell their apartments quickly. Often this can mean they sell at a loss and lose thousands of dollars. There are different ways you can create solutions to this problem and profit by doing so.

Let the apartment room by room

One solution is to rent out the apartment room by room or by the day like a hotel, instead of renting out the whole apartment.

This can provide accommodation for business people, travellers, people looking for affordable temporary accommodation who also want to be able to cook their own meals and do their own washing etc.

To set up an apartment for this strategy, you will need to install good locks on the doors to each room so that tenants feel secure if they are sharing common areas with others. You will also need to employ a cleaner to clean the property regularly or a live-in manager who rents one of the rooms (at a discount), while he/she keeps the rest of the rooms in the apartment clean and also manages the short-term rental tenants.

Marketing

By far the most important step in this strategy is to set up the marketing right from the start, to ensure you get your customers. If you have no clients you will make no money.

To do this you can set up your own website. Sites such as sitebuildit.com offers an affordable DIY solution, or you can get someone, such as Headrush.co.nz to create one for you.

You should also advertise through specialist websites such as eBay or similar. Place classified ads in the local newspapers and specialist magazines or on backpacker notice boards where travellers may be looking for short-term accommodation solutions. This can also give you a lot of exposure.

As with any marketing effort for any business, you will need to measure what advertising is giving you the highest number of leads. Measuring is a very simple process. As soon as you get a phone call, email or walk-in, the first thing you will ask is: 'How did you hear about us?' Keep a note of the answer you get. Then focus your marketing budget on the resources that are providing you with the highest number of leads.

Ensure you have the correct entity

Make sure your apartment is owned in the correct entity (seek good asset-planning advice on this). Because this strategy is run like a small business you are likely to have tax considerations that you need to plan for.

In some countries, if the revenue you are making exceeds a certain amount, you have to be GST registered. This is not necessarily a bad thing as if you set up your company before you purchase the property you can claim GST on the total purchase price of the apartment, and on all other expenses to operate your business. You will also need to check the covenants on the apartment block to make sure that you can run this type of business there.

GST

Talk to your mortgage broker before you buy because if the bank knows that you are purchasing the property through a GST-registered company or trust they may lend on only the purchase price minus the GST, whereas you want them to lend to you on the GST-inclusive amount. We have found that banks may only agree to lend you the GST-exclusive amount in the first instance. After a few months, however, they will be happy to give you a further advance based on the total value of the property including GST. It makes no sense but banks set their own rules and we just work with them.

Find tenant buyers for cheap vacant apartments

Another strategy that provides a solution to the problem of an oversupply of apartments is the lease option downwards strategy that will create a massive opportunity for savvy investors.

These low-yielding apartments are often left vacant because of lack of tenant demand. This will mean there will be lots of uneducated investors wanting to sell their apartments and this creates a drop in prices.

Investors that know how to apply the lease option downwards strategy will buy the empty or low-yielding apartments at a considerable discount from a motivated vendor and would be able to transform the equity created in the discounted purchase into monthly cashflow from the tenant buyer. Remember that the tenant buyer will pay a monthly premium to keep the option agreement valid. (This is explained in more depth in Chapter 29.)

Check new building regulations

New building regulations setting limits for minimum apartment size are being introduced all over the world. They will play a big part in future developments and can create opportunities for investors.

Apartments with very small floor areas will quickly become a thing of the past, because in many places developers will not be allowed to build small apartments any more. This means a demand for small apartments will be created because they will be scarce.

Most investors see these new regulations about apartment size as something to fear and believe they will need to sell their smaller apartments. But there is opportunity in every change if you know how to use it.

So if you can identify a locality that has an oversupply of apartments and where building codes are becoming stricter in terms of apartment size, start buying apartments (with floor areas below the new code) at a discount today. Smaller apartments will command cheaper rentals; if there are not many of them around they will become more popular with tenants. Your yields will increase and so will the value of your property because of the simple rule of supply and demand.

SUMMARY

The way to look at an oversupply of apartments is as a massive opportunity rather than a problem. Look for the twist, go against popular belief and see the great opportunities that change or a new market environment can create. Always look for the solution to the change rather than seeing it as a problem. Remember that problem plus solution equals profit.

Summary of steps

1. Find a location with an oversupply of apartments.
2. Check building codes for minimum apartment size.
3. Negotiate a big discount on purchase price.
4. Decide whether to rent out each room on a short-term basis or lease it down.
5. Create cashflow and keep buying more apartments.

Chapter 35

Cash recycling

TRANSFORM $200K INTO $5 MILLION IN 2.5 YEARS

'Lack of money is the root of all evil.'
— George Bernard Shaw

Cash recycling is a strategy that has the potential to accelerate your portfolio size and take it to a whole new level. The simplicity of this strategy is amazing. It offers fantastic results just by targeting the quintessential problem of running out of deposit money. It provides a way of recycling your deposits quickly and effectively.

In a classic buy-and-hold investment you will need around six months to be able to refinance your property in order to get your deposit back out of the deal. Six months is way too long for most investors, but what if you could do it within weeks? Then your investment portfolio could grow to amazing new heights, and this strategy will do just that for you.

How does it work?

Buy with cash

You can use this strategy if you have a large cash reserve, say more than $250k. You can then look to buy a property to purchase outright in cash. Cash means no mortgage. It could be money from your savings account or a loan from your family, but you just *cannot* get a mortgage. The reason is that when you are buying with cash you are more likely to easily negotiate a better deal on the property. Aim to buy the property at 10 to 20% below valuation.

Add value

Next do some basic value adding, such as painting, changing light fittings, door handles, tidying up the garden and fixing any small problems. Then get a new registered valuation done on the property. Once you have done this show your mortgage broker or bank that you have done improvements to the property and that it has been revalued at a higher price.

Get a loan against the newly revalued property

Get a loan against the property with its new valuation. You will find you have made a no-money-down deal, especially if you bought the property at a good discount. If the loan is up to 80% of the new value, this should be at least the same as the full purchase price that you paid for the property.

Now you own property and you have no money left in it. Then you can go and do it again.

Why buy with cash?

Remember that it does not have to be cash in the hand; it can be existing equity which you can convert to cash easily.

There are benefits to buying a property outright with cash.

- You can portray your offer as a cash offer. Vendors like this and you will be able to obtain a higher discount.
- Banks will be happier to lend on a property you own without a mortgage than on a property you want to buy.

It is a matter of risk level once again. If you have bought a property and assumed the risk yourself, you are less likely to become a problem later on.

Example

Buy at a discount then add value

You negotiate a 20% discount on a do-up property because you are a cash buyer. The market value of the property is $200k and you purchase it for $160k. Then you spend an extra $2k painting the place and doing minor cosmetic improvements.

Get a new valuation

After painting you get a valuation from a reputable valuer recommended on the Richmastery site. The new registered valuation comes a bit higher than you anticipated – it is now worth $210k!

Head to the bank

You take your new valuation of $210k to the bank and ask for an 80% loan on valuation. Do not tell the bank when you purchased the property unless they specifically ask. If you are asked, do not forget to tell them that you renovated the property and that is why you achieved such outstanding equity growth. The bank will then be happy because you meet their requirements and they will approve lending of at least 80% of the new valuation price. You just got $168k back! That means that you actually got paid $6k to buy a deal ($168k – purchase price of $160k – renovation cost $2k = $6k surplus).

Huge potential

Now you know why this strategy is so exciting. The potential is huge, especially when you find the right deals with a good amount of equity. Applying this strategy is definitely not complicated. You just need that initial lump of cash and you are ready to build your property portfolio in record time.

Some of you will be thinking: 'Yeah, but I do not have a lump sum of cash.' Well, the answer is simple – make one. Stop making excuses and start making some money. Enrol in the Richmastery Lease Options course (see www.richmasteryleaseoptions.com), which will point you in the right direction.

SUMMARY

Your buy-and-hold portfolio will never be the same again! Now you can accelerate your way to wealth with this new exciting strategy. The objectives of the strategy are simple yet powerful. You can increase your cashflow, replace your income, and get the freedom and time that you deserve. But the best thing about it is that with the cash-recycling strategy you can accomplish those goals in record time.

You will only need two main components to apply this strategy: a lump sum of cash; and a good mortgage broker (see Richmastery website for recommendations). If you have these two components and are motivated to get started, you can reach your milestones much faster than you ever thought possible. Find the cash and the broker and get cracking today.

Summary of steps

1. Get a substantial sum of cash (probably the hardest part of applying this strategy).
2. Find a property priced around 20% under market value.
3. Buy the property using cash.
4. Do minor renovations.
5. Apply to a lender for a mortgage for the new valuation price after renovations (which also will include your discounted purchase).
6. Keep repeating steps 1 to 5 as many times and as quickly as possible.

Chapter 36

Reversionary deals

GET 60% EQUITY ON EVERY PURCHASE

'It is common sense to take a method and try it. If it fails, admit it frankly and try another. But above all, try something.'
— Franklin D. Roosevelt

Reversionary property investment (RPI) is not a well-known strategy but has made thousands of real estate investors millionaires. It is a common strategy in the United Kingdom, and is becoming more and more common in the United States. There are some people applying it in Australia and New Zealand, although it is still relatively unknown. This means there is a huge gap in the market, allowing you to benefit greatly.

How does it work?

You simply purchase residential properties from elderly homeowners who need to raise capital or cashflow. When you settle on your purchase, your solicitor grants them what is called a peppercorn lease. They continue to live in the property, but now as your tenants. They pay only a nominal (peppercorn) rent and to compensate you for this, you buy these properties at a discount of up to 60% off the market value.

The deal states that when the elderly tenant (former owner) leaves the property, for whatever reason, you can then rent it at full rent market value or sell it for the full open market value. So, you profit from the 60% initial discount and 100% of the property's equity growth from the time you bought it.

How does it benefit the investor?

Helping those in need

The best thing about this strategy is its simplicity and that you actually are helping out people in need to access the equity in their property at the time of life when they need it.

You only need a relatively small deposit

Reversionary property is discounted by around 60%. This leaves you with a low initial capital cost and a massive medium- to long-term capital growth. Your deposit will be substantially smaller than in a conventional buy-and-hold strategy.

Your tenants pay for all repairs and maintenance

Your tenants are the elderly vendors from whom you've bought the property. Under the terms of the lease they are legally required to maintain and repair the property and pay all expenses and outgoings. Not only that, but many of your tenants use some of their new capital to refurbish and improve your property.

You can sell at any time

Although ideally a medium- to long-term strategy, you can sell your reversionary property to other investors who will honour the peppercorn rent of the tenant, at any time. Obviously the price is subject to market conditions, but you should still make a very healthy profit, even if you decide to sell the property before your tenant leaves.

Your selling price will take into account not only any increase in the value of the property, but the increase in the age of the tenant. The older the tenant, the smaller the discount, so as a seller of a reversionary property you will be benefiting greatly as time goes on.

Increase your equity

The main benefit of using this strategy is being able to create a huge amount of equity in your portfolio. It is definitely not a short-term strategy, although you could see massive returns in months.

Even if property prices never increase again, you'll make over 100% profit on the capital growth. This little-known investment strategy virtually guarantees you'll make effortless profits during good or bad economic times.

Complete package deal

The beauty of this strategy is that you can use it to buy property investments as a complete deal (you get the house and the tenant in one strike). You'll now be able to buy superb houses and flats, at under half price. Not only that, but they're already fully furnished and completely fitted out – and already tenanted.

Many of them come with pre-arranged mortgages so, if you want, you can buy them with low monthly payments out of your income. Please check with your mortgage broker to see which lenders will offer mortgages on these deals. They will more than likely be specialist lenders; the traditional lenders will not usually even know that these types of deals exist and may consequently be cautious. Having a good mortgage broker on your team is once again a major benefit, while having an average broker will definitely slow you down.

Minimal time and low risk

You will not need any management or estate agents and your own input in time and energy with this strategy is absolutely minimal.

This strategy is one of the easiest and lowest-risk ways to invest in residential property, with one of the highest potential returns.

Example 1

Here is an example of how this strategy can work over time.

An investment of $47,500 was made in 1992.

The same property is worth $290k today – a net profit of 510%!

If the property was sold today, and the $290k was reinvested using the same formula, in 10 years and assuming equity growth of only 6% per annum, this initial investment would be worth around $1,235,000. This represents a net profit on the initial investment of $47,500 of 2500%!

Example 2

David had an investor friend, Gill, who bought a reversionary property from a 62-year-old gentleman, Barry, who was living by himself. Barry's life partner had passed away around three years earlier and he wanted to release some equity to enjoy the rest of his life. Gill bought the property for $180k when its market value was around $360k. Barry then only had to pay $10 of nominal rent to live there after he sold the investor the deal.

Gill expected to have Barry as a tenant for over 10 years but she got a great surprise three months into this agreement when Barry told her that he was leaving the property. Gill asked him why he wanted to leave the premises and if he knew what it meant. Barry answered: 'I am in love.' He had met a woman and was planning on moving in to her place. He was more than happy to leave Gill with $180k worth of equity because he was in love.

That is a great payday, isn't it? $180k in three months! Gill did help him financially to move to his new girlfriend's place and gave him a nice 'farewell gift' for them to enjoy together. We are not saying that this will happen in every RPI that you purchase, but it may ... or maybe you will get stuck with a tenant paying pretty much no rent for 20 years. The trick of making this strategy work is to have a balanced portfolio so that you can pay for the mortgage and to look at it as a medium- to long-term strategy.

Do your research

There are some facts you need to be aware of when entering an RPI deal. The first one has to do with the average age at which people in your area die or go into retirement homes. The average age of death for males in many countries is around 75.9 years of age; for females it is 82.1. You should also know that after the death of a partner, the other partner is not expected to live, on average, longer than three years.

You need to take these facts into account when you do your numbers and decide whether or not you should buy an RPI. These are just averages and you will get people on both ends of the scale.

If you think that this is a morbid way of investing then we suggest that you reconsider the way you think about it. Look at it from the perspective of the elderly person needing to release some equity from their home and wanting to live in it for as long as possible before having to go to a retirement home. You can really help them achieve this by creating these kinds of deals. But for you as an investor, the numbers need to make sense, and that is why you study the numbers that we have just given you.

So obviously our main goal as investors is for the tenant to move out of the property as soon as possible so that we can have complete access to the equity. But let your tenants live a peaceful life in the place they are proud to call their home (even if you own it).

How does it fit into my strategy?

RPIs are not for everyone. They are part of a healthy portfolio as a medium- to long-term strategy. You should only purchase an RPI when you have enough cashflow from other properties to support the mortgage that you will most likely acquire to purchase the deal.

As you can probably tell by now, they are an outstanding way of getting equity instantly and profiting from property with a minimal outlay. Add the fact that you are helping people out to live in their home until they physically have to leave and you have a clear winner.

SUMMARY

If you want to create a lot of equity quickly in your portfolio reversionary deals are right for you. They will make you very rich, although you will not know when it will happen. You should look at these deals as a long-term deal. They are very money hungry, so before you apply them make sure you have other cashflow-producing properties to take care of the repayments of the mortgage you will acquire to purchase your reversionary deal.

Summary of steps

1. Find an elderly vendor who needs cash but wants to stay in his/her property as long as possible.
2. Offer the vendor an RPI deal.
3. Create a massive amount of equity in your portfolio.
4. Wait for the vendor/tenant to leave the property.
5. You will now own a property you can really profit from.

Part Four

Mapping your path to real estate success

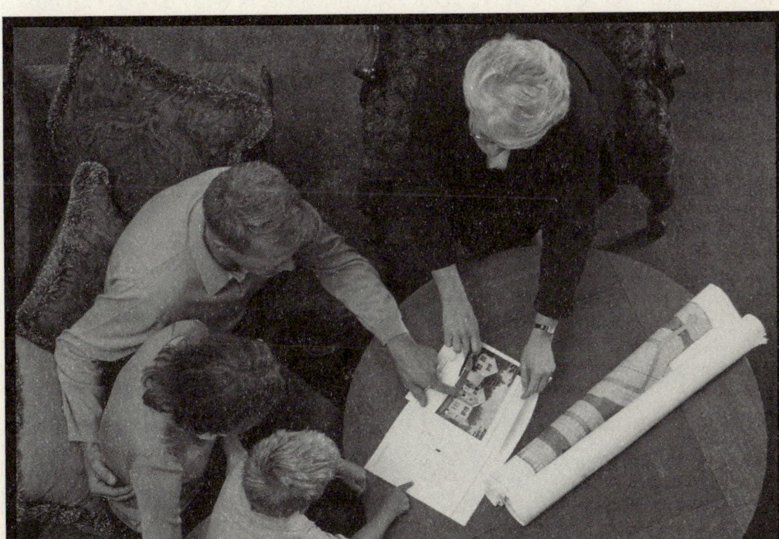

Chapter 37

Goal setting

TECHNIQUES OF SUCCESSFUL INVESTORS

> ***'What other people think about me is none of my business.'***
> **— Phil Jones**

This is the most important chapter in the book. The way you feel about property investing will define how sophisticated and successful you will be as a professional property investor.

SMART goals

The best way to approach property investing is with **SMART** goals. SMART stands for:

Specific

Measurable

Achievable

Realistic

Time-controlled

S – Specific

Let's give you an example of not being specific when setting goals. We have heard lots of people say that their goal in property investing is to make a lot of money. That says absolutely nothing to us – what is a lot of money to you? \$30k, \$250k, \$10 million per year? Do you want it to be passive income or do you want to always be involved? You should know the answer to all of these questions before you even look at your first property.

M – Measurable

When we talk about being measurable we are talking about something that can be accounted for and matched against. For example, 'I want to buy five houses in the next 13 months.'

A + R – Achievable and realistic

You need to make sure that your goals are achievable and realistic so that you do not panic or get bored. You do not want to make your goals so high that you feel discouraged, or so low that you get bored. Finding this balance will take some time but once you get it right you will always keep raising the bar and pushing yourself to the next level.

T – Time-controlled

This is a key concept. If you do not define time boundaries you will get frustrated and quit. You should also set different goals for different time frames; what you want to achieve in the first six months will be very different to what you will want to obtain in five years.

Remember one thing when you are doing this exercise. People tend to overestimate what they can accomplish in a short period (up to six months), and they usually underestimate what they can achieve in longer periods.

Set goals and plan

The best thing for you to do now is to go to a quiet place. Just clear your head and think what your goals are and whether you believe you can achieve them through property. Once you have your goals ready, you have to develop a plan. If you fail to plan, you plan to fail. Planning will design the path you will take to achieve those goals you just set.

Know why you want to get there

It is not enough to just set goals; you need to attach passion to them or they will just become dreams. When you attach feelings to your ideas, they become stronger. You actually use more of your brain when you attach feelings to ideas.

So when you are writing down your goals know *why* you want to get there. It is a major part of this process and therefore part of your future success.

A toolbox with which to accomplish your dreams

This book was intended to give you more options to help you create your pathway to achieve your goals. After having read all the strategies, you will now have a better 'toolbox' with which to accomplish your dreams. Your plan will definitely guide you along the way, and you should always try to stick to it. We intentionally write 'try' because some new paths will open along the way, and maybe these new paths will take you to your goal more quickly or in a more pleasurable way.

Remember as well that you will find obstacles along your anticipated path. It will not be a smooth ride for you. Things will come up to distract you, and you will probably have to withstand quite a lot of negativity from some of your peers and even other investors. Don't get upset when everything around you seems to be slowing you down. You know where you want to get to and why you want to get there.

Take action

Once you know where you are headed and how and why you want to get there, you will be ready to take the most important step: *take action*.

We have seen so many investors who have written down everything they want to achieve, how to achieve it, where to achieve it – they have really done their homework – but they still do not buy any property. We call this 'paralysis by analysis' and it is a symptom far too common in western society. And we mean what we say when we write 'symptom': a symptom is usually caused by a disease. The disease in this case is cultural conditioning. This makes us believe life is about playing everything 'safe' – even if we now know that what we believed was 'safe' is in fact not safe at all.

Life is not about safety; it is about growing, achieving, and sharing with others. We need to constantly challenge ourselves to keep living a happy life. The biggest killer of our mature population is retirement. Your brain is a wonderful tool that needs nourishment; you ought to provide that, in the way of challenges! You need to get out of your comfort zone and venture into the joy of uncertainty. Here is where the real rewards grow. This is the only reason why there are not more millionaires. Most people are just too scared to even try to get there.

The main thing that we hope you will take from reading this book is that you must do something different now to change your outcome. Remember if you finish reading this book and within the next couple of hours do nothing about it, you just wasted a lot of valuable time and the money you invested when you purchased it.

Get moving

To get the most out of this or any other real estate book you must **get moving**. Movement is necessary because it creates momentum. Even if it is just a small act like getting property investor business cards from Headrush.co.nz, this small act will get you moving in the right direction. Promise yourself that you will apply at least one of the principles taught in this book for the next week every single day.

Make a spreadsheet about it now (this can be your first step of the seven-day process), and start filling in what you do each day. It is amazing that within a few days you will have accomplished more than you thought possible. Put some offers in, meet some agents and follow them up, analyse areas, and get a Richmastery Property Mentor! See www.richmasterymentoring.com. They are worth their weight in gold.

Create momentum

When you create momentum you are unstoppable. It works like starting an exercise programme. Most people hate the first day; they are unfit and they sweat and feel pain in muscles they did not know they even had. They get home and the pain gets even worse. The second and third day in the gym are not any better and they feel discouraged because they do not see any amazing results. The only results they get are soreness and missing out on TV dinners at home. After around a week of their exercise programme they start to feel better about themselves, they have more energy and they can see results! Wow!

Now this is what we call momentum. You get hooked on the feelings and more importantly the results. The same outcome applies to property investing: you do your first deal and then you see the money and finally realise that you do not ever need to work for anyone else! You are the master of your destiny, and that feeling is amazing. You also start seeing the money coming into your account. Just imagine adding zeros to your account balance. Then you feel really empowered.

Make it work and take responsibility

Are you excited yet? The analogy of working out in the gym is great for another reason. Most people give up on their fitness routine after around six to eight weeks. The reason is very simple – you reach a plateau. You have now been exercising religiously for five weeks, the changes in your body are amazing and you feel great. The problem is that in one week you have two birthday parties and you have to drive for a whole day to attend a business meeting. Your exercising sessions get reduced to nil during that week.

The other problem is that your metabolic rate has also increased and you are now hungrier than ever. Within that week you seem to gain your whole gut back and feel absolutely exhausted. And then you tell yourself the same old lie you have told yourself all your life: 'This doesn't work.'

You should be telling yourself this instead: 'I did not want it enough to make it work.' Exercising works and so does building wealth through real estate investing. You just need to make them work.

See problems as opportunities

You will have problems that you will need to overcome in your investing career. Look at them not as colossal mountains but as great opportunities to grow as a person and an investor. Just like the parties and business meetings in your exercising routines, you will suffer from lack of funds and unexpected costs in your investing career.

All these problems are solvable and you won't even remember them in a couple of years. The problems that we thought were huge in our humble beginnings are now just dinner table jokes about how silly we were to even consider them problems. Also like the metabolic rate going up or down, you will also have to live with the ups and downs of property cycles. Learn the advantages and disadvantages of them and employ strategies that will let you profit in them. Don't swim against the current, go with it.

Keep trying new things

Most people also plateau for a different reason: boredom. With exercise, you keep exercising at the same intensity and using the same routines for months. After a while you see no new results and exercising is not a thrill anymore. Lack of excitement equals lack of energy. Soon enough you will be so discouraged and unhappy that you will stop your routine altogether. Your brain is too smart to keep boring itself to tears.

When investing in real estate the same principle applies. You need to keep evolving as an investor or you will lose your passion that is the fuel that will get you the success you are after.

Keep trying new strategies, new markets, new property types! All these new elements will make you feel excited and will keep your motivation levels high and healthy. Your brain will tell you: please give me more of this because I am having fun!

Learn and grow

Thrill equals action, and soon enough you will get stunning results that will catapult you into even more excitement because you will start playing with more zeros and different property and investment types. It all comes down to one of the main basic human needs: growth. Our minds and bodies are thirsty for growth. Growth is exciting, it pushes us out of our comfort zone and gets us to achieve new goals in our life. Learning, reading, meditating, teaching, thinking, inventing, writing – all these activities will help us grow as healthy individuals.

Investing in real estate is a process that you must learn to enjoy. Maybe not for itself, but for the results it will produce for you. If your reasons are strong enough you will have the energy and enthusiasm to overcome any hurdles you may encounter. Find those whys and you will be truly unstoppable.

What is your focus?

Self-belief and identity

Most people when asked who they are automatically answer that they are their profession or what they do. We are comfortable with our identity, and it's hard to deny our identity.

Say a kid was always lazy when he was growing up. The idea was reinforced by family and friends for years. His identity was then formed. He was lazy and started acting as a lazy man would. Your brain hates going against your identity because if you don't even know who you are, you are really in trouble.

The opposite is also true. Quite average people, who are told they are smart and intelligent, start to create that identity. They will start copying the behaviour of smart, intelligent people. And guess what? If you copy everything a smart and intelligent person does you will become smart and intelligent! Believe that you are already successful and do what successful people do – the rewards will soon follow.

Focus on what you can achieve

You have to decide whether you will be a can or a can't. Read this last sentence out loud and tell us what you want to be. Focus on what you can achieve and you are certain to get there.

We have way too many people who tell us that they cannot find positive cashflow properties, that they cannot find any profitable renovation deals, that they cannot become wealthy through property investing... We tell them right away that they are completely right. You will probably be shocked to hear this but here is our reason for this statement. When you focus on not being able to find property, your brain automatically stops trying to find it. Therefore it is a self-fulfilling prophecy. Your focus determines your outcome and until you change your focus your outcome will be the same.

You need to decide

The word decide comes from a Latin root that means to cut off. In your life you are always deciding. You are always cutting off paths that you may have followed. Even when you think that you will put off a decision and sleep on it, you are really making a decision. You decided to cut off the possibility of deciding right now instead of tomorrow.

Life is full of big and small decisions. You need to decide on all of your options. Because you have read this fascinating book, now you are presented with a massive decision: Do you become a successful real estate investor or do you keep doing whatever it is you do?

It is up to you to decide the right path, the path that will satisfy your reasons and fulfil your goals. You already know which one it is. Most people know what to do but they don't do what they know.

A friend always kept repeating this sentence:

If it is to be it is up to me.

He always said that these are the 10 most powerful two-letter words to form a sentence in the English language.

Just think about it: everything you focus on you will achieve. Decide to go for it full steam ahead and never look back. Now you have made your decision towards achieving success.

Do you desire it enough?

The word desire also comes from the Latin, meaning 'of the Father', and to desire used to mean to pray. Regardless of your religion, you will understand what it means. Your desires are the reasons you have that will make a successful life. They are the 'whys' that will fill you with unlimited energy to get the most out of every minute.

Knowing what you want

Find your desire and you will find the right path to achieving your goals. You will need time to find what your heart truly desires. Meditation will help you get there. Another way of finding your desire is to do some *active thinking.* We call active thinking the process in which you sit down by yourself and try to find the answer to a question. As soon as you have an idea, you must write it down and eventually you will get the answer you were after.

The processes of active thinking and meditation are unpredictable, and the results could come to you in minutes or months. Keep working on it because when you finally get there your life will never be the same again.

Burning desire

In Napoleon Hill's best-selling book *Think and Grow Rich,* available from www.richmastery.com, he also talks about what desire means. He describes it by explaining where the phrase 'burning desire' comes from. A general and his army were about to take on an adversary who far outnumbered them. When they arrived at their destination he ordered all his men to burn the ships that they had travelled in. Doing so would prevent them from even thinking of retreating or defeat. They now knew that to survive they had to beat their enemies, even if they were outnumbered. It goes without saying that they did win the battle.

It is amazing that when we give 100% of everything we have and there is no other escape plan, more than likely we will find a way to achieve our goals. What ships do you need to burn in order to achieve your goals? What comfort zones will you have to escape? Take the time to identify them and then let go of them to reach a better lifestyle.

Challenge yourself

Do not feel fear about letting go, remember that we are the happiest and we achieve the most amazing results when we grow and we challenge ourselves. No one remembers when you did not take action, but you will always commemorate the times when you did what you knew you had to do. It does not matter whether you won or lost; the only thing that matters is that you gave it your best shot and did not let life pass you by.

Adjust your income to fit your lifestyle

Most people do the opposite of this. They adjust their lifestyle to fit their income – that is why they moan about how miserable life is. They take the role of victim instead of victor. It is a much easier role to play since you don't have to do anything. You just let life do unto you. On the other hand, you can play the role of victor. You will see any adversity that life brings you as an opportunity to grow and contribute. You will see challenges as gifts so that you can be the best you can be and make a difference in the world.

Victim or victor?

Victims moan; victors enjoy. You need to decide on which side of the court you will be playing.

An older lady won $2 million in a lottery. You would think that she would be over the moon about the event, but instead she was really upset about it. After being asked why she was upset she answered that she felt hard done by.

She said that there was another person choosing the same six numbers on the same day and if that person had not played she would have won $4 million instead of $2 million.

Hopefully now you can see what I mean by a victim. Probably you know someone close to you who lives life as a victim. Maybe that person is so close to you that he or she is reading this same page of this book right now! Probably we are wrong to say that because a victim would already have thought of an excuse to not keep reading this section of the book.

Making positive associations

We are not saying that you should always be positive about everything that happens around you. That would just be unhealthy and fake. What we are trying to say is that you can see each individual event that happens around you for what it really is. Just ask yourself this question the next time that you feel hard done by: 'What else could this mean?' Come up with several new positive answers and you will be amazed at how much better you will feel about it.

Stress and victim behaviour comes as a result of associating a highly negative connotation with an event. When you associate other more positive meanings with it, the event itself seems to lose importance.

Let's do a quick exercise. Can you remember a time when you felt really stressed about something that just seems like a light joke today? I am sure you have hundreds of these experiences. They all happen because of your associations. From now on you have to see events for what they really are, just events. The feelings that you attach to these events will determine how you feel about them.

Let us give you another example of this very important concept. In some cultures and religions, people actually celebrate death. They associate a feeling of freedom and happiness with the event. They still miss the people that die, but they do not feel sad about it since they know that the departed have just started another stage, a stage that comes right after death.

In most Western countries the feelings associated with death are very different. You are supposed to feel sad, guilty, lonely, depressed, upset, etc... The funny thing about this example is that they both refer to exactly the same event. Different cultures, however, have completely different feelings about it.

which one do you think behaves as a victim and which one as a victor? It is up to you to decide.

In any investment that you enter you will have to face challenges. They will come from unexpected places and usually whenever you are not ready for them. Start acting as a victor and you will conquer them. Act as a victim and you are sure to never evolve and live a miserable life.

Look the part

Most people are so scared about property investing that they never get started. Their fear can be smelled miles away by vendors, real estate agents and others involved in the property-buying process. This is the main reason why you must fake it until you make it.

You need to act like a professional so that you are treated like a professional. When you act, behave and ask questions as a professional property investor, you will experience a different level of service and – most importantly – *success*.

Professional real estate investors are not arrogant or ill-tempered. Most successful professional property investors that we know are usually even-tempered and humble individuals who always try to create win-win solutions in every scenario.

You do not even need to wear flashy clothes or drive a Porsche. You just need to look the part and wear tidy clean clothes. We have seen people wearing dirty and wrinkled T-shirts when meeting up with their solicitors or estate agents. This just shows a complete lack of respect for them and what you do. If you do not care about yourself, how much will you care about others? Think how a professional investor would present themselves and mirror that.

Don't ever lie

If you lie, you will always eventually get caught out, and your name and integrity are the most important assets in this world. Faking does not mean lying. When you fake something you are just imitating something that you want to be like. When you imitate and behave like successful people do, you get what successful people get. This is why the Ricmastery mentoring programme is such a powerful tool for investors. You can imitate successful property investors so that you achieve the same results.

Do not be afraid to copy what other people do or the systems they implement. If they make them work so can you. If they profit from them so can you. Just emulate their systems and open your bank account to let the money come in.

Always think of your reasons

If in doubt, go back to the reasons why you got started. The answer will then show itself. Most people get so involved in the detail of the process that they lose track of the big picture. The big picture is the compass that will guide you to your destination. Without it you will feel lost all the way to nowhere.

We love the word nowhere. Whenever we see it or listen to it we think NOW / HERE – because you can go nowhere or NOW you can get started HERE. Once again the decision is up to you.

Failure is easier to live with than regret

This is the statement that changed our lives. Hopefully it can do the same for you too.

What do you want your epitaph to say? Will it be something like this?

Here Lies David Leon,
He had a nice life, family and friends
And he never had many problems.

Or would you rather have something like this?

Here Lies David Leon
He enjoyed every second of his exciting life
The people around him will always remember him
for his intoxicating energy.

You choose what will appear on yours. Remember this: you never know when your epitaph will be written, so start acting today! Socrates once said: 'To move the world, we must first move ourselves.' Take action, do all you can while you are here, enjoy every second of the ride and share it with others. Use this little formula and you will be successful not just in property investing but in your life.

Chapter 38

Getting started

THE ROAD TO FINANCIAL FREEDOM

'Your mind will achieve what it focuses on.'
— Deepak Chopra

If you are not sure what your next step is now that you have come to the end of the book, here are some tips.

Connect with the right people

The first step is to get out there and start talking to people. Remember that the personal relationships you make will help to make you wealthy. Choose wisely the people you spend most of your time with. Make friends with people who will push you out of your comfort zone. The Richmastery Forums are a great place to start.

Get a mentor – see www.richmasterymentoring.com

Get some mentors, people who are where you want to go and who can take you there more quickly and safely. They have already been through the problems that you will surely face in your investing career.

Mentoring and coaching are the best methods to get the results you want in record time. Make sure that you pay a fair price for your mentor. This way you will ensure that they will really be working for you and you will not feel bad about calling them or visiting them for advice and expertise.

You will notice that when someone helps you out for free you do not attach any value to the experience and you will barely take any action at all. When you pay for a professional mentoring or coaching service you will take the necessary steps to at least recuperate your investment. This by itself will create the momentum that we talked about in the previous chapter that is essential to getting started and to achieving great success in this or any kind of investment.

Invest in yourself

Keep investing in yourself. Reading this book has been a positive, active step in the right direction towards achieving your goals. Keep reading books, attend seminars, and visit websites that can give you useful information so that you can keep growing as an investor.

Our websites are updated regularly with products and new strategies so that everyone can benefit from the amazing rewards of personal growth and wealth creation. Go to www.richmastery.com to see a schedule of events and seminars that you can attend to learn useful strategies in wealth creation. Also check out www.david-leon.com.

On the Rewards Page in this book (see front or back) you get two free tickets to a Richmastery seminar. Please use them and keep gaining knowledge. Attending seminars and continuing your education is well worthwhile. You will only need to apply one strategy or idea or tip that you learn to make the course or book pay for itself, and you will keep the knowledge forever. It is a no-brainer. Invest in yourself first and reward yourself forever. Go to the Rewards Page now!

Start making some offers on property

You will be amazed to see just how many great deals there are out there, but you have to start taking some action to find them.

Add a due diligence clause

Remember to add a due diligence clause to the standard sale and purchase agreement. This way you will always be able to get out of the deal if there are reasons why you should not complete it. Here is a due diligence clause that we use:

Due Diligence

This agreement is entirely conditional upon the purchaser approving (in the purchasers' sole and unfettered discretion) all matters that the purchaser considers may touch, concern, or affect the property or the commercial viability of the transaction within 21 [*on some deals you may need to negotiate this number; at the very least you will want seven days*] complete working days after the date of this agreement by both parties. If notice is not received in writing by the Vendor's Solicitor or agent by 5pm on the 21st complete working day after the date of this agreement of the purchaser's approval of the property, then the contract will be at an end. This condition is inserted for the sole benefit of the purchaser.

Just include this due diligence clause as an additional clause on the sale and purchase agreement, and start faxing off offers to real estate agents.

By the way, you do need a fax at home, or close to wherever you spend most of your day. Faxing offers back and forth will make you millions and save you a massive amount of time.

Relationship with agents

Some agents do not like the process of getting offers via fax on properties that investors have not even seen. Well ... tough. If they do not want to play ball find someone else in the office who will present your offers. Make him or her aware that you will do so and that you will also inform his or her manager and also the seller that he or she refused to take an offer. As they are obliged to present all offers this will mean action is assured.

Don't be afraid of a small confrontation with agents. Often the agents you have an argument with early in your relationship with them will become the most valuable ones in your power team. Being a straight shooter has its benefits and builds trust.

Personal contract

Now you are going to write a personal contract. This contract will help get you started in the property-investing world. Please complete it and make it happen.

> I, *your name*, promise to purchase one more property with the objective of renting it for profit within the next 90 days.
>
> *Date* *Signature*

These are the simple steps to follow to keep achieving wealth for the rest of your life. Keep investing in yourself and the rewards will be infinite.

So what are you doing still reading this book? Go out there and get started NOW! Life is too short to waste; start really living today!

P.S. Hit the computer and download the bonuses featured on the Rewards Page now!

About the authors

Phil Jones

After starting with just $25,000 in 1999 Phil Jones has accumulated a multimillion-dollar property portfolio. Along with his wife Corinna, he founded Richmastery Ltd in 2001 to empower and educated other investors.

Richmastery has now trained over 46,000 investors in New Zealand and Australia, and Phil has become a respected and sought after speaker.

Phil founded the *Kiwi Property Investor* magazine and built it to be the number one-selling magazine in the Business Category in New Zealand before transferring his interests in the magazine in October 2004.

He is the author of best-selling books *How to Get Rich Rewards in Real Estate in 3 Years, Real Money Real Estate* and *1324 Ways You Can Get Massive Profits in Real Estate by Adding Value and Renovations.* He pioneered the world's first property analysis software, called RevIQ, with the ability to download live real-estate information. This software product is endorsed by international accountancy firm BDO and Australasian data specialists RP Data.

Phil and Corinna have two children, Cheinnelle and Jack. Phil's passion for real estate and his wish to help equip others to use it as an investment vehicle to achieve financial freedom is the driving force behind Richmastery Ltd.

See www.philjonesblog.com

David Leon

After starting with a debt of $15,000 in 2001, David has accumulated a multi-million-dollar portfolio spread over England, Spain and New Zealand. David founded Wealth Intelligence with a very simple objective: 'to teach worldwide proven strategies to improve people's happiness'. He has now trained over 11,000 people in seven countries in the art of improving wealth, health and general success. (Visit www.david-leon.com for more information on Wealth Intelligence.) David is very passionate about real estate investing, and also enjoys investing and setting up businesses. His two new business ventures are The Nabu Foundation (www.nabufoundation.com) and IBroker (www.Ibroker.co.nz). The Nabu Foundation's mission is to give everyone the tools to maximise their body and mind performance. IBroker aims to maximise the returns for everyone who is trying to get finance. It has a revolutionary system that will transform the way the industry operates.

Andrea Crabb

Andrea Crabb co-authored *How to Get Rich Rewards in Real Estate in 3 Years* and *1324 Ways You Can Get Massive Profits in Real Estate by Adding Value and Renovations*. She works as communications manager and writer for Richmastery Ltd, bringing to the roles more than 10 years' experience in the media industry. After completing a BA in English Literature and a Diploma in Journalism, Andrea worked as a television researcher, freelance print journalist, broadcast journalist and radio producer before working as a researcher and assistant producer on numerous international television documentaries for renowned networks such as National Geographic Television and Discovery Channel. She worked as a public relations consultant and as communications manager for Sky television before joining Richmastery Ltd. Andrea is also a property investor.

Special Rewards

To help you get the most out of this book we provide you with the following five Special Rewards. Please make sure you use them and enjoy them.

1. FREE Real Estate Investing Pack worth $249

The pack contains:

- Real Estate Toolbox on CD
- House Plan & Landscaping Software
- Buy or Rent Calculator
- Richmastery Newsletter
- Ebook – How to Create Multiple Streams of Income
- Report – How to Master and Repair Your Credit
- Home Inspection Kit ... and more

Go to: www.richmastery.com/fortune and get your FREE $249 Pack now!

2. FREE Bonus Downloads worth $199

These *essential agreements and documents* enable you to correctly execute many of the strategies contained in this book. You MUST download these agreements as they will increase the rate of your investing success and reduce your risk significantly. Go to: www.richmastery.com/fortune

3. FREE Online Investor Support

Join the Richmastery Forums at www.richmasteryforums.com, a live, fun online meeting place used by thousands of investors to meet, chat, support, share information and help one another achieve investing success.

4. FREE Property Analysis Software

The number 1 tool that EVERY successful investor should be using is RevIQ Property Analysis Software, a critical decision making tool that can save or make you thousands when buying, selling, renovating, flipping or doing lease options. Download a free 14 day trial from: www.reviq.com/bonus

5. FREE Live Event

We want to give you two tickets valued at $79.90 to Richmastery's four-hour *How to Profit from Property* Live Event so you can build on the exciting knowledge you gain from this book. If you'd rather watch the DVD of this event, there's $20 off its price. For your FREE tickets and DVD Discount go to: www.richmastery.com/fortune

Only 50 Members World Wide

PRESIDENTIAL INNER CIRCLE

Corinna Jones with Bill Rancic

Phil Jones with Ivanka

THE WORLD'S MOST INTIMATE AND EXCLUSIVE PRIVATE CLUB

Imagine having unprecedented access to an inner sanctum of exceptional masters and an intimate camaraderie with an extraordinary collection of some of the most unique and powerful investors and individuals who gather together to share and discover closely protected wealth secrets on how to reach the pinnacle of financial and personal growth.

The Presidential Inner Circle is a unique and exclusive opportunity that is strictly limited to fifty serious members worldwide who will experience a range of privileges, access and discovery that is unattainable outside of this select private group.

Your Presidential Inner Circle Masters are...

Phil and Corinna Jones with 42nd US President Bill Clinton

Phil and Corinna Jones with Donald Trump

EXQUISITE ELITE MEMBERSHIP PRIVILEGES...

12 Days of Unprecedented Access

Exclusive Invitations to a minimum of 12 unbelievable days a year (which at times could be divided into separate unique journeys) in the company of the two amazing and respected Presidential Inner Circle hosts in some of the most spectacular, discrete and breathtaking destinations in the world. From gliding through the Hawaiian Islands on a luxury cruise ship to partaking in a refined, intimate gourmet dinner at a secret Queenstown Lodge, your moments as a Presidential Inner Circle Member will be treasured, memorable and powerful.

Exceptional World Class Connections

Membership entitles you to uncompromising access to some of the Worlds Most Influential and recognised individuals, celebrity's, financial and personal development leaders. Some of which will be flown in to Presidential Inner Circles retreats for members sole and distinctive advantage. Whether it's breakfast with Bill Clinton or a chat by the pool with Steven Covey, your time together in the Presidential Inner Circle will be priceless and unforgettable. If you want to be wealthy and successful this is your chance to be assisted and personally guided by the best!

Restricted Invitation Only Events

Your Hosts commanding network of associates and the Clubs powerful leverage will open doors and get you access to people, events, opportunities and resources that previously were impossible for you to obtain. This will help put you on the fast track to unlock your infinite potential, unlimited wealth and your dream lifestyle.

Bi Monthly 2 Hour Masters Coaching

Members bask in 2 hours of Confidential Coaching with two of the Presidential Inner Circle Hosts and Masters and your brains trust of member peers, bi monthly. Coaching is delivered by private group teleconference phone call.

Limited Edition Presidential Inner Circle Connoisseur Collection

Each Member will receive a unique and memorable Presidential Inner Circle Connoisseur Collection gift pack featuring a range of hand selected items to commemorate your Membership at the club.

Masters Personal Protégés

Members receive a once-in-a-lifetime opportunity to be personal protégés of not one but two internationally-renowned masters of property, business, investment and personal development through the Presidential Inner Circle, reaping you rich rewards and exceptional value.

Unmatched Private Contact

Members support is delivered weekly through a private vault only accessible to members and protected by the highest Presidential Inner Circle internet security protocols. This gives members direct access to support and unmatched interaction with the Club hosts on a weekly basis. And enables members to share private investment opportunities with one another and plan, discuss and seek further information on matters from retreats, events, conference calls or market issues.

Explosive Peer Camaraderie

The dynamic intensity, passion, energy, brainstorming and incomparable wisdom that will radiate from this group of 50 of some of the worlds finest individuals that share a common bond forged in the Presidential Inner Circle cannot be overstated. Their collective power, lessons, skills and value will deliver an incredible enrichment and supremacy that cannot be found elsewhere and that all will significantly benefit from.

Investment Advantage

Your special time in The Presidential Inner Circle provides you with the potential to access select business opportunities that may become available through socialising with others in the group.

Rapid Growth Propulsion

Rapidly propel your knowledge and growth to superior levels unattainable elsewhere outside the Presidential Inner Circle. The unique environment and people in the Presidential Inner Circle will guarantee that your time as a select member will be nothing less than extraordinary.

Personal Attention, Service and Support

Club CEO Corinna Jones personally handles all support and assistance to Club members, ensuring you receive total satisfaction and the care, comfort, time and attention your membership status deserves. Club standards are so high that each Club member will be provided with Corinna Jones's personal mobile number for emergency support Monday to Friday between the hours of 9am and 5pm and at any time whilst you are travelling on Club events.

Preferential Priority

Members who wish to bring their spouse into the Club at any time will receive preferential priority with their spouse automatically being placed at the top of the club waiting list so that their participation in the club can be achieved at the earliest possibility.

Destination Refinement

Presidential Inner Circle members get to vote each year on the favoured locations they would like events to be held at. Club Hosts will accommodate member's preferences wherever possible.

Annual Membership Investment

The annual membership investment provides members with access to all Presidential Inner Circle Club services, events and benefits throughout the year. Costs for attending events includes but is not limited to travel costs, food, accommodation, event entry costs (where they exist) and conference call costs are to be paid directly by each member.

The Presidential Inner Circle is not for everyone, nor is it meant to be, it is after all.. The Worlds Most Intimate and Exclusive Private Club limited to only 50 members. If however you know the Presidential Inner Circle is for you or you would like to know more, we invite you contact: concierge@presidentialinnercircle.com or visit:

www.presidentialinnercircle.com

Exceptional Acquaintances - Unparalleled Influence - Elite Connections

Unprecedented Opportunity - Exclusive Access - Incredible Discovery – Private Investments

Success is no accident

How To Guarantee That You Make Money Every Time You Invest In A Property

Successful property investors know that if they buy a bad deal it stays with them for a very long time. Just one bad purchase will stall your investing plans and cost you thousands! Thats's why the most important weapon in your investor toolbox is your Real Estate Analysis Software. RevIQ is the most advanced analysis software in Australasia.

• Make informed decisions • Be safe & save money • Feel Confident
• Know Exactly what you are doing • Take the Risk out of investing

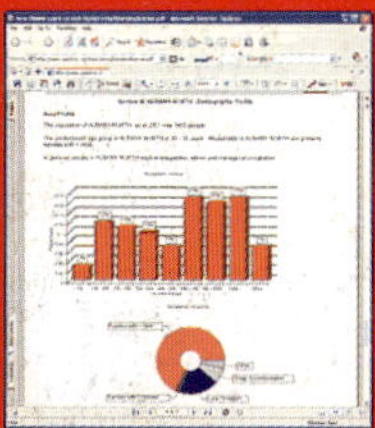

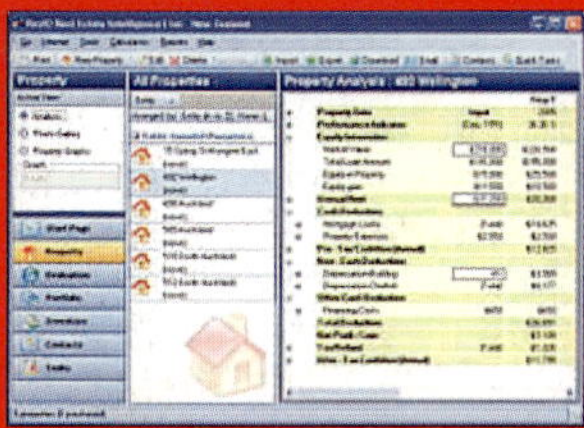

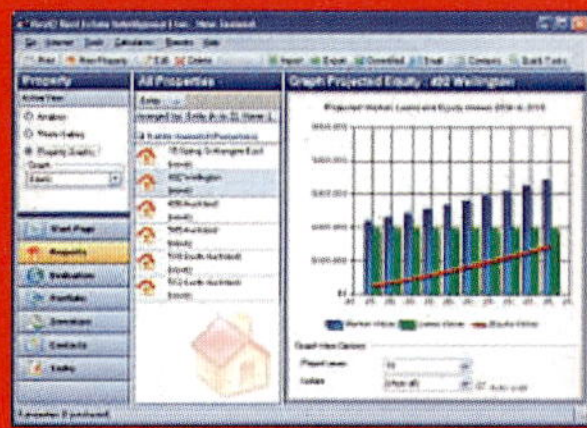

RevIQ IS NOT JUST ANOTHER ANALYSIS PROGRAM

Massive wealth accumulation is made easy using RevIQ's advanced suite of tools including Portfolio Reporting, Borrowing Analysis, and a multitude of other features including a host of calculators, reports, graphs and online news feeds.

ONLINE DATA DOWNLOADING INTERNET EVALUATIONS

RevIQ's exclusive online internet downloading gives you access to impressive detailed internet evaluations on any property in Australasia. Includes Market Rental Data, Demographics, Sales History, and up to the minute valuation information.

• Fast and Easy - Download data reports in seconds
• Gives you incredible confidence - No more guess-work!
• Save time and money and have piece of mind
• Go into every deal armed with all the facts - be a power negotiator

Free 14-Day Trial!

Download or order trial CD from

www.reviq.com/bonus

Australasia's 1st Real Estate Analysis Software with Online Data Downloading

www.reviq.com
REV IQ
Real Estate Intelligence...LIVE

Many of the investors in this book refer to Richmastery Analysis Software, this software is known as RevIQ

Phil Jones has proven his position as one of Australasia's most successful property investors. In 1999 he entered the property market with little more than $25,000, and in less than two years he amassed a substantial multi-million dollar property portfolio. Passionate about the lifestyle property investing creates, Phil created Richmastery Limited in 2001 - and devotes most of his time to equipping and empowering others and growing his investment knowledge.

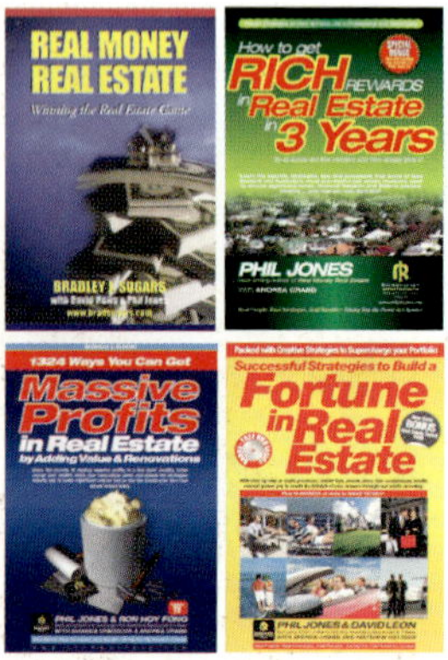

David and Steve are two of the most respected real estate educators and investors in Australasia. Steve's book From 0 to 130 Properties was rated by Dymocks and Money Magazine as the Top financial book for 2004. The book outlines how Steve McKnight, together with his business partner David Bradley, created a real estate investing philosophy, which they implemented to achieve their goal of financial freedom in just three-and-a-half years. $1,000,000 in Property in One Year – written as the property market slumped, outlines more of McKnight's practical investing philosophies for maximising wealth and minimising losses. This fantastic resource is packed with knowledge and will leave you feeling touched, moved and inspired.

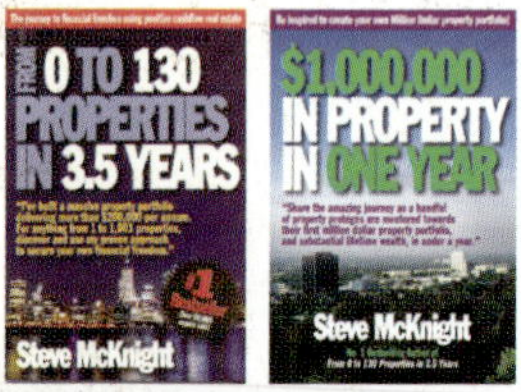

7 Reasons Why Anyone Serious About Property Investment And Creating Wealth Has Got To Attend This Course ...

1 *16 Proven Strategies to purchase property NO MONEY DOWN.*
Learning these advanced strategies of how to buy property can accelerate your wealth creation. These techniques alone could be worth many times your ticket price.

2 *Turn $1000 into $30,000 of additional Property Value*
Amazing but true! Learn 21 tactics you can immediately use to add value to a property and create wealth.

3 *Create a $100,000 Income from 10 Properties*
Learn how to generate a $100,000 income each year for the rest of your life from 10 property deals.

4 *Property Rules of the Rich*
Learn the rules the super-wealthy use to guarantee their property success so you can too!

5 *How you could become Debt Free in 3 to 7 years*
Follow our unique process and you can achieve outstanding results.

6 *9 Ways to Win at Auctions*
Not only can you win at auctions but we will show you how to purchase property at a discount at auctions.

7 *Design your Personal Wealth Roadmap*
You will take away your own personal structured functional plan that will show you how you can achieve your desired level of wealth.

What Must You Do This Instant to begin Expanding Your Money at a Significant Rate?

Information is Power! Getting Rich Can Be Easy, the problem is most people don't know how. At the Richmastery Property Academy we will teach you how, show you how and make sure you know how to significantly expand your money.

But there is one thing you need to do! Book for the course. Nothing happens in life unless you MAKE IT HAPPEN. This could be the unique opportunity you need to break the financial chains that have shackled your life and make an investment in your greatest asset - YOU!

If you want to learn the most effective wealth creation techniques, make sure you learn the best ones! Available through the Richmastery Property Academy.

You will do things at the Richmastery Property Academy that no other course does, learn lessons no other course teaches and get access to information virtually no-one else is prepared to tell you. The Richmastery Property Academy is NOT a seminar, it's an event that will challenge, empower, change and equip you with cutting edge knowledge, resources and tools. Invest in yourself, invest in your future, invest in your life, BOOK NOW for the Richmastery Property Academy.

Millionaires Teach You The Secrets To Unlimited Property Wealth

A 3 DAY JOURNEY THAT REWARDS YOU FOR THE REST OF YOUR LIFE...

"This is probably the most valuable thing I have done this decade! And I wouldn't have done it if it hadn't been recommended by at least 6 people."
Shelley Gilchrist

"Unbelievable, felt like a finishing school of all the wisdom I had always wondered about."
Jason Gilbert

***Fantastic Presentation** - I have never been to nything before that has already & is going to ave a profound influence on my life"*
erald Klyn

Fantastic!!! Learnt as much in 3 days as I did n a 3 year commerce degree."
latthew Stewart

Excellent seminar! I have learnt more in this eminar than all the other investing seminars I ave ever attended."
liff Ah Kit

"Phil is a financially savvy investor who is experiencing massive success because he has put the knowledge gained from some of the world's best entrepreneurial teachers into action! He walks the talk, and has amassed sensational property and business portfolios. Now you can share in his expertise and that of the teachers who have taught him, so you too can enjoy the incredible results he has."
Brad Sugars - Multi-Millionaire, Entrepreneur, Author, Investor

The 8 Rules of the Rich, when it comes to property investing and how you apply them
The Richmastery 18 step system of exactly how to invest in property
The 7 universal characteristics of Millionaires
The 5 laws of the Wealthy - written over 2000 years ago
How to put together your own Wealth Creation Plan and implement it.

DAY 1

- **The Winning Mindset**
- **Removing Your Biggest Obstacle**
- **Money Psychology of the Rich**
- **Top 100 Investment Hot Spots in NZ & Australia**
- **The Economic Clock**
- **Analysing the Property Cycle**
- **Millionaire Bank Account**
- **11 Rules for Dealing with Banks**
- **8 Keys to a Successful Meeting with the Bank**
- **How the Rich Borrow to Make Money**
- **Richmastery Property Game**
- **Young Investors' Panel**

WHY PROPERTY?

- Why invest, what drives the market, why will values continue to rise?
- What are the no-risk strategies to investing
- Australian versus New Zealand investing - the differences
- The 4 ways property pays YOU - if you buy right!
- The secrets to financing your property investments
- How you generate more income and reduce personal debt rapidly
- How you get banks to treat you like a sophisticated investor (even if you aren't)
- How you buy property NO MONEY DOWN!
- How to borrow more than the purchase price of the property with the bank's approval
- Vendor finance, how do you find it, how do you negotiate it
- The type of mortgage that successful investors use

THE ESSENTIAL TOOLS OF THE PROPERTY INVESTOR

- The software tools that the wealthy use to analyse their deals, manage their portfolio, obtain finance, manage cash-flow, rental income and tenants. You will get the opportunity to use these tools first hand at the event, and become fully confident with them
- Setting up office, the equipment and systems you need in place to succeed

DAY 2

- **Advanced Renovation Strategies**
- **Commercial Property - No Money Down**
- **Maximising Depreciation**
- **How to get a 20% return on property in a range of market conditions**
- **Property Development**
- **How you can structure Holiday Homes as Investments**
- **Secret Leasehold Bargains**
- **Millionaire Advisors**
- **Richmastery Property Game**

THE TYPE OF PROPERTY TO BUY

- Setting up your investment rules
- How to build a portfolio that balances capital growth and cashflow
- How to find deals 20%+ below current market valuation
- The lies told about negative cash-flow property
- Location, location, location and cash-flow versus capital growth
- Depreciation, negative gearing and accounting made simple
- The deals that allow you to increase cash-flow and value substantially
- Quick cash deals
- How to do your own development deals
- How to completely redecorate, re-carpet and replace all the light fittings and curtains in your property for less than $1,000
- Freehold, cross lease, leasehold, sub dividing and strata titles
- How you create the time to become an investor, while still doing your day job

THE AGENT, THE CONTRACT & THE NEGOTIATION

- How a Real Estate agent thinks and how to use them to your advantage

You Could Make Hundreds Of Thousands Of Dollars Using These Strategies

- What do you believe? What lies are told?
- Common mistakes buyers make and how to avoid them
- Analysing a deal in less than five minutes, how you set the purchase price target
- Valuing a property yourself - the tools and information to use
- Preparing the contract, the clauses you can use to always have the advantage (and an escape)!
- The negotiation process, how to win, and when to walk away. You will investigate, analyse and negotiate the purchase of a property as part of your training while at the course, using real contracts, and clauses
- How to structure access, settlement and possession to suit you

DAY 3

- **9 Strategies at Auctions**
- **Vendor Conditioning**
- **The Art of Negotiation**
- **Asset & Tax Planning**
- **Advanced Mortgage Strategies**
- **Powerful Sale Agreement Contract Clauses**
- **13 Step Letting Process**
- **Professional Property Management Tips**
- **Millionaire Advisors**
- **Interviews with Successful Investors**
- **Richmastery Property Game**

HOW TO STRUCTURE YOUR INVESTMENTS

- How to protect your personal property - even from banks
- How to minimise your personal tax rate to as low as 0% - legally
- How to get your tax refund monthly instead of at the end of the year
- Cashflow and financial management

HOW TO BUILD A TEAM OF EXPERTS THAT PERFORM TO MEET YOUR NEEDS

- Finding and managing a great accountant
- Find and dealing with an excellent solicitor
- How to work with your valuer, and get the property valued correctly

MANAGING THE TENANTS

- Finding a good property manager
- Doing it yourself successfully and how to get started
- How to get tenants queuing up to rent your property
- How to select the best tenant, and the best tenancy agreement to use
- Repairs, advertising, managing the tenant, documents and contracts to use and the tenancy tribunal

GETTING INTO COMMERCIAL PROPERTY

- What to look for when buying commercial property
- The advantages commercial property has over residential
- The 3 sectors; commercial, industrial & retail
- Leasing - tenants, contracts & legal issues
- Financing your investments - how to maximise your borrowing ability
- Taxation, legislation and accounting

THE ORDER AND DAYS SUBJECTS ARE COVERED ON MAY VARY

How a 26 year old has purchased $983,000 worth of property & makes over $137,000 equity in under 1 year!!!
"Using 3 of the strategies I have purchased more than 4 properties in 12 months giving me yearly passive cashflow of ove $53,000 and immediate equity of $137,000.
Jo Waters

"Thoroughly useful, learned heaps, the best seminar I have attended."
Pat Hutchinson

"Thank you for a very real education at the Academy, it is truly my turn to create and take action! I wonder if people really do understand how cheap your education opportunity really is? I do sincerely thank you both for the opportunity you have provided me with"
Steve Holmes

"***An awesome 3 days***, *excellent presenters & role models."*
Greg Roche

"It has given me the insight I have been looking for!"
Werner Weijerman

"***Great!*** *Nothing covered that wasn't helpful. The 3 days flowed seamlessly from one action to the next"*
Glenice Whittle

RICHMASTERY
Educators Investors Experts

RICHMASTERY
PROPERTY ACADEMY
Where the Mastery of Millionaireship begins

RICHMASTERY
Educators Investors Experts

An Outstanding Return on Investment!

There are **NO MORE EXCUSES!** The Richmastery Property Academy represents an opportunity to increase your personal wealth. The value is reflected in the results other graduates have achieved by applying the strategies and principles they have learnt. Implement one of these strategies and you could more than regain your initial investment in this course ... combine as many as 7 or 8 strategies and your return on your investment could be very substantial.

This is the only course of its type in Australasia, there is **no other** 3 Day Property Academy and **no other** course with even half the number of experts the Richmastery Property Academy provides. The Richmastery Property Academy **SELLS OUT *every year*** because it is recognised as being the best property event learning for New Zealand and Australian Investors.

The only question that remains now is ... will you be joining us at the Richmastery Property Academy? You could be the next graduate sharing their success story with others, or will you choose to do nothing, get nothing, and continue to wallow in the financial wilderness lacking strategies and advice that could transform your life. There are NO MORE EXCUSES! Take control of your life, invest in the Richmastery Property Academy and give yourself a ... **GIFT FOR LIFE!**

Here is what you receive at the Richmastery Property Academy...

- 3 Days (over 40 Hours) of superb property investment education that could change your life
- Access to one of the most comprehensive line ups of Property Investing Specialists ever assembled in Australasia
- Richmastery Millionaire Advisors
- Richmastery Young Investors
- Full Support from Experienced Richmastery Crew
- FREE Financial Assessment
- Personalised Wealth Creation Plan
- Special Academy Discounts
- Full 140 Page Academy Manual
- Handouts
- Meals & Refreshments provided (morning tea, lunch, afternoon tea)
- 100% Money Back Guarantee (conditions apply - see www.richmastery.com)

7 years Investing Experience in 1 Property Game

The Richmastery Property Academy is unique! We don't just fill your head with a whole lot of nice intellectual theories, we teach you step by step processes on how to build a large, robust, low risk property investing portfolio. We immerse you in the Richmastery Property Game where you actively perfect and apply the strategies needed in a simulated market environment.

The Richmastery Property game is the glue that brings everything taught together in one simple cohesive understandable plan.

The Game Features.... an intense high pressure market place featuring slippery real estate agents, motivated sellers, dodgy deals, exceptional property bargains and our own friendly auctioneer! Anything can happen at any time - so you need to be ready to act at a moments notice. You will compete against others to negotiate, buy and build a significant property portfolio and deal with unexpected market booms and recessions.

Each game session mirrors a year in the property marketplace. After 7 sessions you can accumulate as much as 7 years simulated experience in only a remarkable 3 days!

The Richmastery Property Game will educate, equip and prepare you to deal with any unforeseen property twists and gives you the experience and confidence to come out on top every time.

Book Now! Go to

www.richmasterypropertyacademy.com

or phone 1800-427-424 (Aus) or 0800-742-462 (NZ)

to reserve your seat TODAY!

Knowledge Is The Only Barrier To Success - When You Have The Knowledge All Barriers Disappear